On Bigotry

On Bigotry
Twenty Lessons on How Bigotry Works and What to Do About It

Nicholas Ensley Mitchell

BLOOMSBURY ACADEMIC

NEW YORK · LONDON · OXFORD · NEW DELHI · SYDNEY

BLOOMSBURY ACADEMIC
Bloomsbury Publishing Inc, 1385 Broadway, New York, NY 10018, USA
Bloomsbury Publishing Plc, 50 Bedford Square, London, WC1B 3DP, UK
Bloomsbury Publishing Ireland, 29 Earlsfort Terrace, Dublin 2, D02 AY28, Ireland

BLOOMSBURY, BLOOMSBURY ACADEMIC and the Diana logo are
trademarks of Bloomsbury Publishing Plc

First published in the United States of America 2025

Cover design: Chloe Batch
Cover image © Anadolu Agency/Getty Images Plus/Samuel Corum

Library of Congress Cataloging-in-Publication Data to come

ISBN: HB: 978-1-5381-8976-4
      ePDF: 979-8-7651-5497-7
      eBook: 978-1-5381-8977-1

Typeset by Deanta Global Publishing Services, Chennai, India
Printed and bound in the United States of America

For product safety related questions contact productsafety@bloomsbury.com.

To find out more about our authors and books visit www.bloomsbury.com and
sign up for our newsletters.

For Herman, Florence, Morris, and Elaine

CONTENTS

Preface: Childhood's End — ix

Acknowledgments — xv

Introduction — 1

PART I
HOW DO BIGOTS THINK ABOUT THE WORLD? — 21

Lesson 1 — Bigotry Makes You Immoral — 27

Lesson 2 — Bigotry Destroys a Person's Ability to Think — 35

Lesson 3 — All Forms of Bigotry Are Intertwined — 41

PART II
HOW DOES BIGOTRY TEACH PEOPLE TO THINK? — 49

Lesson 4 — Bigotry Is Taught — 55

Lesson 5 — Bigotry Always Seeks New Targets — 63

Lessons 6 and 7 — Bigotry Is Paranoid, and Bigotry Makes You Violent — 71

CONTENTS

PART III

HOW BIGOTRY DISGUISES ITSELF | 81

Lesson 8 Bigotry Presents Itself as Philosophy | 87

Lesson 9 Bigotry Presents Itself as a Concern | 95

Lesson 10 Bigotry Presents Itself as Science | 105

PART IV

HOW DOES BIGOTRY TEACH PEOPLE TO ACT POLITICALLY? | 113

Lesson 11 Bigotry Does Not Give Up Easily | 121

Lesson 12 Bigots Will Take Advantage of Members of Their Targeted Groups Who Advocate for Their Own Inferiority | 129

Lesson 13 Bigotry Does Not Compromise | 141

Lesson 14 Bigotry Demands Action from Bigots | 149

Lesson 15 Bigotry Loves Moral Panics | 157

Lesson 16 Bigots Want You to Think They Are Unintelligent | 165

Lesson 17 Bigotry Loves False Moral Equivalence | 173

Lesson 18 Bigots Always Claim That They Are the Real Victims | 181

Lesson 19 Bigotry Gaslights Everyone | 189

Lesson 20 Bigotry Cannot Be Disproven | 197

Conclusion: The World Is a Punk Bar | 203

Index | 215

About the Author | 227

PREFACE
CHILDHOOD'S END

One of the cross-cultural realities of the human condition is that all cultures recognize childhood as the period when future adults are ignorant of the world and, therefore, innocent. This is why we make funny faces at a staring baby to make them smile and why, when a toddler hands you a toy phone, it is a customary reflex that you answer it. This is why we carve out playgrounds and make special items such as toys for children. The recognition of the sanctity of childhood is what gives holidays their special flair and why parents delay telling a child that Santa Claus is not real for as long as they can. Understandably, parents want to extend their children's childhoods for as long as possible.

All childhoods are destined to end, because that, too, is the human condition. Children grow into adolescents and begin learning about the world, their innocence naturally fading and being replaced by awareness. In an ideal world, this would always be the case, but we do not live in an ideal world. We live in a real one. In the real world, childhood is a privilege snatched away early or denied entirely to many for the most horrific reasons, of which you, the reader, may already be aware: war, neglect, mental and physical abuse, poverty, and both man-made and natural disasters. This book focuses on one of those horrors: bigotry (CDC, 2024; Jones et al., 2020).

To illustrate what I mean, I invite you to walk with me as I describe the moment when my childhood started to end.

In the fall of 1991, Louisiana sat at the center of the world's political gaze. The former grand wizard of the Ku Klux Klan, David Duke, was engaged in a runoff election for governor with the former governor of Louisiana, Edwin Edwards, who later went to prison but remained very popular. As John Maginnis (1992) detailed in his classic text, *Cross to Bear*, the election laid bare all of Louisiana's class, religious, and racial divisions for the entire world to see. This is when I discovered that bigotry existed. I was nine years old.

I was born and raised in Baton Rouge. My hometown is perched on the bluffs overlooking the Mississippi River, in what is famously called "cancer alley," because of its proximity to many of Louisiana's ubiquitous chemical plants, the lights of which glitter in the darkness on clear nights. I have previously described Baton Rouge in an essay for Blavity thusly: "From the west bank city of Port Allen, it stretches jaggedly along the eastern shore, alternating between squalor, industry, administrative buildings, the city's version of opulence, and is bookended by the stateliness of two different universities—one historically Black and the other predominantly White. It is simultaneously an industrial city built around one of the largest oil refineries in the world, a college town, and the state capital" (Mitchell, 2020, para. 9). It is the sort of Southern gothic place where Faulkner and Caldwell would set their stories.

I grew up in a Black, middle-class family. Like many members of the Black middle class in the American South, my mother and father were both civil servants. I grew up in an integrated neighborhood that, at the time, was on the outskirts of town. I spent many summer days playing in the woods, by creeks, and near bayous with both White and Black friends. I am also a product of Roman Catholic schools. In 1991, I was a student at a racially integrated elementary school, which nuns administered at the time. In many ways, my childhood was the idyllic Southern variety that country musicians sing about, and I look back on it fondly.

It is a strange thing to be able to remember when your childhood ended, not totally, but in part. I cannot recall the exact date, but I mark it by my first sight of a billboard off the highway on the way to my grandparents' house. The fall of 1991 remains etched into my memory. The billboard was bright red with a white circle in the middle, and a black symbol that nine-year-old me did not understand. It had the words "No Nazis, No Duke" printed on it. I had forgotten about this billboard for decades until I was visiting a friend who managed a nightclub, and in the back office one night, they produced an old picture of the billboard to ask me if I knew anything about it. Seeing the image of what adult me knew was a swastika flooded my mind with memories of the fall when I'd first laid eyes on it.

In my research to figure out where the billboard was, I discovered from a photo in the *New York Magazine* that it hung on Interstate 10 North right before the Louise Street exit by the on-ramp from Dalrymple Drive (Corkran, 1991; Kilgore, 2019). The billboard sat on the lip of Old South Baton Rouge, the historically Black neighborhood where my mother grew up and my grandparents lived. I saw this sign every week when my mother or my father took me to visit my grandparents.

That billboard marked the beginning of my education about bigotry and the end of my childhood. So, what did I learn? First, I learned there were people who hated me because I was Black. Second, I learned that one of them was running for governor. I was only nine, but I understood what a governor was. Finally, I learned about the Ku Klux Klan and the Nazis. I describe this moment as when my childhood started ending because I had to absorb the fact that there were people out there who did not like me, my parents, and my grandparents simply because we'd been born with extra melanin in our skin. It had never occurred to nine-year-old me that such a thing was possible because I did not understand what race meant. Of course, I noticed that my White friends looked different from me, but that carried all the importance of noticing that flowers were different colors. My mind was occupied with comic books, professional wrestling, and memorizing the patterns to beat Dr. Wily in Mega Man. In the fall of 1991, I discovered that people would hate me for something I could not change.

Do I fault my parents and my grandparents for telling me these things? No. There was a real possibility that David Duke was going to be the governor of our state. My parents and grandparents were products of Jim Crow America, and they knew what internalized racism does to a person. They also knew that the only way to inoculate a person against that is to tell them that bigotry exists and that you should never apologize for "how God made you," to quote my grandmother. My teachers did not hide who David Duke and the Ku Klux Klan were. The first time I ever heard the word *racism* was from a Sister who said, "Racism is a sin." I would later discover the nuns had nothing but contempt for David Duke, which always brings me a smile as someone with a deeply ingrained fear of an angry nun.

Some readers may assert that my parents, grandparents, teachers, and the nuns should never have broached the topic of racism with children as young as I was because of concern for preserving our childhood innocence. As I stated earlier, childhood is a beautiful thing that people rightfully want to extend as long as they can. I understand this complaint, but I disagree with it. The people who cared for me and educated me as a child introduced me to the existence of bigotry because this was and remains necessary knowledge. Being informed is a form of intellectual, moral, and emotional inoculation because it protects you from the dangers posed by those who will physically and emotionally hurt you based on your appearance, your religion, whom you love, and the disposition of your body. Being informed about bigotry also can protect you from becoming a bigot yourself, because you recognize it as being mean or wrong or, to cite the nun I learned this from, a sin.

There are many reasons I can invoke to justify writing a book such as this. Politically, the United States is at a moment when the influence of open bigotry is experiencing a resurgence in rhetoric and policy. Ideologically and philosophically, bigotry continues to be a pertinent and influential force that people try to intellectualize to make it more palatable for ordinary people. Educationally, clashes over the meaning of diversity, equity, inclusion, multiculturalism, how to teach about gender, and how to teach about America's history of racism are all skirmishes in a larger conflict over who is part of American civilization and who is not. This is not a partisan issue; the recent spikes in islamophobia and antisemitism stand as stark evidence of how bigotry is truly a diverse ideology that appeals to people across the political spectrum.

All these interests justify writing this book, and perhaps it is also a bit of the Catholic school kid in me remembering all the social justice classes I took. However, the reason I have chosen to commit this public pedagogy to paper is simple and moral. As you read these words, somewhere on the planet, a parent is explaining to their child that people hate them for being different and that they must remember this knowledge to remain safe. That child could be White or a person of color. They could be of any religion or no religion at all. They could be able-bodied or have a disability. They could be neurotypical or neurodiverse. They could be straight or queer. They could be cisgender or gender nonconforming. They could be poor or financially secure. They could be privileged or marginalized. In the end, the details do not matter, aside from them being the target of bigotry for being different. I think of that child trying to process this new information in a mind that, up to that point, had only been concerned with what we all hope children are concerned with—dreams, joys, and simple delights. I think of the parents watching, perhaps not the light fade from their child's eyes completely, but watching that light dim a bit. I think of how bigotry ends so many childhoods, and I am filled with sadness, outrage, and familiarity. For me, that is reason enough to write this book.

Note: Reference to specific commercial products, manufacturers, companies, or trademarks does not constitute its endorsement or recommendation by the U.S. Government, Department of Health and Human Services, or the Centers for Disease Control and Prevention.

References

Corkran, L. (1991). *White nationalist David Duke campaigns* [Photograph]. Getty Images. Retrieved November 13, 2024, from https://www.gettyimages.com/detail/news-photo/highway-bilboard-protests-former-ku-klux-klan-member-david-news-photo/542365290

Jones, C. M., M. T. Merrick, and D. E. Houry. (2020). Identifying and preventing adverse childhood experiences: Implications for clinical practice. *JAMA*, 323(1), 25–26. https://doi:10.1001/jama.2019.18499

Kilgore, E. (2019, July 23). Democrats should attack Trump's racism, but that won't be enough to beat him. *New York Magazine*. Retrieved September 3, 2024, from https://nymag.com/intelligencer/2019/07/is-attacking-trumps-racism-enough-to-beat-him.html

Maginnis, J. (1992). *Cross to Bear*. Dark Horse Press.

Mitchell, N. E. (2020, February 3). *Young, black, and southern: How being born in the U.S. after Jim Crow expands my perspective on race*. Blavity. Retrieved September 3, 2024, from https://blavity.com/young-black-and-southern-how-being-born-black-in-the-us-after-jim-crow-expands-my-perspective-on-race

U.S. Centers for Disease Control and Prevention. (2024, October 8). *About Adverse Childhood Experiences*. Retrieved December 1, 2024, from https://www.cdc.gov/violenceprevention/aces/index.html

ACKNOWLEDGMENTS

The book is the product of decades of long conversations in bars, dorm rooms, restaurants, parks, classrooms, parking lots, and living rooms. I can't list all the names of the many people who supported me as I wrote this book . . . but I will try.

To Karl, Bart, Brenna, Megan B., Auw, Allen, Meagan S., Will H., Victoria, Max, Ryan, Meagan M., Claire, Toni, John, Thomas, Will L., Ashley, Blake, Jessa, Alex, Jonathan, Kate, Rodneyna, Cat, Vaughn, Channing, Melissa, Ryan S., Michelle, Phil, Adam, Mike, Doug and Anni, Kayla, Brenton, Austin, Terry, Meagan M., Blake T., Bethany, Jay, Gary, Lauren, Josh, Luke, Madison, Lee, Erin, Rhiannon, George, Neva, Joey, Jordan, Jacob, Grady, Donney, Ansel, Liz, Jarvis, Ward, Christie, Mase, and Jason, who were thought partners at the various stages of this book moving from idea to manuscript, thank you.

Thank you to the nuns, brothers, and laypeople who taught me that bigotry is wrong.

I owe the University of Kansas and my mentor, Steven White, an outstanding debt for listening to me and providing feedback as I wrote the many drafts that became this book.

Thank you to Heidi Hallman for teaching me how to write a book proposal.

I must also thank the School of Education and Human Sciences at the University of Kansas for supporting me in this endeavor.

I would have never finished this book without Jane Loper, who proofread and provided feedback for the world's slowest writer with a weak grasp of the rules of grammar.

To my agent, Sha-Shana Crichton, for making this happen.

I owe a special thanks and debt to Roland Mitchell and the School of Education for providing me with a writing space and access to the library at Louisiana State University over the summer of 2024. To Alyssa Palazzo and Jessica Thwaite for everything they did to get this project from manuscript to book.

To Rae Taylor, Alfred Kammer, David Hansen, Michele Casavant, Lisa Wolf-Wendel, Kelli Feldman, Dean Richards, Jaclyn Dudek, Ngondi A. Kamaṭuka, Carrie La Voy, Amanda Mollet, Bryan Mann, Zak Foste, Lena Batt, Jennifer Ng, Reagan Mitchell, Anna Yonas, Imogen Herrick, and Petra Hendry for introducing me to critical knowledge that helped me think through bigotry.

And to my Rachel for her love and support.

INTRODUCTION

To the reader,

You are responsible, in every sense of the word, for confronting and ending bigotry in American society. No, you are not personally responsible for every act of bigotry committed in the past and happening right now. Guilt always lies with those who committed the crime, and it does not pass down in families like a curse. If you have committed no acts of bigotry, you are guilty of nothing. However, you are responsible for ending bigotry, because we are all responsible for making the world, regardless of where we live in it, a better place than we found it. Responsibility is not guilt, but an acknowledgment of the world as it is, and what role we must play to correct and improve it. If you disagree with this moral, political, and philosophical claim, this book is not for you. If you agree with the first sentence, I hope the following pages will serve you well and that you enjoy reading them as much as I enjoyed writing them.

The purpose of this book is to expose how bigots think so you will recognize bigotry when you see it and rebuke it with the contempt that bigotry always deserves. This book will not teach you how to debate with bigots. There is no reason to debate bigots because we have already heard everything that bigots, regardless of their stripe, have to say for themselves, across time. We heard everything the Nazis had to say for themselves during the Nuremberg trials. We heard everything the segregationists had to say for themselves during the civil rights movement. We heard everything the homophobes had to say for themselves during the outbreak of HIV and the debates over same-sex marriage. Bigots remix the same claims, "We are superior, and they are inferior," repeatedly, from era to era.

One of the goals of this book is to demystify bigotry for you, the reader, which is why I have written in the public pedagogy style of Jason Stanley's (2020) *How Fascism Works: The Politics of Us and Them*, Timothy Snyder's (2017) *On Tyranny: Twenty Lessons from the Twentieth Century*, and Kathlyn Gay's *Bigotry and Intolerance: The Ultimate Teen Guide* (2013). It is also a work of critical pedagogy in the tradition of Paulo Freire's (1970/2018) *Pedagogy of the Oppressed*. I draw on these two traditions and their respective styles because I am a firm believer that philosophy and the social sciences should be accessible to everyone rather than buried under academic terminology, and I believe that people cannot combat the forces that seek to divide them until they understand how these forces work. To that end, I like to think of this book as more of a field guide for understanding bigotry than a philosophy text.

My understanding of bigotry draws on the work of the numerous scholars, writers, theologians, research centers, and leaders I cite throughout this book. I owe an outstanding intellectual debt to Jan Gross's (2002) *Neighbors: The Destruction of the Jewish Community in Jedwabne, Poland*, Eric Yamamoto's (1999) *Interracial Justice: Conflict and Reconciliation in Post-Civil Rights America*, Charles Mills's (1997/2014) *The Racial Contract*, Carole Pateman's (1988/2018) *The Sexual Contract*, Monique Wittig's (1992) *The Straight Mind and Other Essays*, Susan Stryker's (2008/2017) *Transgender History: The Roots of Today's Revolution*, Elizabeth Young-Bruehl's (1998) *The Anatomy of Prejudices*, Gordon Allport's (1954/1979) *The Nature of Prejudice*, and Erec Smith's (2020) *A Critique of Anti-Racism in Rhetoric and Composition: The Semblance of Empowerment*, whose ideas and arguments have greatly impacted my understanding of how bigotry functions and are the intellectual foundation of my definition of and my eleven assertions about bigotry presented later in this section. What all these works have in common is an understanding of bigotry as more than the ramblings of ignorant people. Bigotry is bigger and more dangerous than that. It is a code of behavior that people live by. It is a worldview that has multiple manifestations but a common code of hate to which no community, regardless of their history as perpetrators or victims, is immune. The north star of my thinking and the foundation of this book is the claim that bigotry is not inherent; it is taught, and everything taught has a curriculum we can scrutinize (Hendry, 2011; Kliebard, 1982; Pinar et al., 1995; Rosiek & Kinslow, 2016; Watkins, 1993, 2001; Wozolek, 2021).

I have broken the curriculum of bigotry, meaning what it teaches those foolish enough to adopt it, into a series of twenty lessons. We already know the sort of America in which bigotry wishes to thrive because we have history to inform us. Throughout this book, I will explore bigotry's historical and contemporary manifestations in both the world and American society. In the conclusion, I will describe what people can do to rebuke bigotry. I hope that after reading this book, you will understand how bigotry thinks about the world, how it presents itself, and what it does to the individual. You can then be an advocate for accepting difference while being a bulwark against the forces of bigotry that have a vested interest in keeping you confused while they act. In the same way that you become financially and politically literate through exposure to how economics and politics function, this book seeks to help you become literate in how bigots think, and the rhetorical tactics bigotry uses to justify itself.

Before we explore how bigotry teaches bigots to think, it is crucial to define *bigot* and *bigotry*. *Merriam-Webster* (n.d.-b) defines a *bigot* as "a person who is obstinately or intolerantly devoted to his or her own opinions and prejudices; especially: one who regards or treats the members of a group (such as a racial or ethnic group) with hatred and intolerance." *Bigotry* is defined as "obstinate or intolerant devotion to one's own opinions and prejudices: the state of mind of a bigot" (Merriam-Webster, n.d.-a). Simply put, a bigot is a person who hates people for being different, and bigotry is how they justify their hatred. Bigotry comes in many forms. Racists hate people who have a different skin color. Xenophobes hate foreigners. Antisemites hate Jews. Islamophobes hate Muslims. Sexists hate people of different sexes. Homophobes hate people who are gay, lesbian, or bisexual. Classists hate people of another social or economic class. Transphobes hate transgender people. The common thread between all these groups is a hatred of difference, and that hatred is why, to quote my grandfather, bigots are *fucked-up people*.

Bigotry, if given enough time, makes people cruel in ways both profound and petty. Jim Crow America is an excellent example of how this scale of cruelty played out in real life. Profound cruelty was Black people, like Emmett Till, being lynched by White people and their murderers never being imprisoned. Petty cruelty, as Manning Marable (Hoffman, 2022, 08:22) pointed out, was the everyday ritual of segregation that said a Black person could not try on certain clothes in a store, or he could purchase food from a diner but not eat inside. The desire to be cruel consumes bigots and makes their range of possible actions predictable. We see this in how transphobes want to deny transgender youth access to gender-affirming care that may help them find joy in life, because it is cruel to deny people access to care that may help them live fuller, happy lives; inflicting harm is the purpose (Serwer, 2021). The irony of bigotry is that it makes figuring out what social justice is elementary. Social justice is the opposite of what bigots think and want to do.

In this book, bigotry is also understood as an ideology that influences how people see and interact with society. In this sense, I define *bigotry* as the intellectual and moral commitment to the belief that the proper arrangement of society is one in which those deemed superior are allowed to harass, discriminate against, oppress, and harm those whom they deem to be inferior, degenerate, or threatening. Bigotry can be directed externally, toward groups to which the bigot does not belong, or internally, toward the bigot's own group.

Every lesson presented in this book applies to both internal and external bigotry. I have developed eleven assertions about bigotry that have guided the writing of this book:

1) Bigotry corrupts everything it touches.

2) Given enough time and opportunity, a bigot will unambiguously confirm their bigotry toward groups they deem inferior, threatening, or degenerate in word, action, or both. This is the iron law of bigotry.

3) Bigoted laws and societies result from bigoted individuals in power.

4) Bigotry *is not* inherent to any group.

5) *No group* is immune to bigotry.

6) All bigoted behavior exists on a spectrum that ranges from the petty to the profound.

7) You can be a victim of bigotry and a bigot at the same time.

8) Being a bigot is a point of identity in the same way that religion and politics are.

9) All bigots see themselves as superior to the targets of their hate.

10) Bigots of every variety are obsessed with gaining and maintaining power and become agitated when they think they are losing it.

11) The victims of bigotry understand how bigotry functions better than bigots do because they have to navigate it to survive it.

INTRODUCTION

Anti-bigotry is the opposite of this. Simply stated, anti-bigotry can be described as the intellectual and moral commitment to oppose bigotry in all its forms, regardless of who engages in it and why (Boston University Center for Antiracist Research, 2022). I will use the terms *anti-bigot* and *opponents of bigotry* interchangeably because the only requirement for being an anti-bigot is to oppose bigotry.

It is impossible to create a comprehensive list of the categories of bigotry in the United States because the list of targets is always evolving. It is with that recognition that I present this list of categories of bigotry largely taken from Boston University's Center for Antiracist Research (2022):

- Ableism

- Ageism

- Anti–Asian/Asian-American racism

- Anti-Black racism and colorism

- Anti-fat bigotry

- Anti-Indigenous bigotry

- Anti-Latinx racism

- Anti–Pacific Islander bigotry

- Antisemitism

- Classism

- Heterosexism and Transphobia

- Islamophobia

- Linguicism

- Religious intolerance

- Sexism

I have taken the liberty of adding anti-White racism to the Center's original list of fifteen categories. My reason for doing this is tied up in my commitment to anti-bigotry. Popular culture debates whether White people, as a group, are subjected to systemic and institutional bigotry, but it is clear that White people can be subjected to interpersonal bigotry by people of color for many reasons. As anti-bigotry rejects all forms of bigotry, regardless of who does it and why, one cannot call themselves an anti-bigot or an anti-racist while also being anti-White. It is important to note that opposing White supremacy is not the same as engaging in anti-White racism. The former is anti-bigotry. The latter is bigotry. It is also important to note that while these categories of bigotry are presented as separate for the sake of discussion and education, in reality, these categories often overlap or intersect. For example, anti-fat bigotry and classism can combine to create a prejudice against overweight, poor people getting access to government programs like SNAP because of an assumption that they are fat because they are lazy.

I am not writing from a detached, objective perspective. I am writing from the position of an anti-bigot who has been subjected to the cruelty of bigots more than I care to recall, but also as a person who challenges bigotry, regardless of the form it takes, every chance I get, and as an academic who studies bigotry. In the interest of keeping it real, I need to state that I am a Southerner born after the fall of Jim Crow. I am a member of the "first generation of African Americans born outside of slavery" and segregation in the history of the United States (Mitchell, 2019, para. 3). I am forty-two years old as I write these words. I grew up in the ruins of Dixie, surrounded by plantations that, as I have grown older, strike me as the perfect metaphor for the South. Southern culture presents itself as well-mannered and well-kept. Still, beneath the alabaster columns and stately trees, the ground is saturated with ancient blood, and the danger of open, bigoted violence lingers in the air like humidity. This is a land where individuals of all races must pick their words carefully. The restless specters of slavery and Jim Crow haunt the South.

INTRODUCTION

There is still significant segregation there, but there is also great integration and an abiding belief that the future can be better than the past. This reality is why I am also a proud Southerner.

Everything I have just written about the South is also true of America, as a whole. The most significant proof that the unquiet ghosts of our collective awful past still haunt our present is the ubiquity of bigots and bigotry in every facet of American life. From cops kneeling on the neck of George Floyd while he pleaded for his life (Mitchell, 2021), to the sheer amount of multidirectional bigotry unleashed across the political spectrum in the wake of the 2024 presidential election, it is fair to say that America has a bigotry problem. The critical question is, *What are we, those who are not bigots, going to do about it?*

My journey into the study of bigotry and the path that has led me to write this book began at the most unusual place: a college football game. Louisiana State University sits along the eastern bank of the Mississippi River, straddling the flood plain and the highland in the southern part of the state capitol of Baton Rouge. The campus itself has a gothic quality. It is a mix of Great Depression–era buildings and the lush canopy of oak, magnolia, crepe myrtle, and cypress trees, among which they are built, that is stark under the azure Louisiana sky. At night, the campus becomes a mosaic of amber streetlights and jagged shadows streaking the pavement, swallowing some corridors in an inky blackness so deep that one could stand in it and not be visible to passersby. This is the backdrop of the football game I attended in the autumn of 2005.

I was a twenty-three-year-old master's student in the history department. I had attended LSU as an undergraduate and was a native of Baton Rouge, so I knew and still know the campus well. On this particular day, I was tailgating with my friend Jackson. He was a year younger than me, with curly brown hair, blue eyes, and a wiry build, thanks to his years as a wrestler in high school. We often attended football games with the friendly exchange of his tailgate food for my access to a clean bathroom, as I had the key to the building where the history department resided. So, overall, a fair trade. Jackson was, and remains, one of my closest friends; he and I had bonded over a mutual affection for Aqua Teen Hunger Force cartoons and Strong Bad's emails.

The year 2005 was a challenging time in Louisiana, following Hurricanes Katrina and Rita. Baton Rouge was overflowing with displaced people from both southeast and southwest Louisiana. In the weeks after the hurricanes, LSU had taken in many college students and their families. It was common for the normally serene campus to be interrupted by the sound of helicopters flying to and from the Bernie Moore Track Stadium (All hands, 2015). By October, those sounds had disappeared, though, as people looked for a distraction from the physical and emotional devastation around them. Many people on campus bore the weight of having had the traumatic experience of being displaced, searching for and finding friends and loved ones, and searching for and never finding friends and loved ones in the aftermath of the twin disasters.

Despite sitting next to one of the blackest neighborhoods in the state, LSU was predominantly White. Less so in 2005, because of the influx of displaced Black students from New Orleans universities, following Hurricane Katrina, including the local historically Black colleges. Baton Rouge is a Southern industrial city, and like other Southern industrial cities, it was starkly segregated by race and class. In those days, LSU leaned very much into its Southern college image. As a graduate student, I had little contact with undergraduates outside my friends behind me in college. Still, I had been told about the complaints of the new Black LSU students, concerning the ubiquity of purple and gold confederate flags at campus tailgates.

The purple and gold confederate flag was a regular topic of debate among students and faculty on LSU's campus in the 2000s. Having grown up in Baton Rouge, I had learned to note it as a red flag of bigotry, denoting the racism of the owner. A history professor once told me that its origin was an insult to the University of Mississippi, but it had lost that meaning by the time I arrived on campus. It was now seen as something of a pathetic whimper for "traditional" Southern masculinity, often called "the surrender rag." The absurdity of waving a symbol associated with the Ku Klux Klan, to cheer on a football team that was almost entirely Black, was not lost on my classmates or on me. But, then again, perhaps that was the point: to remind those Black players and Black students whose campus it was. Despite its image as the Creole State, best known for Mardi Gras, Louisiana is a land of harsh race relations, always teetering on the edge of violence. This was the case in 2005 and still is. Hurricane Katrina had ratcheted the already strained race relations to its breaking point.

I am one of the millions of Black millennials whose political awakening began with watching the government and media response to Hurricane Katrina. Journalist Jelani Cobb (Life Stories, 2021, 52:27) was correct when he said that the hurricane had the same impact on Black America that 9/11 had on the United States as a whole because it changed how we related to society and the government. Yet, for me, the actual moment of complete awareness happened the first time I heard survivors of the storm described as "refugees," and how Black people trying to survive were called "looters" while White people doing the exact same things were never described in such disparaging terms; they simply found food in all that devastation (Mikkelson, 2005; Ralli, 2005). Seeing your government abandon people, some of whom you know personally, many of whom look like you, while many of your fellow citizens harangue the survivors as thieves for stealing things that had to be thrown away due to exposure to floodwaters, changes you. Hurricane Katrina was my intellectual turning point, and I have never turned back.

So, against the backdrop of a city with awful race relations hosting a massive influx of people traumatized by a disaster that had reminded the world of America's racial inequities, I was not surprised when I heard that some of the Black students planned a protest and march for game day. Protesting and college go together like bayous and humidity, so I figured it would be a small affair that would generate some debate on the letter to the editor's page of the local newspaper, and one of the many message boards of the pre–social media explosion internet, but nothing more.

A unique part of Louisiana culture is how much time people spend in mob settings. The state's most famous cultural event, the Carnival season, is a series of street parties around parades that increase in size and frenzy, leading up to Mardi Gras day. At its most intense, game day on the LSU campus is a Mardi Gras street party without the parade. For miles around the stadium, fans and students cook, eat, and drink for hours on end. The air is thick with the smell of various Cajun and Creole delicacies and the cacophony of multiple playlists ranging from Lil Boosie to the always-popular "Callin' Baton Rouge" by Garth Brooks. All this revelry then piles into Tiger Stadium. In 2005, the stadium looked like the Roman Colosseum. It was a worn dark gray and covered in a patchwork of intact and broken dorm-room windows. On Saturday nights, it illuminated the darkness for miles around, and when at its capacity of over ninety thousand, the roars that rose into the sky could be heard for just as far. The thing about a mob is that it takes on its own mood. I had never been among thousands of people who all turned angry at the same time until I saw what the protest looked like coming down the avenue (Clough, 2005; Gibson, 2005).

"Oh, wow," I said to myself as I watched the lengthy line of students march through the campus streets toward the football stadium, chanting and holding signs calling for the university to ban the confederate flag, not just the purple and gold version, on campus. From my vantage point, I could see the reaction of a segment of White fans to this group of Black students exercising their First Amendment rights: first shock, then disgust. I could hear taunts of, "If you don't like it, go to Southern!" yelled at the visibly unbothered protestors. Looking back on it, I think this upset the jeering White fans the most. Not just that Black students had dared to disrupt the sanctity of game day, but that they did not care whom they offended.

Jackson and I attended the game and saw a smaller group of students protesting in the stands (Gibson, 2005). The student section at an LSU football was massive, and it often moved as a single unit in rhythm with the band. However, this time, the student section did not know what to make of the protestors as I do not think they had ever seen a protest in the stands of a sporting event before. I could feel the glare of the ninety-thousand-plus fans bearing down on these Black students, who, in return, never backed down or stopped their chants. I am still impressed by how much willpower it must have taken not to give in to the angry stares of an entire stadium. After the game, Jackson and I bid goodbye to our friends and exited the stadium. Considering LSU had won the game, I noticed the crowds were uncharacteristically somber.

A question for you, the reader, which cites an old Bugs Bunny cartoon I used to see on television regularly as a boy: "Have you ever had the feeling that you're being watched?" It is one of those feelings you cannot shake once it settles. As Jackson and I made our way through the streets back to his truck, I started looking around to dispel the feeling, thinking I had gotten too much sun or had one too many drinks and was just a little buzzed. I did not expect to notice angry eyes in angry faces staring at me.

"Hey, man. Am I losing my mind, or are all these pissed-off White folks looking at me?" I asked as a knot of realization set into my stomach.

"Yep," Jackson answered in his characteristically flat and unbothered tone. I gave him a sideways glance as we moved up the hill leading away from the stadium. The strobes of police lights illuminated his face long enough for me to read his expression. Regardless of the tone of his voice, the way his eyes were darting around the broad avenue, scanning the masses of people, told me everything I needed to know. He could sense something was moving through the throng of LSU fans, and he was worried. I noticed his eyes looking at me every few seconds, but then a realization hit me with the force of a physical blow, causing the knot in my gut to tighten, my heart to quicken, the night to brighten from my eyes dilating, and my muscles to begin to tremble from adrenaline. Jackson was not looking at me. He was looking past me to make sure no one was moving toward me in my blind spot.

We arrived at his truck and quickly realized there was no way we could get off campus. A river of headlights snaked away from us and lit up the darkness under the oak trees. Crowds of people moved past me: parents with children, college students, older people, and teens all going about their business, but always among them, I could see the angry White faces here and there. Amid all this, I could hear my grandfather's voice coming from the recesses of my mind.

My grandfather was one of those Southern men who spent a lifetime working in industry, in his case as a laborer in the local refinery, long enough for Standard Oil to become Exxon. His voice was as raspy as his hands were rough from decades of working around caustic chemicals. He was born into the deep madness of Jim Crow America, he'd fought in the Second World War, and he had seen things, some of which he swore he would never talk about.

One day, as we sat on the porch of his shotgun house when I was in high school and just starting to go to parties, he told me, "Nicky, you keep your eyes on them White boys, especially when they get that liquor in them." I asked him what he meant, and he responded as he peered over his thick lenses at me, "Sometimes, these White boys catch a mood where they get angry at you. Maybe you did something, but most times, you didn't do anything. You must pay attention to how they look at you because when they get in a foul mood, White boys can be as dangerous as anything on this earth and will hurt you or worse." I had grown up in the integrated South, in that liminal space between the suburbs and the country. I had White friends and, at the age of sixteen, a White romantic prospect, so I did not understand why White folks whom I knew and had grown up with would hurt me.

"Why would folks who don't even know me try to hurt me, Bobo?"

My grandfather pushed his glasses back up on his nose and sighed deeply. He paused for a moment, and then he spoke. "Because racism has robbed them of their humanity and replaced it with hate. All that hate makes them beasts. Not all White folks, mind you, but the racist ones, most assuredly. And beasts look for any reason to attack what they hate. Bigots are fucked-up people. Pay attention to how they look at you, Nicky. The eyes never lie because they can't hide that malice. If you ever see that look, you run. You hear me? Ain't no one bad enough to fight a mob of White racists alone. Your job at that moment, and I pray to God you never have to do this, is to survive the night."

I turned to Jackson and said, "We got to get out of here, man."

Jackson looked at me and quickly said, "You ain't lying, but where are we gonna go?"

"Shit," I mumbled to myself.

"Doesn't Mary live on campus?" Jackson asked me. We stared at each other for a few seconds, and then I started fumbling for my phone. Modern cell phones do not have great reception in a large crowd. In 2005, it was even worse. The ringing was crackly, but I felt a sense of relief when I heard Mary's voice answer.

"Hey!" she said in her characteristically chipper voice.

"Hey, yo! What are you doing?" I tried to mask my anxiety as Jackson stood on the side rails of his truck, scanning the crowd for trouble.

"Just hanging out in my dorm."

"Would it be cool if Jackson and I came by to wait out the traffic? It's kind of crazy out here," I said with a fake chuckle as I glared back at a middle-aged White man who was staring at me, with all the menace I could muster.

"Sure! I'll wait outside for y'all."

I hung up the phone, looked up at Jackson, and said, "We are heading to her dorm." Jackson nodded, and we headed out.

Adrenaline is a hell of a hormone. I had been a football player in high school and had engaged in my fair share of male peacocking as a fraternity boy. But this was the first time I had ever actually been afraid. I thought I knew what an adrenaline rush felt like, but nothing had prepared me for the flood that accompanies knowing you are in danger. My entire body tightened, and I could feel my fingernails digging into my hands. A few angry faces moved toward me, but thankfully, they were easily steered away by their friends. After what seemed like hours, I could see Mary sitting on the stone bench outside her dorm in pajama pants and a T-shirt.

She jumped up and swiped us in. Jackson sat perched on the edge of a lobby couch as he took off his hat and exhaled. I sank into the sofa, and Mary walked up with a puzzled look. "Are y'all okay?" she asked.

"Yeah, we're cool," I replied as I tried to summon all the early 2000s R-and-B smoothness I could, to mask the adrenaline that had made me twitchy.

"Uh-huh," she said as she sat next to me, propping up her arm on the back of the couch and resting her head on her hand. She put her hand on my shoulder in that "It's okay to tell me" way people do. I exhaled and told her what had just happened. She tried to maintain a stoic demeanor as she listened, but her eyes betrayed her real emotions.

Mary was White, from rural Louisiana, so she was no stranger to racism. But, like me, she was a stranger to *this*. When she finally spoke, she said, "Okay, well, y'all get comfortable because y'all aren't fucking leaving this dorm until the roads are clear." Part of me wanted to protest, but I knew she was right because my grandfather had been right. I am not a small man now; I was even larger in my youth, but few people, if any, can fight a mob. So, I did what my grandfather told me to do. I survived the night.

It is important to state that there was no race riot on the LSU campus that night. In retrospect, this event was my first significant experience with a large gathering of racists in one place. People whose experiences that night are different from mine have the right to disagree with me about how intense the racism was; this was mine. Still, this terrifying episode in my life also encapsulates why Louisiana, the South, and LSU hold a special place in my heart. I met many of my closest friends and my fiancée there. I received all my degrees, including my doctorate, from LSU, and this book was largely written on that campus. Yes, there was great bigotry active that night, to be sure, but there was also great opposition to the bigotry in the air. This is true of America in general. The events of that October night in 2005 set me on an intellectual path from which I have never deviated. I still look back on that night because I have been chasing an answer to two questions for a long time: *What does bigotry do to a person to turn them into bigots?* and, *What are the rhetorical tactics that bigotry uses to present itself as anything other than hatred?* This book is my attempt at an answer.

As a Black Southern man born after Jim Crow who has attended predominantly White schools, while also being a professor at a primarily White university, it would be intellectually dishonest for me to argue that there has been no progress across multiple fronts over the last one hundred years. Even to call it progress is disingenuous because it has been nothing shy of a cultural revolution. The America we currently inhabit is the product of the collective revolutionary energy of freedom movements such as the civil rights movement, the women's rights movement, the queer liberation movement, and the daring work of Holocaust educators. The concerns over social justice, human rights, and knowledge about the warning signs of resurgent bigotry have been taught to a critical mass of the population as a safeguard for the inevitable day when bigotry begins to try to reassert itself into the cultural mainstream. On the wall of the Holocaust Memorial Museum Hall of Remembrance in Washington, DC, is a quote from former president of the United States and supreme allied commander of the Allied forces during the Second World War, Dwight Eisenhower, which reads:

> The things I saw beggar description . . . The visual evidence and the verbal testimony of starvation, cruelty, and bestiality were so overpowering . . . I made the visit deliberately, in order to be in a position to give first-hand evidence of these things if ever, in the future, there develops a tendency to charge these allegations to propaganda. (Carl Cox Photography, 2005)

The inevitable day future Eisenhower dreaded has arrived, because while those freedom movements pushed the power of bigotry to the fringes of American society and culture, bigotry did not vanish. Now it is on the move again. We see it move in places like Charlottesville, Virginia, where antisemitic racists marched through the UVA campus chanting, "Jews will not replace us," only to instigate a deadly race riot the next day. We even see it with, in fulfillment of Eisenhower's concerns, politicians and activists banning history books and rewriting the history of slavery and Jim Crow in states like Florida (Planas, 2023).

I do not and will not pretend that the lessons, arguments, and examples presented in this book are comprehensive. I fully acknowledge that it is likely that I missed parts of how bigotry teaches bigots how to think and see the world. I hope people use these lessons to identify other emerging and overlooked manifestations of bigotry not addressed in this book. It is my desire that this book will spark conversation within communities, friend groups, and families about the threat bigotry poses to America's stability as a country, and how people should respond to bigotry when they encounter it. I do not advocate for violence, and anyone who interprets this book to be a call for violence has given in to bigotry themselves. I am committed to Proverbs 3:31. The English Standard version reads, "Do not envy a man of violence and do not choose any of his ways"; another translation of "man of violence," found in older versions of Proverbs, is "cruel" or "oppressor" (Biblehub.com, 2024). We will not rid our communities of bigotry through bigotry. The tactics of the anti-bigot are confrontation, denunciation, and ostracism if need be. We are allowed to defend ourselves, but seeking out violence is not a viable tactic because it is morally wrong. This book seeks to expose the ways of bigots so that you may recognize and reject them. It is with this commitment in mind that I thank you, the reader, for taking the time to have this conversation with me.

Let us begin.

References

All Hands on Deck: LSU athletes, coaches bring campus together in the wake of Hurricane Katrina. (2015, August 30). *Reveille*. Retrieved January 31, 2025, from https://lsureveille.com/164230/katrina/all-hands-on-deck-lsu-athletes-coaches-bring-campus-together-in-the-wake-of-hurricane-katrina/?return

Allport, G. (1979). *The nature of prejudice* (25th anniversary edition). Perseus Books. (Original work published 1954).

Bible Hub. (2024). *Proverbs 3:31*. Biblehub.com. Retrieved September 3, 2024, from https://biblehub.com/proverbs/3-31.htm#lexicon

Boston University Center for Antiracist Research. (2022). *Moving toward antibigotry: Collected essays from the Center for Antiracist Research's Antibigotry Convening*. Boston University Center for Antiracist Research.

Carl Cox Photography. (2005). *The quotation by Gen. Dwight David Eisenhower on the exterior of the Hall of Remembrance facing Eisenhower Plaza, the U.S. Holocaust Memorial Museum* [Photograph]. United States Holocaust Memorial Museum. Retrieved September 3, 2024, from https://collections.ushmm.org/search/catalog/pa1159986

Clough, M. (2005, October 25). Protests escalate over purple and gold Confederate flag. WAFB. Retrieved September 3, 2024, from https://www.wafb.com/story/4022337/protests-escalate-over-purple-and-gold-confederate-flag/

Freire, P. (2018). *Pedagogy of the oppressed* (50th anniversary edition). Bloomsbury Academic. (Original work published 1970).

Gay, K. (2013). *Bigotry and intolerance: The ultimate teen guide*. Scarecrow Press. https://play.google.com/store/books/details?id=lX_HF06fGe4C

Gibson, G. (2005, October 23). Students march for ban on Confederate flag. *Reveille*. Retrieved September 3, 2024, from https://www.lsureveille.com/students-march-for-ban-on-confederate-flag/article_55f850d7-798d-53c3-af2d-594282e8d715.html

Gross, J. (2002). *Neighbors: The destruction of the Jewish community in Jedwabne, Poland*. Penguin.

Hendry, P. (2011). *Engendering curriculum history*. Routledge.

Hoffman, D. (2022, November 12). *A firsthand account of the Jim Crow South from historian who lived it* [Video]. YouTube. Retrieved September 3, 2024, from https://www.youtube.com/watch?v=nPBttI52sPw

Kliebard, H. (1982). Curriculum theory as metaphor. *Theory into practice* 21(1), 11–17. https://doi.org/10.1080/00405848209542974

Life Stories. (2021, October 8). *Jelani Cobb interview: Race, politics, Obama, & the complexities of identity* [Video]. YouTube. Retrieved September 3, 2024, from https://www.youtube.com/watch?v=_xy_0S6UTMM&t =2266s

Merriam-Webster. (n.d.-a). Bigotry. *Merriam-Webster.com dictionary*. Retrieved November 19, 2024, from https://www.merriam-webster .com/dictionary/bigotry

Merriam-Webster. (n.d.-b). Bigot. *Merriam-Webster.com dictionary*. Retrieved November 19, 2024, from https://www.merriam-webster .com/dictionary/bigot

Mikkelson, D. (2005, August 31). *Were Hurricane Katrina "looting" photographs captioned differently based on race?* Snopes.com. Retrieved September 3, 2024, from https://www.snopes.com/fact-check/hurricane -katrina-looters/

Mills, C. (2014). *The racial contract*. Cornell University Press. (Original work published 1997). https://play.google.com/store/books/ details?id=GnmuAwAAQBAJ

Mitchell, N. E. (2019). Context matters: Race and the importance of historical framing. *JustSouth Monthly*, 96. Retrieved November 19, 2024, from https://jsri.loyno.edu/sites/loyno.edu.jsri/files/justsouth_monthly _june_2019_mitchell.pdf.

Mitchell, N. E. (2021, July 19). *Black childhood's end: Reflections on the anniversary of the lynching of George Floyd, the conviction of Derek Chauvin, and the source of Black rage at police killings*. The North Star with Shaun King. Retrieved September 3, 2024, from https://www.thenorthstar .com/p/black-childhoods-end-reflections/

Pateman, C. (2018). *The sexual contract* (30th anniversary edition). Stanford University Press. (Original work published 1988).

Pinar, W., W. Reynolds, T. Slattery, and P. Taubman. (1995). *Understanding curriculum: An introduction to the study of historical and contemporary curriculum discourses* (vol. 17). Peter Lang.

Planas, A. (2023, July 20). New Florida standards teach students that some Black people benefitted from slavery because it taught useful skills. *NBC News*. Retrieved November 13, 2024, from https://

www.nbcnews.com/news/us-news/new-florida-standards-teach-black-people-benefited-slavery-taught-usef-rcna95418

Ralli, T. (2005, September 5). Who's a looter? In storm's aftermath, pictures kick up a different kind of tempest. *New York Times*. Retrieved September 3, 2024, from https://www.nytimes.com/2005/09/05/business/whos-a-looter-in-storms-aftermath-pictures-kick-up-a-different.html

Rosiek, J., and K. Kinslow. (2016). *Resegregation as curriculum: The meaning of the new racial segregation in U.S. public schools*. Routledge.

Serwer, A. (2021). *The cruelty is the point: The past, present, and future of Trump's America*. One World.

Smith, E. (2020). *A critique of anti-racism in rhetoric and composition: The semblance of empowerment*. Lexington Books.

Snyder, T. (2017). *On tyranny: Twenty lessons from the twentieth century*. Crown.

Stanley, J. (2020). *How fascism works: The politics of us and them*. Random House.

Stryker, S. (2017). *Transgender history: The roots of today's revolution* (Revised edition). Seal Press. (Original work published 2008).

Watkins, W. H. (1993). Black curriculum orientations: A preliminary inquiry. *Harvard Educational Review* 63(3), 321-339. https://doi.org/10.17763/haer.63.3.26k2433r77v631k2

Watkins, W. H. (2001). *The White architects of Black education: Ideology and power in America, 1865–1954*. Teachers College Press.

Wittig, M. (1992). *The straight mind and other essays*. Beacon Press.

Wozolek, B. (2021). *Assemblages of violence in education: Everyday trajectories of oppression*. Routledge.

Yamamoto, E. K. (1999). *Interracial justice: Conflict and reconciliation in post-civil rights America*. NYU Press.

Young-Bruehl, E. (1998). *The anatomy of prejudices*. Harvard University Press.

Part I

HOW DO BIGOTS THINK ABOUT THE WORLD?

Some years ago, I toured the Holocaust Museum and the African American History Museum in Washington, DC, on the same day. The exhibits told a harrowing story of humanity's inhumanity to other human beings. Of all the artifacts and videos that I saw, the two that stand out most to me were a train car used to transport Jewish people to the concentration camps and a re-creation of the bowels of a slave ship used to bring Africans, including my ancestors, to the plantations of the Western Hemisphere. Staring into the darkness of these vessels, separated by centuries in service but dedicated to the same brutal ideology of bigotry, I wondered: How did people convince themselves to do this?

I believe this question haunts anyone who has ever studied genocide. Questions often beget other questions, so in recent years, I have asked myself how a culture turns its back on any sense of morality to engage in something it knows is wrong. In 1996, the scholar and founder of Genocide Watch, Gregory Stanton, wrote a paper where he described eight stages of genocide, which would later be expanded to ten. His original list of the "genocidal process" in order was:

- Classification

- Symbolization

- Dehumanization

- Organization

- Polarization

- Preparation

- Extermination

- Denial (Stanton, 1996)

Stanton described denial in these terms:

> Every genocide is followed by denial. The mass graves are dug up and hidden. The historical records are burned, or closed to historians. Even during the genocide, those committing the crimes dismiss reports as propaganda. Afterward such deniers are called "revisionists." Others deny through more subtle means: by characterizing the reports as "unconfirmed" or "alleged" because they do not come from officially approved sources; by minimizing the number killed; by quarreling about whether the killing fits the legal definition of genocide ("definitionalism"); by claiming that the deaths of the perpetrating group exceeded that of the victim group, or that the deaths were the result of civil war, not genocide. In fact, civil war and genocide are *not* mutually exclusive. Most genocides occur *during* wars. (1996, p. 4)

Why would those who commit genocide go to such extreme ends to hide evidence of it? Why would they change histories, destroy accounts, and teach their children lies about the past? As a Black Southerner, I am well acquainted with how societies engage in denial about how brutal slavery and Jim Crow were, but that does not answer the question. Perpetrators of genocide deny the evidence because they know it was wrong, and they seek to hide their guilt.

The question of why people would do this in the first place lingers over all forms of bigotry. How does one arrive at the point where seeking to harm people for being different from you even makes sense? There is no shortage of scholarship trying to answer this question. Daniel Goldhagen (1996) wrote in *Hitler's Willing Executioners*:

> The program's first parts, namely the systematic exclusion of Jews from German economic and social life, were carried out in the open, under approving eyes, and with the complicity of virtually all sectors of German society, from the legal, medical, and teaching professions, to the churches, both Catholic and Protestant, to the gamut of economic, social and cultural groups and associations. Hundreds of thousands of Germans contributed to the genocide and the still larger system of subjugation that was the vast concentration camp system. (p. 8)

A bigoted society is a prerequisite for such extreme horrors as genocide. This means that for bigotry to exist on a systemic or culture-wide level, there must be a "critical mass" of individual bigots willing to support it (Mitchell, 2018, p. 5). Institutional bigotry, systemic bigotry, and culture-wide bigotry, like we have seen in apartheid South Africa, Nazi Germany, and America during the Jim Crow period, cannot sustain themselves if there is no mass buy-in among the population. But how does an individual rationalize this to themselves? As a curriculum theorist and critical pedagogue, my answer to this question is that the first form of indoctrination that bigotry provides is an intellectual ordering of the world, and this allows people to rationalize their bigotry.

Part I of *On Bigotry* contains the first three lessons:

- Lesson 1: Bigotry makes you immoral.

- Lesson 2: Bigotry destroys a person's ability to think.

- Lesson 3: All forms of bigotry are intertwined.

I have chosen to elevate these three topics to the beginning, because if we accept that the notion commonly attributed to G. M. Gilbert was correct, when he said that evil is the absence of empathy in describing how the Nazis could justify the evil of the Holocaust, and that genocide is the most extreme form bigotry can take, then it stands to logic that the first capacity that bigotry seeks to rob people of is their ability to engage in moral discernment, which is the ability to tell right from wrong.

In a 1998 interview, Toni Morrison said:

> You cannot enslave people or kill races of people . . . whole races in a continent . . . you cannot do that as a human being unless you have persuaded yourself that it is . . . that A) they are not people or their lives are not worthy or that you have a mission to do that. No human being could do that. You cannot do it unless you believe it is better for those people to be dead. If you can get in an airplane in Brazil and fly around and shoot Indians for sport, now you have to persuade yourself that they are sport. Now, I don't know if that's malice or psychosis, but it exists. And the people who do it know it. They know that they are living a lie. (The Post Archive, 2019, 14:07)

If we accept that Toni Morrison is correct that the prerequisite for hunting human beings in sport is that you must convince yourself that they are sport, then it stands to logic that bigotry seeks to rob people of their ability to think, which is the ability to separate fact from fiction and the rational from the irrational. If we also remember that the Nazis were bigots in every way that one could be and that the victims of a society where difference was a capital offense included Romanies, people with disabilities, communists, Jehovah's Witnesses, and queer people, then it stands to logic that bigotry teaches people to hate groups in all their totality and complexity.

References

Goldhagen, D. (1996). *Hitler's willing executioners: Ordinary Germans and the Holocaust*. Alfred A. Knopf.

Mitchell, N. E. (2018). Remembering the past: Truth and white privilege. *JustSouth Quarterly*, Summer 2018. Retrieved September 4, 2024, from https://jsri.loyno.edu/sites/loyno.edu.jsri/files/JSRI%20Newsletter_justsouth_quarterly_%20Summer_%202018_Mitchell.pdf

The Post Archive. (2019, May 22). *Toni Morrison—intro and interview*. [Video]. YouTube. Retrieved September 4, 2024, from https://www.youtube.com/watch?v=WoTELoC8Q0M

Stanton, G. (1996). *The eight stages of genocide (working paper)*. Genocide Watch. Retrieved September 4, 2024, from http://www.genocide-watch.com/images/8StagesBriefingpaper.pdf

BIGOTRY MAKES YOU IMMORAL

The first mental faculty that bigotry seeks to alter is morality because brutalizing humans is easier if you think of them as less than human and if you think the harm you inflict is morally required.

Merriam-Webster (n.d.) defines *morality* as "a moral discourse, statement, or lesson; a doctrine or system of moral conduct; and conformity to ideals of right human conduct." Synonyms are *virtue* and *decency*. Because bigotry is based on the hatred of people for simply being different, it turns virtues into defects and decency into depravity. Given enough time, it surrounds an individual with a wasteland of moral devastation, with the people closest to them bearing the brunt of the emotional and physical damage.

In his October 2022 column for the *American Conservative*, Matthew Schmitz wrote about the practice of "Friendsgiving" among millennials in a larger commentary about the endemic loneliness facing urbanites. He wrote, "Friendsgiving, likewise, is the feast for those who feel the absence of family, who have moved far from their parents and are not parents themselves" (Schmitz, 2022, para. 10). This article generated a great deal of blowback on social media as being a bit harsh. I found his statement to be an accurate description of "Friendsgiving," but lacking real context about why some people have replaced Thanksgiving with this new take on an old holiday.

For those unaware, Friendsgiving is a gathering of close friends on or around Thanksgiving where people make dishes and eat together in something akin to a potluck dinner. I first encountered the idea of "Friendsgiving" as an undergraduate in the fall of 2003. I was invited to one such gathering the day after Thanksgiving and was told by my friend Alex to bring ice because, "I know you can't cook, and I'm not eating anything you make, so bring ice. We always run out of ice." Despite this clear slander on my culinary skills, I did what Alex told me and brought a couple of pounds of ice to his apartment. I was expecting two or three friends from the area of campus we frequented, affectionately known as "the benches," but to my surprise, there were about ten people there. The spread was sparse but prepared with love; someone had made a turkey, and there were a few pies and a large Tupperware container of stuffing. We all sat around for a few hours, eating, laughing, and playing video games. After dark, a few of us found a local bar to grab a post-Friendsgiving drink.

I sat at the table with Alex as he nursed a cheap beer. "Did you expect so many people?" I asked.

"I did," he responded, pulling a cigarette from the pack tucked in his pants pocket.

Confused, I wondered aloud if those folks had no family to go home to, and Alex replied as he blew smoke into the air, "None that would let them in the door." He could tell from the look on my face that I did not understand what he was getting at. "A lot of families kick their gay, lesbian, and bisexual kids out," he said in his most flat tone, as if he were telling me something as obvious as stating that the earth is round. "If they are lucky, they find family. Friendsgiving is for the found family. It's for the family you pick."

The only response I could muster was, "Damn." I realized how lucky I was that my biological family were not the sort of people who would cast me out for any reason, let alone my sexuality, but Alex's words stuck with me. I would discover a few weeks later that

Friendsmas followed up Friendsgiving in December. In the years after, as an undergraduate, I would ask my mother to make to-go plates for my friends who had nowhere to go for the holidays so they could eat something not from a drive-thru. Even at forty-two, Friendsgiving and Friendsmas are still significant events in my life, full of smiles, hugs, delicious foods, and faces that I only see at these gatherings but miss with all my heart in between.

Not all my college friends I met at "the benches" were outcasts from their families, but some were. We found each other and formed bonds that remain as I write these words. What Matthew Schmitz missed about Friendsgiving is that it is the answer to loneliness, just like Friendsmas. As Alex said, these two new holiday practices are outgrowths of the ancient practice of finding family. In these dynamics, complete strangers become older and younger siblings. I am pleased to say that in addition to my biological sisters and brother, I have an assortment of found siblings of various races, genders, and sexual orientations; some of them have had children who, with no hesitation, call me Uncle Nik.

In the landmark 1990 documentary about the New York Drag Ball Scene, *Paris Is Burning*, the concept of "a house" is described:

> A house, let me put it down sharply, they're families. You can say that. They're families for a lot of children who don't have families. But this is a new meaning of family. The hippies had families, and no one thought nothing about it. It wasn't a question of a man and a woman and children, which we grew up knowing as a family. It's a question of a group of human beings in a mutual bond. (Empire State University, 2017, 24:39)

A house is a found family. It is the opposite of loneliness. It is the rejection of a culture that often punishes those who are different with loneliness. It is also a tactic and a site of resistance in a world that is openly hostile to you, because there is safety in numbers, and it creates a world that hate cannot penetrate. Some may claim that society has moved past the stigmatization of LGBTQ+ youth, but a 2022 Trevor Project report stated that "14% of LGBTQ youth reported that they had slept away from parents or caregivers because they were kicked out or abandoned, with 40% reporting that they were kicked out or abandoned due to their LGBTQ identity" (DeChants et al., 2021, p. 4). The fact of the matter is that many queer kids are still looking for a home after being driven from theirs.

A question I have often asked myself is, what sort of person banishes their child because they are different or, as I would discover later, because they date someone who is of a different religion or race? What sort of person can break that bond over something truly incidental? The answer is a bigot. Bigotry destroys morality in the saddest and most profound ways.

A bigot is taught to place their bigotry at the very center of their entire worldview and web of human connections so that all other human relations are subordinate to it. For example, a racist will destroy his own family and cast out his children for having crossed the color line. A transphobe will banish her child for living his truth. In this sense, the bigot is unwilling to exercise the unconditional love necessary to be a parent. But the bigot is rarely content to be a bigot in the confines of their own home and social network.

It is the lack of morality that leads a bigot to harass or physically harm people actively. They will interject themselves into the object of their hatred's everyday life because their morality is so twisted that they feel that harassing Black people barbecuing in a park, an unfamiliar Black child swimming in a pool, or the accepting family of a transgender child for daring to affirm their gender, is required of them. Never forget that the actual function of bigotry is to be able to brutalize or kill people labeled as inferior, threatening, or degenerate (Mitchell, 2020). This is why a man like Dylann Roof was able to massacre Black parishioners in South Carolina after attending Bible study with them (Drash, 2015). This is why racists were able to attack elderly Asian-American people during the height of the COVID-19 pandemic (Takamura et al., 2022). This is why transphobes in states like Texas are using the power of the state to harass transgender families for seeking gender-affirming care for their children (Klibanoff, 2022). This is why misogynists like Elliot Rodger killed six people in California in 2014 (Branson-Potts & Winton, 2018). Bigotry teaches the bigot to build his entire moral universe around hatred of the other.

The sheer number of historical examples are far too numerous to name. Martin Luther King Jr. couched the goals of the civil rights movement and the opposition to integration in explicitly moral terms. He wrote in his famous *Letter from a Birmingham Jail*:

> Hence segregation is not only politically, economically and sociologically unsound, it is morally wrong and sinful. . . . Is not segregation an existential expression of man's tragic separation, his awful estrangement, his terrible sinfulness? Thus it is that I can urge men to obey the 1954 decision of the Supreme Court, for it is morally right; and I can urge them to disobey segregation ordinances, for they are morally wrong. (King, 1963, para. 13)

King's reasoning for this was simple: segregation caused harm to the segregated and morally devastated those who did the segregating. There are many ways to describe Jim Crow, but it is fair to describe it as "state-sponsored sadism" (Mitchell, 2023, para. 2). The endemic bigotry that ruled Jim Crow America convinced millions of White Americans that it was morally acceptable to inflict all manner of horrors on people of color, including murder, lynching, and rape.

I separate lynching and murder for a reason. A lynching is, above all other things, an act of terror because it is a spectacle. We see this with the lynching of Leo Frank in 1915 for a murder he did not commit, the lynching of Emmett Till in 1955 for a flirtatious remark to a White woman that he never made, and Matthew Shepard, who was lynched in Laramie, Wyoming, his body left tied up in a barbed-wire fence in 1998 because he was gay. Still, some of the most glaring historical examples of how bigotry destroys morality can be seen in any number of lynching photos and postcards taken throughout the twentieth century. In 1919, Will Brown was lynched in Omaha, Nebraska. He was hanged, his body dragged behind a car, set on fire, and then dragged behind a car again. Members of the mob posed with his corpse for a photograph as a hunter would with his prey (Menard, 2010).

What is most striking about the photograph, other than Brown's burning corpse, are the White men and boys posing with wide smiles. Bigotry had taught these men that Black life could be snuffed out with the same level of detachment as one has when hunting a deer. These men were proud of what they did. These men enjoyed what they did.

James Baldwin said it best in his 1963 interview with Dr. Kenneth Clark:

> There are days—this is one of them—when you wonder what your role is in this country and what your future is in it. How, precisely, are you going to reconcile yourself to your situation here and how you are going to communicate to the vast, heedless, unthinking, cruel white majority that you are here. . . . I'm terrified at the moral apathy, the death of the heart, which is happening in my country. These people have deluded themselves for so long that they really don't think I'm human. And I base this on their conduct, not on what they say. And this means that they have become in themselves moral monsters. (Baldwin, 1963, 05:28)

Anyone who can disown their child and love them only on the condition that they appease their bigotry can easily find themselves standing in a crowd, ignoring the screams as a human body is torn apart because their morality has been destroyed by bigotry. As Baldwin put it, all that is left is a "moral monster."

References

Baldwin, J. (1963, June 24). *A conversation with James Baldwin* [Video]. WGBH. Retrieved September 4, 2024, from http://openvault.wgbh.org/catalog/V_C03ED1927DCF46B5A8C82275DF4239F9

Branson-Potts, H., and R. Winton. (2018, April 26). How Elliot Rodger went from misfit mass murderer to "saint" for group of misogynists—and suspected Toronto killer. *Los Angeles Times*. Retrieved September 4, 2024, from https://www.latimes.com/local/lanow/la-me-ln-elliot-rodger-incel-20180426-story.html

DeChants, J. P., A. E. Green, M. N. Price, and C. K. Davis. (2021). Homelessness and housing instability among LGBTQ youth. *The Trevor Project: West Hollywood*. Retrieved November 14, 2024, from https://www.thetrevorproject.org/research-briefs/homelessness-and-housing-instability-among-lgbtq-youth-feb-2022/

Drash, W. (2015, December 17). Inside the Bible study massacre: A mom "laid in her son's blood." *CNN*. Retrieved November 14, 2024, from https://www.cnn.com/2015/06/19/us/inside-charleston-bible-study-massacre/index.html

Empire State University. (2017, April 4). *Paris is burning* [Video]. Retrieved September 4, 2024, from https://learn.sunyempire.edu/media/Paris+is+Burning/1_jifxjkx2

King Jr., M. L. (1963, April 16). *Letter from a Birmingham jail*. Africa Studies Center at the University of Pennsylvania. Retrieved September 6, 2024, from https://www.africa.upenn.edu/Articles_Gen/Letter_Birmingham.html

Klibanoff, E. (2022, May 20). Texas resumes investigations into parents of trans children, families' lawyers confirm. *Texas Tribune*. Retrieved September 4, 2024, from https://www.texastribune.org/2022/05/20/trans-texas-child-abuse-investigations/

Menard, O. (2010). Lest we forget: The lynching of Will Brown, Omaha's 1919 race riot. *Nebraska History* 91, 152–165. https://history.nebraska.gov/document/lest-we-forget-the-lynching-of-will-brown-omahas-1919-race-riot/

Merriam-Webster. (n.d.). Morality. *Merriam-Webster.com dictionary*. In Retrieved November 19, 2024, from https://www.merriam-webster.com/dictionary/morality

Mitchell, N. E. (2020). A lesson from George Floyd: A man was lynched today. *JustSouth Monthly*, 108. Retrieved November 19, 2024, from https://jsri.loyno.edu/sites/default/files/2021-03/justsouth_monthly_june%202020_mitchell.pdf

Mitchell, N. E. (2023, December 28). *Bigotry masquerading as philosophy was a 2023 low point*. MSNBC. Retrieved September 6, 2024, from https://www.msnbc.com/opinion/msnbc-opinion/hamas-israel-antisemitism-islamophobia-rcna131486

Schmitz, M. (2022, October 17). Pumpkin spice loneliness. *American Conservative*. Retrieved September 4, 2024, from https://www.theamericanconservative.com/pumpkin-spice-loneliness/

Takamura, J. C., C. Browne, R. Jeung, A. J. Yellow Horse, D. Kwok, and D. Howard. (2022). Asian American elders: Caught in the crosshairs of a syndemic of racism, misogyny, and ageism during coronavirus disease 2019. *Public Policy and Aging Report* 32(3), 87–93. https://doi.org/10.1093/ppar/prac011

LESSON 2
BIGOTRY DESTROYS A PERSON'S ABILITY TO THINK

Bigotry claims to possess knowledge about individuals that they cannot possibly have because those individuals belong to a group. It replaces critical thinking and the nuance required to discuss the historical context of an event with platitudes and irrationality that justify a bigoted worldview.

Bigotry is the opposite of intellectual, reasoned thought because it makes claims about the world without evidence and encourages irrational behavior. In the absence of evidence, bigotry embraces stereotypes as proof of its claims and will distort or ignore any contradictory information challenging those claims (Allport, 1954/1979). We see this with every form of bigotry. A Jewish Ponzi-scheme architect becomes proof of the Jewish domination of banking. A Black murderer becomes proof of Black criminality. A queer sex predator becomes proof of queer predation. None of these examples proves anything, because while everyone is capable of crime, most people never commit crimes. The majority of Jewish people are not bankers, the majority of Black people never commit murder, and the majority of queer people never commit sex crimes. All of this is empirically true, but bigotry does not accept empirical data because that would mean that bigots would have to think about what they say and believe. Instead, bigots deal in pathologies based on stereotypes and empty platitudes presented as data.

Regarding irrationality, it is a well-established fact in the social sciences that programs such as Temporary Assistance for Needy Families (TANF), which provides money to unemployed and low-income families, lose White support if they are believed to also benefit racial minorities (Wetts & Willer, 2018) even though many people who receive social safety net benefits are White (Shapiro et al., 2017). This trend is so well documented that some activists and intellectuals claim it is why the United States does not have a national universal healthcare system subsidized by taxes. While this assertion remains a topic of debate among political scientists and public health scholars, we are confronted with a particular manifestation of anti-intellectual bigotry—the masochistic kind. It takes a special dedication to bigotry to be willing to inflict harm on yourself as long as the group that you hate also suffers.

There may be no more glaring example of this lesson in action than the raging debates over diversity, equity, and inclusion. It is important to state that the national conversation over DEI is not a simple binary of bigot versus anti-bigot that matches up neatly with those for and those against universities, private companies, and the civil service attempting to comply with civil rights laws. It is intellectually dishonest to ignore the people who support and engage in DEI but are also harsh critics of how it is implemented. The people who take this position, who are a diverse range of people from across the political spectrum, and I count myself among them, are not bigots, and their voices are necessary for creating a working DEI framework.

The same cannot be said for those who completely oppose diversity, equity, and inclusion policies and practices in universities, private, and public institutions. It cannot be denied that some people claim to be anti-DEI because they think it is shorthand for opposing specific policy, not necessarily the values listed in the acronym. However, it is disingenuous to pretend that elements of the anti-DEI movement do not openly oppose all efforts to promote diversity, equity, and inclusion in any area of American life. Some anti-DEI activists have even gone so far as to attack the Civil Rights Act of 1964, the law that ended Jim Crow, because it created the DEI apparatus they loathe so much (Pierce, 2024). In their minds, any person from a marginalized group with a job or admitted to a prestigious university was given these opportunities solely because of some nefarious DEI plot rather than being qualified. We saw this assumption rear its head in the national debate about Harvard and the University of North Carolina considering race as part of holistic admissions.

Bluntly stated, if a person assumes that, for example, every Black person or woman whom they see in a high-profile position, such as a CEO, president of a university, or even an airplane pilot, only got those positions because they were a "diversity hire," then they are an anti-Black bigot, a misogynist, or both. The reason for this is straightforward—they claim knowledge they cannot possibly have. Barring the accuser having access to human resources information from the airline that employs the pilot, the only knowledge they have about the pilot is their race or sex. To assume that a race of people or an entire gender is unqualified for the jobs they hold because of their race is not only irrational, but textbook racism and sexism.

Another example from recent history of how bigotry destroys a person's ability to think is the entire Birtherism movement that rose after the election of Barack Obama in 2008. On its face, the assertion that the first Black president was not born in the United States was absurd. Yet many people even believed, including Obama's successor in the White House (Habeshian, 2024), it was plausible that the United States government, including all its intelligence agencies, the military, and the state governments of Hawaii and Illinois, had missed or ignored that Obama was born outside the country and was ineligible to be president. Birtherism is irrational, but people believed it because they wanted to believe it. Belief, in this case, was that it was impossible for a Black American to be qualified to be president of the United States, so he must be a foreigner; it was more important than evidence; it was more important than thinking.

One of the frustrations anti-bigots of any variety express when dealing with bigots is how easily they dismiss proof that they are wrong. This is because bigotry intellectually operates much like a fundamentalist cult. Skepticism, reason, rationality, evidence, data, and deliberation are discouraged within bigoted movements. In its place is what philosopher Hannah Arendt called the banality of evil, meaning that evil relies on easily recited platitudes and beliefs to justify itself. She coined this term in her work on the 1961 trial of Adolf Eichmann in Jerusalem for his role in the Holocaust. She wrote:

> To be sure, the judges were right when they finally told the accused that all he had said was "empty talk"—except that they thought the emptiness was feigned, and that the accused wished to cover up other thoughts which, though hideous, were not empty. This supposition seems refuted by the striking consistency with which Eichmann, despite his rather bad memory, repeated word for word the same stock phrases and self-invented clichés (when he did succeed in constructing a sentence of his own, he repeated it until it became a cliché) each time he referred to an incident or event of importance to him. Whether writing his memoirs in Argentina or in Jerusalem, whether speaking to the police examiner or to the court, what he said was always the same, expressed in the same words. The longer one listened to him, the more obvious it became that his inability to speak was closely connected with an inability to *think*, namely, to think from the standpoint of somebody else. No communication was possible with him, not because he lied but because he was surrounded by the most reliable of all safeguards against the words and the presence of others, and hence against reality as such. (Arendt, 1963/2006, pp. 67–68)

This is ironic, of course, because Arendt (1959) herself relied on platitudes and showed her inability to think from the standpoint of someone else in her opposition to the integration of Central High in Little Rock, Arkansas. This shows us that one should never assume that education is automatically a bulwark against bigotry, because many of the greatest architects of bigotry have been highly educated men and women; education and thinking are not necessarily interchangeable. Still, Arendt was correct. In the end, bigotry is banal, but banality doesn't preclude genius in the pursuit of humanity's worst impulses. This is why argumentation is such an effective tool for exposing bigotry. Because bigotry is inherently banal, it is incapable of explaining itself.

References

Allport, G. (1979). *The nature of prejudice* (25th anniversary edition). Perseus Books. (Original work published 1954).

Arendt, H. (1959). Reflections on Little Rock. *Dissent* 6(1), 45–56. https://www.dissentmagazine.org/article/reflections-on-little-rock/

Arendt, H. (2006). *Eichmann in Jerusalem: A report on the banality of evil.* Penguin. (Original work published 1963). https://play.google.com/store/books/details?id=yGoxZEdw36oC

Habeshian, S. (2024, January 11). Trump's history of launching "birther" conspiracy theories against rivals. *Axios.* Retrieved November 14, 2024, from https://www.axios.com/2024/01/12/trump-nikki-haley-birther-conspiracy

Pierce, C. (2024, January 15). Conservatives sure have an interesting way of observing Dr. Martin Luther King, Jr.'s birthday. *Esquire.* Retrieved September 4, 2024, from https://www.esquire.com/news-politics/politics/a46393481/mlk-day-turning-point-usa/

Shapiro, I., D. Trisi, and R. Chaudhry. (2017). *Poverty reduction programs help adults lacking college degrees the most.* Center on Budget and Policy Priorities. Retrieved September 4, 2024, from https://www.cbpp.org/research/poverty-and-inequality/poverty-reduction-programs-help-adults-lacking-college-degrees-the

Wetts, R., and R. Willer. (2018). Privilege on the precipice: Perceived racial status threats lead White Americans to oppose welfare programs. *Social Forces* 97(2), 793–822. https://doi.org/10.1093/sf/soy046

ALL FORMS OF BIGOTRY
ARE INTERTWINED

All forms of bigotry are interconnected because people exist in multiple communities. A racist is also a sexist, homophobe, transphobe, and xenophobe.

Every generation of college students in America has an issue or two that were the major political issues of the day that people debated on campus. For elder millennials (I was born in 1982) in college in the 2000s and early 2010s, they were the war in Iraq and gay marriage. I was an undergraduate when *Lawrence v. Texas* struck down sodomy laws as unconstitutional in 2003, which meant that the police could no longer arrest and imprison people for being in same-sex relationships.

The Gallup poll (2025) in August 2005 showed that for the question "Do you think marriages between same-sex couples should or should not be recognized by the law as valid, with the same rights as traditional marriages?" 59 percent of respondents said "should not be valid," while 37 percent said "should be valid." When the Supreme Court ruled in June 2015 in *Obergefell v. Hodges* that the Constitution protected the right of same-sex couples to get married, the July Gallup poll (2025), for the same questions, showed that 58 percent of respondents said "should be valid," with 40 percent disagreeing. I have vivid memories of the debates around gay marriage that played out in the campus newspapers and on the early evening commentary shows on cable news in the twelve years between the *Lawrence* and *Obergefell* decisions.

One moment that stands out was the comparison of the gay rights movement to the civil rights movement. The nature of the debate at the time was that some African American activists felt it was wrong to compare the two movements because, as the logic went at the time and as some people still argue today, Black folks cannot hide their Blackness, but gay people can hide their gayness (Bates, 2015). Essentially, the argument was that by staying in the closet, gay people could escape discrimination. As a younger man, I saw some logic to this argument until I read Lorde's (1983) short essay "There Is No Hierarchy of Oppressions."

The essay laid bare what, or who, had been largely ignored in the debate over comparing the two rights movements: queer Black folks. While it is something of a cliché, it is true that no group is a monolith. Black is not a monolith, and neither are queer folks. The monolith metaphor is typically invoked when describing diverse opinions within a community. However, it can be, and should be, applied to the diversity of community within a community. Let us take Black people as an example. It is wrong to pretend that queer issues, disability issues, religious issues, women's issues, and poverty issues are not Black issues, because Black people belong to all these groups.

This reality is what Lorde (1983) is talking about, and the realization changed my mind on the separateness of the gay rights movement and the civil rights movement. The success of the civil rights movement impacted her life in the same manner that the success of the gay rights movement did because she was a Black lesbian. I have come to realize it is foolish and cruel to demand that a person elevate one set of concerns that apply to them over another set, because it reveals a profound misunderstanding of the nature of oppression. In the history of humanity, there has never been a form of bigotry that only targeted a single group because human beings do not exist in single groups. If you show me an antisemite, I will show you an anti-Hispanic bigot and a misogynist because there are Hispanic Jews and Jewish women. If you show me an anti-White bigot, I will show you a transphobe because there are White transgender men, women, and nonbinary people.

The argument that tried to set the gay rights movement and the civil rights movement as separate political movements willfully ignored the existence of queer Black folks for whom both movements affirmed their full citizenship. At that time, and still today, many people have interpreted intersectionality to be something of a decoder ring, where privilege and disparity can be easily assigned. This is why poor White folks sometimes express anger with the language of White privilege. While it is true that poor White people enjoy White privilege in society, this does not erase the suffering and marginalization they experience because of poverty. Whiteness does not dull hunger pains or the ravages of disease with no affordable treatment. People easily forget that humans exist in multiple communities simultaneously, identity is lived, and that, as Dr. King asserted, we all exist in a web of mutuality (Crenshaw, 1989; King, 1963; Yep, 2016).

In 1865, in Pulaski, Tennessee, six former Confederate soldiers created a social fraternity that they named the Ku Klux Klan (Southern Poverty Law Center, n.d.; Baudouin, 2011). In short order, that group would become famous for the terrorization and murder of former enslaved people and of reconstruction government officials. The federal government's weight would crush the original Klan under President Ulysses Grant. The second Klan would rise in 1915 and gain national power until its implosion right before the United States entered the Second World War. The Klan that exists today is the third iteration of America's oldest terrorism group (Southern Poverty Law Center, n.d.).

If you asked most Americans to name a group the Ku Klux Klan hates, it would be safe to wager that the first group they would mention is "Black people." They would not be wrong. The Klan has a long, explicit history of terrorizing the Black community across the country. This knowledge is so ubiquitous that it is not uncommon to find the GIF of Marsha Brady saying, "Sure, Jan," with Jan replaced by Klan to mock bigots in many comment sections on social media. What is less known is that the Klan did not then and does not now limit their hatred to Black people.

History tells us that while Black people were the first targets of the original Klan and have remained a target for all later versions of the hate group, the list of targets has grown to include Jewish people, Muslims, immigrants, Hispanic people, Roman Catholics, queer people, and transgender people, to name a few (Southern Poverty Law Center, n.d.). We can view this in two ways. First, this is confirmation that bigots will always seek new targets. This is addressed later, in lesson 5. Second, this hatred can be seen as intersectional because groups are intertwined. Within the Black community, there are Jews, Muslims, immigrants, Hispanic folks, Roman Catholics, queer people, and transgender people.

Another example of this is how often anti-queer bigotry and misogyny are intertwined. If we consider the homophobic and transphobic males, their hatred of gay, bisexual, and pansexual men often lies in their perception that the gay, bisexual, and pansexual man is intimate with other men, something the homophobic man believes is the proper role of a woman. They may even extend their homophobic gaze to the mannerisms of a gay, bisexual, or pansexual man and deem them "feminine," which is to say the way they walk, talk, and gesture is something the bigot associates with women. For the transphobic male, transgender women represent something of an intellectual crisis, because the transphobe may not be able to tell, or "clock," the transgender woman and find themselves attracted to them. In this case, the realization that they are attracted to a transgender woman can trigger a violent response that results in grievous harm or the murder of the trans person by the transphobic man. Now, it is important to write at this juncture that this is not me expressing support for the gay or trans panic defense that often gets cited in defense of people charged with the assault or murder of a queer person. What I am saying is that bigotry toward queer people, trans people, and women sits at the center of all of it.

Anti-queer bigotry, anti-trans bigotry, and misogyny are intertwined because hatred toward queer people and trans people are expressions of hatred toward women and broader bigotry toward anyone who does not follow "traditional gender roles." Some readers may dismiss this as "woke nonsense," but the argument I have presented here is the same one that Justice Neil Gorsuch, appointed to the Supreme Court by President Donald Trump, made in the 2020 case *Bostock v. Clayton County*. Gorsuch wrote that:

> An employer who fires an individual for being homosexual or transgender fires that person for traits or actions it would not have questioned in members of a different sex. Sex plays a necessary and undisguisable role in the decision, exactly what Title VII forbids. (*Bostock v. Clayton County*, 2020, p. 2)

Americans tend to think of civil rights as sets of laws affirming the rights of separate groups. This assumption is understandable, given how politics separates people into interest groups and focuses on community interests. I prefer to think of civil rights in the sense that King and Lorde understood them. I view civil rights as a "chain" in which each group (Mitchell, 2022, para. 20) represents a link: Black rights, which are linked to women's rights, which are linked to queer rights, which are linked to disability rights, which are linked to . . . and so forth, and so on. The old metaphor that "a chain is only as strong as its weakest link" applies here. Civil rights are only as strong as the weakest group, and this is compounded by "the fact that we [all] occupy multiple links in the chain simultaneously" (Mitchell, 2022, para. 22). When society allows one link to break, it is the same as saying, "We admit that not everyone deserves complete civil rights protection." At this point, the only thing to be determined is which groups are part of the chain and which links are removed

(Mitchell, 2022). Bigots know this, which is why, as we will discuss in the next lesson, they seek out new targets constantly.

References

Bates, K. (Host). (2015, July 2). African-Americans question comparing gay rights movement to civil rights [Audio podcast transcript]. In *All Things Considered*. National Public Radio. Retrieved September 4, 2024, from https://www.npr.org/2015/07/02/419554758/african-americans-question-comparing-gay-rights-movement-to-civil-rights

Baudouin, R. (ed.). (2011). *Ku Klux Klan: A history of racism and violence* (6th edition). Southern Poverty Law Center.

Bostock v. Clayton County, Georgia, *Altitude Express, Inc. v. Zarda*, and *R.G. & G.R. Harris Funeral Homes Inc. v. Equal Employment Opportunity Commission* 590 U.S. (2020). Retrieved September 4, 2024, from https://www.supremecourt.gov/opinions/19pdf/17-1618_hfci.pdf

Crenshaw, K. (1989). Demarginalizing the intersection of race and sex: A Black feminist critique of antidiscrimination doctrine, feminist theory and antiracist politics. *University of Chicago Legal Forum*, 1989(1), 139–167. https://chicagounbound.uchicago.edu/uclf/vol1989/iss1/8

Gallup. (2025). *LGBTQ+ rights*. Retrieved February 5, 2025, from https://news.gallup.com/poll/1651/gay-lesbian-rights.aspx

King Jr., M. L. (1963, April 16). *Letter from a Birmingham jail*. Africa Studies Center at the University of Pennsylvania. Retrieved September 6, 2024, from https://www.africa.upenn.edu/Articles_Gen/Letter_Birmingham.html

Lorde, A. (1983). There is no hierarchy of oppressions. *Interracial Book for Children Bulletin* 14(3&4), 9. https://digital.library.wisc.edu/1711.dl/ZV6IH7UCTMVC28H

Mitchell, N. E. (2022, April 4). There still is no hierarchy of oppression. *North Star with Shaun King*. Retrieved September 4, 2024, from https://www.thenorthstar.com/p/there-still-is-no-hierarchy-of-oppression

Southern Poverty Law Center. (n.d.). *Ku Klux Klan*. Retrieved September 4, 2024, from https://www.splcenter.org/fighting-hate/extremist-files /ideology/ku-klux-klan

Yep, G. A. (2016). Toward thick(er) intersectionalities: Theorizing, researching, and activating the complexities of communication and identities. In K. Sorrells & S. Sekimoto (eds.), *Globalizing intercultural communication: A reader* (pp. 86–94). Sage.

HOW DOES BIGOTRY TEACH PEOPLE TO THINK?

As a student of the history of ideas, and as an anti-bigot, a document to which I often return is the closing argument delivered by the U.S. chief prosecutor, and later associate justice of the U.S. Supreme Court, Robert H. Jackson, in the ruins of Nuremberg, Germany, on July 26, 1946. The Nuremberg trials marked the first time in modern world history that the military and civilian leadership of a country were charged and convicted of:

- Crimes against peace—defined as participation in the planning and waging of a war of aggression in violation of numerous international treaties.

- War crimes—defined as violations of the internationally agreed-upon rules for waging war.

- Crimes against humanity—namely, murder, extermination, enslavement, deportation, and other inhumane acts committed against any civilian population, before or during the war; or persecution on political, racial, or religious grounds in execution of or in connection with any crime within the jurisdiction of the Tribunal, whether or not in violation of domestic law of the country where perpetrated. (USHMM, 2018, para. 5)

It was the first time that a government would be held accountable for violating the human rights of minorities within their borders and within the territory they controlled.

Jackson's (1946) final lines still strike me as timeless wisdom, transcending decades:

> It is against such a background that these defendants now ask this Tribunal to say that they are not guilty of planning, executing, or conspiring to commit this long list of crimes and wrongs. They stand before the record of this trial as blood-stained Gloucester stood by the body of his slain King. He begged of the widow, as they [the Nazis] beg of you: "Say I slew them not." And the Queen replied, "Then say they were not slain. But dead they are." If you were to say of these men that they are not guilty, it would be as true to say there has been *no war*, there are *no slain*, there has been *no crime*. (p. 107)

Jackson's remark about the "background" and his reference to the main character of Shakespeare's *Richard III*, Richard the Duke of Gloucester—and his denial of the murder of Henry VI to his daughter-in-law, Queen Anne—was a metaphor for the bloody, bigoted history of the Nazi regime that everyone at Nuremberg knew to be factual after the revelation of the Holocaust. His argument was both a moral appeal and a demand that the Tribunal believe the history laid before them that they had seen with their own eyes. Nearly eighty years later, these words still provide us with the language to articulate the scope and depth of the accountability required to address the brutality and dehumanization inherent to all forms of bigotry.

Some will ask why I have chosen the Nuremberg trials as a means of making sense of other forms of bigotry. After all, the Holocaust and, for example, the brutality experienced by African Americans in the United States are different events with radically different contexts. Others will point out that the war crime trials were, in part, over European antisemitism, whereas the antiblackness I refer to exists in an American context, so these are radically different phenomenon. My response to both questions is the same: I see no intellectual differences between European antisemitism and American antiblackness or any other form of bigotry. While the targets and the rhetoric differs, the core ideology remains the same.

Nazism began as an idea. As it spread, it evolved and adapted to the new environments in which it found itself, until it became the dominant ideology through which Germany saw itself and the world. If it sounds like I am describing Nazism as an organism, that is because I am. Like organisms, ideas change in response to the environments in which they exist overtime and combine with other ideas to create more complex concepts and ideologies. This fact makes up the core of the relationship between antisemitism, racism, and every other form of bigotry; the term for an idea that acts like an organism is a *meme* (Dawkins, 1976/2016; Krippendorff, 2013).

You, the reader, may find this odd because the term *meme* is now most commonly used to describe GIFs, images, clips, terms, dances, styles of dress, and phrases that spread via social media. This commonly understood definition does not contradict the academic one (Dawkins, 1976/2016; Krippendorff, 2013). Everything that is commonly understood to be a meme is also an idea. This is especially true with terms and phrases. For example, consider how the term *Karen* spread from a long line of terms in Black English vernacular that refer to a racially hostile White woman, to a catch-all for women who are hostile to people they view as beneath them in social situations (Bates, 2020). The idea began in one specific cultural environment and spread to the culture as a whole, as people were taught what the term meant and how to use it. Acknowledging that memes, or ideas, instruct people in how to think and act is key to understanding bigotry.

I state in lesson 4 that because bigotry is taught, it has a curriculum and a pedagogy that we can observe, document, and study. In philosophical terms, bigotry is a form of gnostic knowledge, which is to say that it deals with identity (Davis, 2008). Because of this, the bigoted curriculum is an identity-oriented curriculum, meaning that it seeks to shape how people define themselves and those around them. In short, bigotry teaches people how to think and how to act in a way that is similar to how religions instruct members of the faith. Like all instruction, it is a process.

It is critical to point out here that I am not arguing that bigotry is a new form of religion. I understand that making such pronouncements about political ideologies has been in vogue now for some time, with some ideologies being described with the suffix "ism" called "new religions," and the followers of some political parties being accused of being members of "cults." I do assert that religion is a meme, meaning an idea that evolves over time, that instructs people how to think and behave. Merriam-Webster's (n.d.) dictionary defines *orthodox* as "conforming to established doctrine especially in religion." *Orthodoxy* typically refers to following established thought, and *orthopraxy* typically refers to correct behavior (Oxford Reference, 2024). Like all religions and secular ideologies, bigotry instructs bigots in its own orthodoxy and orthopraxy. This is the subject of the second part of this book.

Part II of *On Bigotry* contains the following lessons:

- Lesson 4: Bigotry is taught.

- Lesson 5: Bigotry always seeks new targets.

- Lesson 6: Bigotry is paranoid.

- Lesson 7: Bigotry makes you violent.

If we follow the framing of religious studies, lessons 1 through 3 would be understood as articles of faith. They are intellectual and moral commitments to see the world in a certain way. Lessons 4 through 7 are correct thought and correct actions, or orthodoxy and orthopraxy, which form the foundation of how bigots construct their interactions with society and their dedication to spread bigoted ideas and ideology into new environments.

In his 1965 debate with the founder of the *National Review* and one of the most influential conservative intellectuals, William Buckley at Cambridge University, James Baldwin speculated on the intellectual underpinnings of White America's resistance to desegregation and the things they were doing in the name of preserving Jim Crow segregation, such as harming and murdering Black children. Baldwin said:

> The Mississippi or Alabama sheriff, who really does believe, when he's facing a Negro boy or girl, that this woman, this man, this child must be insane to attack the system to which he owes his entire identity. . . . They've been raised to believe . . . No matter what disaster overtakes them, they have one enormous knowledge and consolation which is like a heavenly revelation: at least they are not black. Now I suggest that of all the terrible things that can happen to a human being, that is one of the worst. I suggest that what has happened to white southerners is in some ways, after all, much worse than what has happened to Negroes there. (American Archive of Public Broadcasting, n.d., 16:30)

The Alabama sheriff was not born a bigot or born a person who would view a child protesting their oppression as insane. They were not born with that paranoia that drives them to oppress Black people to preserve their sense of self. They were not born with the intellectual ability to take comfort in the fact that they are not Black. So, what terrible thing, as Baldwin described it, happened to the Alabama sheriff to turn them into a moral monster? They were taught from childhood, or at a vulnerable moment in their development, to think this way by individuals, groups, or their community. The Alabama sheriff, like many bigots, was radicalized (Brunel University, n.d.) to be a bigot by other bigots.

All bigots begin their journeys into bigotry as victims.

References

American Archive of Public Broadcasting. (n.d.). *Debate: Baldwin vs. Buckley* [Video]. Retrieved September 5, 2024, from https://american-archive.org/catalog/cpb-aacip_151-sn00z71m54

Bates, K. (Host). (2020, July 15). What's in a "Karen"? [Audio podcast episode]. In *Code Switch*. National Public Radio. Retrieved September 5, 2024, from https://www.npr.org/2020/07/14/891177904/whats-in-a-karen

Brunel University. (n.d.). *What is grooming and radicalisation?* Retrieved September 5, 2024, from https://reportandsupport.brunel.ac.uk/support/what-is-grooming-and-radicalisation

Davis, B. (2008). *Inventions of teaching: A genealogy.* Routledge. https://play.google.com/store/books/details?id=lRUNqxbs3kUC

Dawkins, R. (2016). *The selfish gene* (40th anniversary edition). (Original work published 1976). Oxford University Press. https://play.google.com/store/books/details?id=o59HDAAAQBAJ

Jackson, R. H. (1946). Closing arguments for conviction of Nazi war criminals. *Temple Law Quarterly* 20(1), 85–107. https://heinonline.org/HOL/Page?handle=hein.journals/temple20&div=17&g_sent=1&casa_token=&collection=journals

Krippendorff, K. (2013). *Content analysis: An introduction to its methodology* (3rd edition). Sage.

Merriam-Webster. (n.d.). Orthodox. In *Merriam-Webster.com dictionary*. Retrieved November 19, 2024, from https://www.merriam-webster.com/dictionary/orthodox

Oxford Reference. (2024). *Orthopraxy.* Oxford Reference. Retrieved November 19, 2024, from https://www.oxfordreference.com/display/10.1093/oi/authority.20110803100255215

United States Holocaust Memorial Museum. (2018, January 5). *Nuremberg Trials.* Retrieved September 5, 2024, from https://encyclopedia.ushmm.org/content/en/article/the-nuremberg-trials

LESSON 4
BIGOTRY IS TAUGHT

No one is inherently bigoted. Like any other form of thought, bigotry is taught to children by their parents and communities.

One of the great lies bigots claim is that bigotry is inherent to humanity. Merriam-Webster's (n.d.) dictionary defines *inherent* as "involved in the constitution or essential character of something" and "belonging by nature or habit." To assert that someone or an entire group of people is inherently bigoted means they are born that way. This is false on its face because people are born with no knowledge of the world or the social divisions that human beings have created, like race, gender, sexual orientation, and nationality. These divisions, and the bigotry attached to them, only exist in the human imagination and must be taught to youth to exist. Claiming that bigotry is natural is an attempt to shield bigoted thoughts and actions from rebuke.

In her 1998 interview with Jana Wendt, Toni Morrison described a harrowing scene she witnessed during the later days of Jim Crow:

During the Civil Rights Movement, there were women who would rush out to the schoolyards when they were trying to integrate schools, and they would push over the school buses that were bringing black children to the school. Push them over and set them afire. And when I saw that I was wondering whether I could ever get a group of black women under any circumstances from any walk of life to hurt some white children, to set a bus on fire full of white children, for any reason. Prostitutes, drug addicts, ministers, teachers, black women of any level. Could I call them all together and say we have got to burn these white children? And I didn't believe I could ever find that. So, I thought those white mothers, they were not just white women, they had actually had children they knew what that was like, but they could do that to those children. They could spit at a child. So, I thought that is the most degrading life I could imagine. Of being an adult who could do that. If I were those white people, the absence of that shame was so profound that the real victim was not those children. It was those women who had given up everything: their motherhood, their womanhood, their citizenship, everything to do that nasty thing. Now, that is a true victim of history. . . . It always is shocking. It's always shocking, and I insist on being shocked. I'm never going to become immune. (The Post Archive, 2019, 19:43)

Morrison is, of course, correct. Bigotry is shocking to watch, and it is critical for anti-bigots never to become numb to bigoted rhetoric and actions. But Morrison is telling this story to prompt us to ask a more profound question: How does a White mother, who has born and raised children of her own, arrive at the point where it makes sense to her to attack a bus full of Black children? How does a man conclude that women are inferior to him despite him having a mother and possibly a wife and daughters? The answer is short and no different from the Alabama sheriff to whom Baldwin alluded. They were taught that this brutal behavior—and the brutal thoughts that justify it—was normal.

Bigotry is a curriculum taught in institutions, communities, and homes. It functions in the same way that all curricula do. Bigotry can be taught explicitly and implicitly as part of the formal school curriculum, the community culture, and the home. It can also be taught in the hidden sense that people glean from example and observation (Pinar et al., 1995).

The instructional process is simple. A bigot teaches an individual that a specific type of difference is negative, inferior, and a threat. Racists do this with skin color. A White racist teaches other White people that darker-skinned people are inferior. So, they deserve to be shunned, oppressed, or harmed. Inversely, the racist of color teaches other people of color that White people are inferior and deserving of the same treatment for which the White racist advocates. Of course, the rhetoric may differ, but that difference is superficial. A White racist may say that Hispanic people are prone to violent crime, while a Black racist may say that White people bring desolation everywhere they go. Still, the bigoted curriculum remains the same: the group subject to bigotry is inherently harmful for some reason, violent in this example, which justifies any bigoted actions toward them.

The impact of taught bigotry extends beyond how people interact in the present. It also shapes how people think about, remember, and teach the past. To return to Stanton's (1996) genocide process, the final stage is denial. Bigots have an investment in perpetuating denial because it keeps people arguing over what happened in the well-documented past, which, in turn, maintains bigotry's influence on the state of community relations while insulating it from direct scrutiny. It should come as no surprise that bigotry, which teaches the lie that people are naturally divided into inferior and superior groups, also teaches outright lies and omissions about history and denies historical facts. Many of these lies and omissions have made it into American elementary, middle, and high school instruction through so-called Critical Race Theory bans and variations of "Don't Say Gay" laws.

Bigotry in the curriculum is why many Americans of all races were unaware that the 1921 Tulsa Race Massacre, in which the prosperous Black Greenwood neighborhood was destroyed in a White supremacist-led pogrom, happened until it was highlighted on HBO's "Watchmen," in 2019. The Tulsa Race Massacre is a significant event, but it's only a grain of sand on the island of knowledge about the bloody and profound history of American bigotry denied to students in this country. The founder of Black History Month and second Black PhD graduate from Harvard University, Carter G. Woodson (1933/2005), called this form of historical omission, and the more significant teaching of bigotry as if it were normal, "miseducation." The bigoted interest in maintaining denial is the reason why certain facts, like the mass lynching of Italians in New Orleans in 1891 and the Red Summer in 1919, are omitted from the official history and civics curriculum across the United States. The people who set the curriculum, often state lawmakers, are compelled to sanitize history for the same reason that the last stage of any genocide or atrocity is denial: if citizens don't know their actual history, they will not be able to recognize the signs of popular politically empowered bigotry rising again. This hinders citizens' ability to fully participate in democracy because they are misinformed about what their culture is capable of, and it allows bigots to go undetected in society and in critical positions of power.

Education is not confined to the classroom or the lecture hall. Curriculum is not restricted to books and PowerPoint slides. Much of what human beings learn about the world and themselves happens as they live within a society. People learn how to interact with other people through observation. For example, a Jewish child has no idea how to behave in the synagogue until their parents tell them and they see how people behave during services. Perhaps the best example of this dynamic is people learning to act in a restaurant and interact with the waitstaff. Like the child in the synagogue, the individual may have been instructed how to behave, but they also learn from being in the environment as they observe how other people behave. The common name for this sort of instruction is "social mores," or acceptable behavior. Bigotry can be, and often is, taught in the same way. People observe how others are treated and mimic accordingly.

A glaring example of this is how men learn sexist behaviors toward women. A group of men catcall a woman walking down the street, and other men join them. Why? Observation of how different men behave has taught them that the sexual harassment of women, with violent undertones and sometimes overtones, is acceptable. Another example is the harassment of transgender youth in schools, by the schools themselves, via laws and policies that forbid teachers to address students by their chosen names and pronouns. A question that should be asked is, *What does this teach cisgender students about how transgender students should be treated?* Suppose a student sees adults in positions of power mistreating people for being different for any reason. In that case, it teaches them that mistreating those groups is acceptable, and a link in the chain of bigoted logic is forged.

Symbols also teach people. Historian Timothy Snyder (2017) wrote in *On Tyranny*:

> The symbols of today enable the reality of tomorrow. Notice the swastikas and other signs of hate. Do not look away, and do not get used to them. Remove them yourself and set an example for others to do so. . . . In the politics of the everyday, our words and gestures or their absence count very much. (pp. 32–33)

To illustrate this, Snyder (2017) points to how the Soviets dehumanized farmers as pigs to justify the seizure of their property during Stalin's early reign in the 1930s, how the Nazis' branding of shops and properties as Jewish signaled them for harassment, harm, and eventual genocide, and how Soviet citizens and Germans accepted this as part of everyday life (pp. 33–35). His examples perfectly encapsulate how symbols teach bigotry. An American example of how bigots in power use symbols to normalize bigotry are Confederate monuments that still dot the landscape in the South.

These monuments were erected primarily during the bloody imposition of Jim Crow, when the federal government gave up on establishing a multiracial democracy and allowed the South, explicitly, and the rest of the country, implicitly, to establish a racial caste system that lasted until the civil rights movement overthrew it. Politically, they were victory trophies of White supremacy over a federal government that ended slavery and tried, albeit briefly, to guarantee the rights of freedmen. Symbolically, the monuments were a curriculum designed to teach people of color that they had no rights, including the right not to be physically harmed or killed, which White people were obligated to respect. This same curriculum taught White people that slavery and segregation were justified and that enslavers and segregationists were moral people rather than bigots engaged in crimes against humanity. In the wake of the Mother Emanuel church shooting in 2015, a multiracial coalition pushed to remove Confederate statues and other Confederate iconography. This effort was renewed in the wake of the race riot in Charlottesville in 2017 and after the lynching of George Floyd in 2020. Just like erecting the Confederate monuments enabled the madness of Jim Crow to rule for decades, their removal enables a possible future free from a world where people are taught to be bigoted.

Some people dismiss the power of symbols to their own detriment. Ta-Nehisi Coates (2017) echoes Snyder's assertion about symbols when he wrote, "It has been said that the first Black presidency was mostly 'symbolic,' a dismissal that deeply underestimates the power of symbols. Symbols don't just represent reality but can become tools to change it" (p. xvi). Symbolic power is just a fancy way of saying "meaning," but the power of meaning is real power in any society. A church is just a decorated building until people imbue it with Christian meaning. A flag is just a piece of colored cloth with patterns sewn into it until people imbue it with nationalistic meaning. Racial, sexual, gender, and religious slurs are just words; bigoted meanings make them slurs. This reveals what bigotry teaches people, which makes it so dangerous. Bigotry teaches a twisted version of meaning that is applied to all of humanity.

Ultimately, social mores and laws instruct people on how others should be treated, just as much as instruction in classrooms and books does. This lesson presented here is not confined to racism, sexism, and transphobia. Consider how poor people and rural people are dismissed as "ghetto" and "rednecks" by the more affluent sections of society, to the point that they are blamed for their own marginalization and denied the recognition of their legitimate grievances. The ability to ignore human suffering does not come naturally to people.

The ability to ignore, dehumanize, and oppress is taught.

References

Coates, T. N. (2017). *We were eight years in power: An American tragedy.* One World.

Merriam-Webster. (n.d.). Inherent. In *Merriam-Webster.com dictionary.* Retrieved November 19, 2024, from https://www.merriam-webster.com/dictionary/inherent

Pinar, W., W. Reynolds, T. Slattery, and P. Taubman. (1995). *Understanding curriculum: An introduction to the study of historical and contemporary curriculum discourses* (vol. 17). Peter Lang.

The Post Archive. (2019, May 22). *Toni Morrison—intro & interview* [Video]. YouTube. Retrieved September 5, 2024, from https://www.youtube.com/watch?v=WoTELoC8Q0M

Snyder, T. (2017). *On Tyranny: Twenty Lessons from the Twentieth Century.* Crown.

Stanton, G. (1996). *The eight stages of genocide* (working paper). Genocide Watch. Retrieved September 5, 2024, from http://www.genocide-watch.com/images/8StagesBriefingpaper.pdf

Woodson, C. (2005). *The miseducation of the Negro.* Dover Publications. (Original work published 1933).

BIGOTRY ALWAYS SEEKS NEW TARGETS

Bigotry targets weaker groups first, to build momentum to attack larger, more powerful groups later; it's all the same hatred.

While lesson 3 is about how bigots see their opposition as an interlocking chain of threats, lesson 5 is about momentum. A common observation among ordinary people who do not pay attention to bigotry until it flares up in ways they cannot ignore is, "how rapidly bigotry spreads." Although this observation is understandable, it is false. Bigotry does not spread rapidly. Another observation common to older Black Southern communities, which I grew up hearing from my parents and grandparents, is that "racism is bubbling beneath the surface" and "the racism is more hidden now, but it is still there." It may appear that bigotry is spreading rapidly, but in reality, it is spreading constantly, and ordinary people notice when it has the required cultural momentum to impact society in horrifying ways.

Arguably, the most enduring articulation of this lesson comes from German Lutheran pastor Martin Niemöller. He was an early supporter of the Nazi party before becoming one of Adolf Hitler's most outspoken critics, which landed him in the concentration camp system in 1938 and eventually imprisoned at Dachau in 1941 until the end of the war (USHMM, n.d.). He famously described the Holocaust in these terms:

> First they came for the socialists, and I did not speak out—because I was not a socialist.
> Then they came for the trade unionists, and I did not speak out—because I was not a trade unionist.
> Then they came for the Jews, and I did not speak out—because I was not a Jew.
> Then they came for me—and there was no one left to speak for me. (USHMM, 2023)

Niemöller's words can be read in two ways. First, as a commentary on how the indifference to bigotry allowed it to spread in Nazi Germany until it plunged the nation into war, genocide, and dismemberment by the Allied powers (USHMM, 2023). This is how I first encountered this passage in high school, and it raises a critical point. Bigotry thrives on indifference and the mistaken belief that forms of bigotry that do not impact us directly are not our problem.

The second reading is something I have arrived at more recently through the study of bigotry and genocide. Niemöller's quote is a plain-text description of how bigotry uses momentum to spread and generate support and complicity for its violent designs. Contrary to popular belief, Jewish people were not the only victims of the Holocaust, nor did the Holocaust happen overnight. Communists, LGBTQ+ folks, Romany, and political dissenters were also targeted. The Nazis used the hatred of these other groups and antisemitism to build the necessary momentum to steadily increase the oppression of everyone whom they considered "undesirable," until they could enact their infamous "final solution." Niemöller's famous quote should be read as wisdom, admonishment, and warning.

Peabody Award–winning video essayist Natalie Wynn echoes Niemöller's dire warning about how bigotry is always seeking to build momentum for nefarious ends in her 2017 video essay on how to recognize alt-right fascists. She said:

The common thread in all fascist strategies is deception and manipulation, often aimed at representing what is essentially an attack on non-white people as a defense of white people and "white culture." The fascist's long-term goal is a homogenous ethnostate, which at some point will require massive ethnic cleansing of one kind or another. But of course, they won't tell you about that unless they think you're also a fascist. The strategic fascist knows it's better to start with realistic, achievable goals, and that means focusing first on stopping non-white immigration, something they'll try to get you—the centrist, conservative, or liberal—on board with by emphasizing the danger and criminality of non-white immigrants and refugees. If they can whip up enough racist sentiment with that rhetoric, they can later turn that energy against the non-white people who are already here. (Contrapoints, 2017, 15:47)

A contemporary, nonviolent example of Wynn's description of how bigotry utilizes momentum in a cultural and political sense is the strange evolution of the word *woke*.

According to Merriam-Webster's (n.d.-b) dictionary, the definition of *woke* is being "aware of and actively attentive to important societal facts and issues (especially issues of racial and social justice)." But this is not the whole story, nor is it the whole definition, because it leaves out the strange space the word occupies in American culture. The concept of people becoming conscious of injustice in society is an old one (DeBerry, 2021). *Woke* is a peculiar word in the current American lexicon. Depending on what side of America's never-yielding culture war the speaker occupies, *woke* is used either as a self-identifier for one's commitment to creating an equitable society or "an insulting or disparaging remark or innuendo" about those who seek to create an equitable society.

There is a term for the latter usage of *woke*: a slur (Merriam-Webster, n.d.-a). As a curriculum theorist, I have an interest in slurs because they are memes (Dawkins, 1976/2016; Krippendorff, 2013) that teach and are easy to observe gain or lose momentum. To use a slur as a slur, one must accept the worldview that the slur endorses. A slur is a virtue signal for like minds.

Damon Young's 2022 article for the *Washington Post* was the focus of outrage from segments of the political right and left because he asserted that "woke" is a dog whistle for "Black" among the then-nascent anti-diversity movement. Like Young, I first encountered the term *woke* as a college student, where it was something of a dismissive catch-all for Black folks who were hyper-politically aware but lacked any real insight or solutions. Later, it emerged as a euphemism on the left for being aware of issues of social inequality because it subsumed a different term that was once common in the Black community, and that term was "socially conscious."

Young (2022) is entirely correct that "woke" is a dog whistle for Black people and Black ideas in the rather diverse anti-diversity movement, and that it is not limited to just the Black community. For the anti-diversity movement, "woke" is a slur for ideas and groups of people that include women, queer people, religious people who adhere to social justice, disabled people, and those who would be considered allies to marginalized people, to name a few. But it is not as simple as sheer bigotry. "Woke" is an action-based slur among the anti-diversity movement, meaning it is reserved for people who commit a particular transgression and hold a particular belief that the anti-diversity movement loathes. That transgression is complaining about social inequality and trying to do something about it. "Woke" is a slur for marginalized people who will not suffer in silence, for their allies, and for those who believe in racial, gender, sexual, disability, and class egalitarianism.

Among the anti-diversity movement, "woke" functions as a slur on an intellectual and interpersonal level. Intellectually, one of the apparent uses of the word *woke*, by the anti-diversity crowd, is as an ideological escape from conversations and debates they do not want to have. An example of this is the 2023 Florida Department of Education justifying blocking AP African American History classes in the state because the course was "woke indoctrination masquerading as education" that violated stated curriculum law (Fawcett & Hartocollis, 2023, para. 11). Branding something as "woke" means that they do not have to even engage with it. Have you just discovered that the Declaration of Independence lists stopping enslaved people from revolting as reason number twenty-seven for the Revolution (National Archives, n.d.)? Call the history book or class that points this fact out "woke." It is the ultimate move of sticking one's head in the sand. In this way, it is a descendant of how the anti-diversity movement used Marxism, the academic lens that focuses on class conflict and the intellectual foundation for communism, as a catch-all for generations, to attack ideas and movements they found threatening, and facts they found inconvenient, including the civil rights movement (MLKREI, n.d.). The tradition continues today with attempts to connect Critical Race Theory, an academic lens that examines how race impacts policy and law, to Marxism, despite CRT forming as a response to the absence of the consideration of race in the critical study of law, including the Marxist perspective.

Some may reject describing "woke" as a slur because the word *slur* often connotates forms of bigotry, and how can one be a bigot toward an ideology? Just as ideas come from people and communities, ideological slurs are just interpersonal slurs cosplaying as ideological critique. There is a long history of slurs being created toward groups of people for their ideas and practices. Catholics were routinely called "papists" by Protestants in America over theological differences, to the extent that John F. Kennedy had to navigate anti-Catholic sentiment while running for president in 1960 (JFKPLM, n.d.). "Cultural Marxism" has always had an antisemitic connotation (Berkowitz, 2003). "Woke," as a slur, stands in this tradition of "you know who those people are" forms of hatred. It's the sort of thing that someone says when they don't want to come out and confirm the depths of their bigotry.

"Woke" is a flexible and intersectional slur because there is no shortage of people from marginalized communities who will denounce "wokeness" as a signal of loyalty to an anti-diversity movement they think might ignore their own diversity, if that group were ever to come to power; this topic is the subject of lesson 12. Of course, "woke" is not always a slur. In some instances, the word *woke* does retain its original Black cultural meanings of being aware of social injustices or engaging in performative politics with no viable solutions. But when U.S. senator Ted Cruz slams the military for being "woke" and "emasculated" in response to a recruitment video (Shepherd, 2021, para. 3), or Ron DeSantis describes his state as a place "where woke goes to die" (Bowden, 2022) in response to American citizens advocating for inclusivity as a virtue in a diverse country, they use it as a slur.

A slur is what Southerners call "a tell." People often hide their real feelings, but if you learn enough about an ideology, you notice its sign words, which can take on the form of slurs. "Woke" is a tell for the anti-diversity crowd. Some people will vehemently oppose this characterization of being anti-diversity because they feel exposed, but to use another Southern expression, "they told on themselves." In the end, once a tell is exposed and cataloged, it becomes something different: a confession.

"Woke" is a meme that reveals an intellectual journey among those who use it as a slur. It is a recitation of the history of how the anti-diversity movement used the momentum they built from attacking one group to attacking another. What was first co-opted to attack and discredit young Black activists was then directed to queer activists, feminists, and eventually White non-queer social justice advocates to devastating social and political effect.

References

Berkowitz, B. (2003, August 15). '*Cultural Marxism' catching on*. Southern Poverty Law Center. Retrieved September 5, 2024, from https://www.splcenter.org/fighting-hate/intelligence-report/2003/cultural-marxism-catching

Bowden, J. (2022, August 25). DeSantis says "woke" 5 times in 19 seconds in culture war laden primary speech. *Independent*. Retrieved September 5, 2024, from https://www.independent.co.uk/news/world/americas/us-politics/ron-desantis-woke-florida-primary-speech-b2152132.html

ContraPoints. (2017, September 1). Decrypting the Alt-Right: How to recognize a f@scist ContraPoints [Video]. YouTube. Retrieved September 5, 2024, from https://www.youtube.com/watch?v=Sx4BVGPkdzk&t=6s

Dawkins, R. (2016). *The selfish gene*, (40th anniversary edition). (Original work published 1976). Oxford University Press. https://play.google.com/store/books/details?id=o59HDAAAQBAJ

DeBerry, J. (2021, November 28). 'Woke' has been weaponized to label those fighting oppression the oppressors. MSNBC. Retrieved September 5, 2024, from https://www.msnbc.com/opinion/woke-has-been-weaponized-label-those-fighting-oppression-oppressors-n1284129

Fawcett, E., and Hartocollis, A. (2023, January 21). Florida gives reasons for rejecting A.P. African American studies class. *New York Times*. Retrieved September 5, 2024, from https://www.nytimes.com/2023/01/21/us/florida-ap-african-american-studies.html

John F. Kennedy Presidential Library and Museum. (n.d.). *John F. Kennedy and religion*. Retrieved September 5, 2024, from https://www.jfklibrary.org/learn/about-jfk/jfk-in-history/john-f-kennedy-and-religion

Krippendorff, K. (2013). *Content analysis: An introduction to its methodology* (3rd edition). Sage.

The Martin Luther King, Jr. Research and Education Institute, Stanford University. (n.d.). *Communism*. Retrieved September 5, 2024, from https://kinginstitute.stanford.edu/communism

Merriam-Webster. (n.d.-a). Slur. In *Merriam-Webster.com dictionary*. Retrieved November 19, 2024, from https://www.merriam-webster.com/dictionary/slur

Merriam-Webster. (n.d.-b). Woke. In *Merriam-Webster.com dictionary*. Retrieved November 19, 2024, from https://www.merriam-webster.com/dictionary/woke

National Archives. (n.d.). *Declaration of Independence: A transcription*. Retrieved September 5, 2024, from https://www.archives.gov/founding-docs/declaration-transcript

Shepherd, K. (2021, May 21). Sen. Ted Cruz insulted a "woke, emasculated" U.S. Army ad. Angry veterans fired back. *Washington Post*.

Retrieved September 5, 2024, from https://www.washingtonpost.com/nation/2021/05/21/ted-cruz-russia-army-emasculated/

United States Holocaust Memorial Museum. (n.d.). *Martin Niemöller: A biography*. Retrieved September 5, 2024, from https://encyclopedia.ushmm.org/content/en/article/martin-niemoeller-biography?parent=en%2F271

United States Holocaust Memorial Museum. (2023, April 11). *Martin Niemöller: "First they came for . . . "* Retrieved September 5, 2024, from https://encyclopedia.ushmm.org/content/en/article/martin-niemoeller-first-they-came-for-the-socialists

Young, D. (2022, September 26). Woke is now a dog whistle for Black. What's next? *Washington Post*. Retrieved September 5, 2024, from https://www.washingtonpost.com/magazine/2022/09/26/damon-young-woke-is-now-dog-whistle-black-whats-next/

BIGOTRY IS PARANOID, AND BIGOTRY MAKES YOU VIOLENT

Bigots are always afraid of retribution from their targets. This drives them to become increasingly cruel as a way of forestalling the inevitable. While the methods may vary, the end goal of bigotry is always to be able to use the power of the state, institutions, and individual action to inflict harm on those they hate.

I have combined these two lessons because they exist in a feedback loop. Being a bigot is a prerequisite for being an oppressor, and to be an oppressor, one must commit to violence to maintain oppression. The impact of this on the oppressor is that they commit to embracing a constant state of paranoia. Bigots exist in a state of fear of revenge at the hands of their victims. Ta-Nehisi Coates described this loop in the context of the Antebellum South:

> One of the corollaries of white supremacy, in this country, is the idea that, should black people ever get power, they will immediately enact revenge among the white populace for all the years of toil, rape, murder, slavery, and terrorism. The notion is at least as old as the antebellum South, and probably older. (Coates, 2012, para.1)

For as long as oppression has existed, so has the fear of revenge. This fear drives oppressors of all varieties to claim the targets of their bigotry want to do the same to them. When taken together, paranoia and violence are a tactic called "accusation in a mirror." Kenneth Marcus (2012) described *accusation in a mirror* as:

> A rhetorical practice in which one falsely accuses one's enemies of conducting, plotting, or desiring to commit precisely the same transgressions that one plans to commit against them. For example, if one plans to kill one's adversaries by drowning them in a particular river, then one should accuse one's adversaries of plotting precisely the same crime. (p. 359)

Ironically, the paranoia-driven violence and the accusation in a mirror are conceits by bigots that they do understand the legacies of bigotry toward the marginalized. One must understand transgression to fear revenge.

On May 14, 2022, a self-described White supremacist murdered ten Black people in a grocery store in Buffalo, New York. He live-streamed the entire massacre and was later arrested. The American tendency is to attribute instances where White racists murder people to them being mentally unstable. This may be the case in Buffalo (Tucker, 2022), but this denies the history of racial violence in the United States and scapegoats those with mental health issues as being a threat to the general public. Philosopher Jason Stanley (2015) wrote, "One main source of the unrevisability of certain beliefs is that they are connected to social practices. The beliefs are ones I need to have in order to remain in those practices" (p. 185). I agree with this assertion. Ideology is a belief that motivates people because ideologies all have a function. They want us to *do something*. With bigotry, this *something* is always brutal and often violent in simple and complex ways (Mitchell, 2020). This is especially true in the case of White supremacy in America, whose bloody path stretches from the ruins of Tulsa in 1921 to the aisles of a Tops Friendly Market in Buffalo, New York, in 2022.

Like many modern mass murders, the shooter in Buffalo left behind a manifesto (Veronica, 2023). For him, it was a long, racist screed, but what jumped out at many people was his strong belief in what is called replacement theory (Jones, 2022). The Southern Poverty Law Center (2020) defines *replacement theory* as "the idea that White people of European descent are being systematically displaced in the Western world" (para. 16). It is not a new idea. Historian Kevin Kruse (2023) points out that the idea was found in Madison Grant's 1916 highly influential racist work, *The Passing of the Great Race*. To understand replacement theory, it is important to understand those who came up with the idea and those who continue to claim *The Passing of the Great Race* as their intellectual foundation: White supremacists (Hoff, 2021).

White supremacy in the United States is as old as the country is, and White supremacists have been consistent in their belief: White people are superior on the earth, and everyone else is subhuman, deserving of no rights or consideration as human beings. It is important to point out that not all White people are White supremacists, and White supremacists are not above using violence against White people who oppose them, because they consider them to be race traitors. This is central to understanding how they see their opposition as an alliance of subhumans and race traitors. White supremacists are also apolitical in the sense that they have no strong political party commitment.

Some will try to argue that White supremacy belongs to one side of the political spectrum or the other. This is a flat-out lie. White supremacy, as an ideology, stretches from the far left to the far right in the United States. Fredrickson (1981) defines White supremacy as:

> The attitudes, ideologies, and policies associated with rise of blatant forms of White or European dominance over "nonwhite" populations. . . . In its fully developed form, white supremacy means "color bars," "racial segregation," and the restriction of meaningful citizenship rights to a privileged group characterized by its light pigmentation. . . . It [White supremacy] suggests systematic

and self-conscious efforts to make race or color a qualification for membership in the civil community. (p. xi)

In this sense, it is a social contract and for most of American history, White supremacy was the chief organizing principle of government, the chief economic organizing principle, and the primary lens for interpreting the Constitution (Mills, 1997/2014). In truth, White supremacy has no political affiliation, as most Americans would understand the concept. It is its own political worldview.

White supremacist communists exist just like White supremacist free-market capitalists. There is no reason that a White supremacist would oppose Medicare for all or the welfare state; just as long as people of color and other undesirables don't have access to it. White supremacy is perfectly adaptable to any political point that exists on the mainstream political spectrum, and this is by design. White supremacy is politically flexible. This is why the political leanings of the shooter in Buffalo are, frankly, irrelevant. Far-left? Far-right? Centrist? For the White supremacist, all these terms are little more than intellectual cosplay to be discarded as the need arises.

White supremacy is also multimedia platformed. While it is true that Tucker Carlson trades in replacement theory (Bond, 2023), the shooter was eighteen years old. What are the chances that he was introduced to this toxic idea on television, as opposed to the darker corners of the internet? White supremacy stopped being about handmade magazines long ago. This is why replacement theory is so unique; it's one of the few beliefs held by White supremacists that cannot be disguised as anything other than what it is. And it has gone mainstream in many ways.

Replacement theory is the purest expression of White supremacy because it unifies all its targets into a single constellation of sadism. It is a grand conspiracy theory. The theory itself is not only racist, but also antisemitic, xenophobic, misogynistic, homophobic, and transphobic, but it also orbits a concern about White birth rates, and this is how it must be understood. White supremacists only consider people with pure White ancestry to be White. Mixed people with one White parent are, in their eyes and in replacement theory, not White. This also fuels xenophobia. The old term was *miscegenation*, and it drove the resistance to integration. But why would it be misogynistic, homophobic, and transphobic? Again, this is because they are obsessed with White birth rates. In the mind of the replacement theory follower, White women who have children with people of color, and the mere existence of gay White men, White lesbians, and White transgender people, are understood to be race traitors because they are not having White babies and are seen as challenging the patriarchy inherent to White supremacy.

The antisemitic aspect of replacement theory is particularly important for a few reasons. First, it shows the enduring power of the ancient bigotry called antisemitism. Second, it is a reminder that antisemitism and racism are complementary ideologies that serve the same destructive goals. Third, while Jews are multinational, multiethnic, and multiracial, White supremacists have long had a particular venom toward Jews of European descent, whom they do not consider to be White. This shows an often-ignored truth of White supremacy—it has a very specific definition of Whiteness that does not mean "descended from the people of Europe." White supremacy deals in gradients of Whiteness where some people are Whiter than others. This is best exemplified by the ideology of the Ku Klux Klan, who hated European Catholic immigrants (Zeitz, 2015), and the Nazis, who tried to exterminate and enslave millions of non-Jewish Eastern and Western Europeans (USHMM, 2024).

To assume that replacement theory does not have such gradients is a profound leap of faith. Despite being an obsession, birth rates are not the main driver of White supremacists or replacement theory. The focus on White birth rates is largely a ploy to cover up what really sits at the heart of the theory and of White supremacy itself—paranoia. Unlike many of the racial conservatives who seek to harness their energy and try to gaslight communities of color about the existence of systemic racism, White supremacists suffer no such delusions. They understand systemic racism has existed in the past, and reimposing it in the most brutal fashions they can imagine is their political goal for the future.

Because of this knowledge, White supremacists are paranoid about what communities of color may do to them if they ever get to be the majority, with the entire power of the American state at their disposal. This paranoia sits at the heart of replacement theory. White supremacists are terrified of the possibility that communities of color will treat them like White supremacists have historically treated communities of color. In short, White supremacists fear revenge. This fear is not new. The Declaration of Independence accused the British of trying to inspire "domestic insurrections," meaning enslaved people's rebellions (National Archives, n.d.). Plantation owners were always afraid of slave uprisings. Segregationists were terrified that integration would usher in a world where Black people would repay the cruelties of Jim Crow.

Confronting replacement theory is a low bar. All one needs to do is denounce it as sadistic babble from an ideology that believes in cruelty as the goal of state and culture. But a great many people are going to fail to leap over this bar.

As I write this lesson, a sanitizing campaign has already begun online with racial conservative public intellectuals and people who ally themselves with racial conservatives to transform what is clearly replacement theory into concerns over demographics or immigration. The demographic spin is intellectually dishonest for one reason—demographics are not destiny. Just because America becomes a majority-minority does not mean that minority communities will vote in certain ways or believe certain things. Republicans of color, like Tim Scott of South Carolina, are in no danger of losing their seats. All of Trump's electoral coalitions were multiracial. The people trying to sanitize replacement theory recognize its electoral power, but they seem to think they can harness this inferno of hatred and not get burned.

In a country addicted to a culture war, those who try to pass off replacement theory as valid political thought have yet to realize they are playing with the intellectual equivalent of a dirty bomb, and when it finally explodes, they, too, will be irradiated. They simply do not understand that White supremacists cannot be bargained with. They do not cut deals. They do not care about ideologies concerning taxes, war, or freedoms. They do not care about political affiliation. They only care about blood, because it is inescapable. It is their only loyalty. Everyone else is trying to replace them. Those who try to sanitize replacement theory have convinced themselves that the screams will never be theirs. If they took the time to read history books, instead of banning them from libraries, they would see how wrong they likely are.

Note: Parts of this lesson were originally published as *The only politics is blood—On replacement theory in America* by Nicholas Mitchell at The North Star with Shaun King, on May 17, 2022. Retrieved September 5, 2024, from https://www.thenorthstar.com/p/the-only -politics-is-blood-on-replacement

References

Bond, S. (Host). (2023, April 25). How Tucker Carlson took fringe conspiracy theories to a mass audience [Audio podcast transcript]. In *Morning edition*. National Public Radio. Retrieved November 15, 2024, from https://www.npr.org/2023/04/25/1171800317/ how-tucker-carlsons-extremist-narratives-shaped-fox-news-and- conservative-politi

Coates, T. N. (2012, September 25). Fear of a Black avenger. *Atlantic.* Retrieved September 5, 2024, from https://www.theatlantic.com/ national/archive/2012/09/fear-of-a-black-avenger/262826/

Fredrickson, G. (1981). *White supremacy: A comparative study in American and South African history.* Oxford University Press.

Hoff, A. (2021). *The passing of the great race; Or the racial basis of European history (1916), by Madison Grant.* Embryo Project Encyclopedia,

Arizona Board of Regents. Retrieved September 5, 2024, from https://keep.lib.asu.edu/items/173053

Jones, D. (2022, May 16). *What is the "great replacement" and how is it tied to the Buffalo shooting suspect?* National Public Radio. Retrieved September 5, 2024, from https://www.npr.org/2022/05/16/1099034094/what-is-the-great-replacement-theory

Kruse, K. (2023, October 23). The not-so-great replacement theory. *Campaign Trails*. Retrieved September 5, 2024, from https://kevinmkruse.substack.com/p/the-not-so-great-replacement-theory

Marcus, K. L. (2012). Accusation in a mirror. *Loyola University Chicago Law Journal* 43(2), 357–393. https://ssrn.com/abstract=2020327

Mills, C. (2014). *The racial contract*. Cornell University Press. (Original work published 1997). https://play.google.com/store/books/details?id=GnmuAwAAQBAJ

Mitchell, N. E. (2020). A lesson from George Floyd: "A man was lynched today." *JustSouth Monthly*, 108. Retrieved November 19, 2024, from https://jsri.loyno.edu/sites/default/files/2021-03/justsouth_monthly_june%202020_mitchell.pdf

National Archives. (n.d.). *Declaration of Independence: A transcription.* Retrieved September 5, 2024, from https://www.archives.gov/founding-docs/declaration-transcript

Southern Poverty Law Center. (2020, March 18). *The year in hate and extremism: 2019*. Retrieved September 5, 2024, from https://www.splcenter.org/news/2020/03/18/year-hate-and-extremism-2019

Stanley, J. (2015). *How propaganda works*. Princeton University Press.

Tucker, E. (2022, June 6). *The Buffalo shooting suspect showed signs of violent behavior and was left untreated. Violence prevention experts say troubled youth like him need long-term support.* CNN. Retrieved September 5, 2024, from https://www.cnn.com/2022/06/06/us/buffalo-case-shows-why-troubled-youth-need-long-term-treatment/index.html

United States Holocaust Memorial Museum. (2024, April 4). *What groups of people did the Nazis target?* Retrieved September 5, 2024, from https://encyclopedia.ushmm.org/content/en/article/what-groups-of-people-did-the-nazis-target

Veronica, N. (2023, August 1). *Buffalo mass shooter's alleged diatribe leaves no doubt attack was White supremacist terrorism.* News4Buffalo. Retrieved September 5, 2024, from https://www.wivb.com/

news/buffalo-supermarket-mass-shooting-tops/buffalo-mass-shooters
-alleged-manifesto-leaves-no-doubt-attack-was-White-supremacist
-terrorism/

Zeitz, J. (2015, September 23). When America hated Catholics. *Politico Magazine*. Retrieved September 5, 2024, from https://www
.politico.com/magazine/story/2015/09/when-america-hated-catholics
-213177/

HOW BIGOTRY DISGUISES ITSELF

In 1897, noted philosopher, civil rights advocate, and one of the founders of sociology, W. E. B. Du Bois published his essay, "Strivings of the Negro People," in the *Atlantic* magazine. It was here that Du Bois first introduced what would become one of his most famous contributions to global culture—double consciousness. He wrote:

> After the Egyptian and Indian, the Greek and Roman, the Teuton and Mongolian, the Negro is a sort of seventh son, born with a veil, and gifted with second-sight in this American world—a world which yields him no self-consciousness, but only lets him see himself through the revelation of the other world. It is a peculiar sensation, this double-consciousness, this sense of always looking at one's self through the eyes of others, of measuring one's soul by the tape of a world that looks on in amused contempt and pity. One feels his two-ness—an American, a Negro; two souls, two thoughts, two unreconciled strivings; two warring ideals in one dark body, whose dogged strength alone keeps it from being torn asunder. (Du Bois, 1897, para. 3)

In short, double consciousness is the ability of a Black person to see themselves through the eyes of another, as well as through their own eyes. In Du Bois's view, this split mentality creates internal conflict within Black people who are burdened with having to anticipate how they will be received as a Black person. Of course, this is not limited to Black people or even to oppressed people. Simply being "the other" in a social situation is enough to trigger double consciousness. Despite Du Bois's remark, double consciousness has been cited as an asset for activism, advocacy, and resisting oppression because it allows the holder to anticipate how they will be perceived by allies and opposition outside their community. It can be understood as a tactic.

In a perverted sense, bigots have their own sense of double consciousness. While bigots have a corrupted sense of morality and intellect, they largely retain the ability to be reflective. Only the most galling bigots will announce themselves as bigots immediately. We see this with neo-Nazis covering their bodies with White supremacist tattoos and wearing clothing emblazoned with racist imagery or text. If this were the behavior of all or even most bigots, then confronting and stopping bigotry would be easy. Unfortunately for society, bigots are well aware of how the public generally perceives them in a negative light. So, they have developed tactics to advance their own advocacy and protect themselves from opposition.

Much of advocacy is rooted in rhetoric and the use of what politicos and academics call "dog whistles." Merriam-Webster (n.d.) defines the political use of the term *dog whistle* as "an expression or statement that has a secondary meaning intended to be understood only by a particular group of people." It is important to note that the entire political spectrum uses dog whistles in their political rhetoric and messaging campaigns. Examples of this are how the Occupy Wall Street movement referred to "the 99 percent" as code for the bulk of the population that was not wealthy. Historically, "We Shall Overcome" was a dog whistle for members and allies of the civil rights movement to indicate that they supported ending Jim Crow laws. Bigots employ dog whistles to appeal to people who may share some of their resentments but who don't want to out themselves as bigots in public.

Perhaps no modern American figure embodies the use of the bigoted dog whistle more than the political consultant and strategist

Lee Atwater (Perlstein, 2012). In a now-infamous interview with political scientist Alexander Lamis, for his classic book on Southern politics, *The Two-Party South*, Atwater described the art of the bigoted dog whistle:

> You start out in 1954 by saying, "Nigger, nigger, nigger," By 1968, you can't say "nigger"—that hurts you. Backfires. So you say stuff like forced busing, states' rights and all that stuff. You're getting so abstract now [that] you're talking about cutting taxes, and all these things you're talking about are totally economic things and a byproduct of them is [that] blacks get hurt worse than whites. And subconsciously maybe that is part of it. I'm not saying that. But I'm saying that if it is getting that abstract, and that coded, that we are doing away with the racial problem one way or the other. You follow me—because obviously sitting around saying, "We want to cut this," is much more abstract than even the busing thing, and a hell of a lot more abstract than "Nigger, nigger." (Lamis, 1990, p. 26)

Atwater described the rhetorical methodology that bigotry employs. If you can disguise bigotry as something else and justify it using rhetoric that appears not to be rooted in bigotry, you can achieve bigoted ends. The goal is to give people plausible deniability. Bigotry is invested in presenting itself as anything other than being an emotional and intellectual commitment to hatred because this allows bigots to seek out converts while protecting themselves from exposure and rebuke by the public at large. I call this practice intellectual cosplaying, and this is the subject of the third part of this book.

Part III of *On Bigotry* contains the following lessons:

- Lesson 8: Bigotry presents itself as philosophy.

- Lesson 9: Bigotry presents itself as a concern.

- Lesson 10: Bigotry presents itself as science.

A historical example of the rhetorical tactic Atwater described is seen in the following quotes from onetime member of the Ku Klux Klan and former state representative in the Louisiana legislature, David Duke, when discussing the National Association for the Advancement of White People, which he founded.

> It's not a question of being against minorities at all. It's simply a question of making sure that our rights are also protected. That if we're going to have civil rights in America, we must have civil rights for everyone and not a chosen few. (NBC News, 2015, 01:02)

On its face, this statement is something that most ordinary people would not oppose. Everyone must have civil rights. But the civil rights of White Protestants, Duke and the KKK's core constituency, has never been in doubt or insecure in the United States. For Duke, this was a way of rebranding his opposition to existing civil rights laws in a way that voters in Louisiana would find palatable in the remark of, "not being against minorities at all," while also hearing the dog whistle of what he meant by civil rights.

What does this look like currently? Broadly speaking, it looks like the weaponization of bigoted ideas across the political spectrum into propaganda that is accessible to everyday people (Morris, 2017, p. 25). An effective propaganda message can take on a myriad of forms. Lessons 8, 9, and 10 attempt to distill the weaponizing of ideas into their most common groupings. Bigots will latch on to any issue and hijack any philosophy in order to craft a useful vehicle for getting its message to the people it wants to convert. In this sense, bigotry is an equal opportunity appropriator.

There is no contemporary issue that illustrates this practice among bigots more than how bigotry quickly infiltrated the debates over the Israeli-Palestinian conflict that began in October 2023. As I write this book, a human catastrophe is unfolding in Israel and Palestine that has unleashed a great amount of antisemitism and Islamophobia throughout American mainstream culture. While the targets are different, the same bigoted assumption sits at the center of both antisemitism and Islamophobia: (1) collective guilt and (2) collective punishment. To be certain, collective guilt sits at the heart of bigotry because it holds every member of a community responsible for the actions of an individual or group. Collective punishment flows from collective guilt in the sense that the whole must be punished for the actions of a few. Collective guilt and punishment is a major intellectual commitment that, unsurprisingly, bigots will not maintain if they ever find themselves on the wrong side of their own logic, regardless of if they pretend to be conservative or progressive (Mitchell, 2023).

For example, among the bigots cosplaying as conservatives, who think collective punishment against Palestinians is justified, you'd be hard-pressed to find one who'd say White supremacist Dylann Roof's slaughter of nine Black people at the Mother Emanuel A.M.E. church in Charleston justifies Black people killing White people who weren't responsible. Likewise, you'd have an equally difficult time finding a bigot cosplaying as a progressive who thinks the deaths of innocent Israelis were justified by Israel's occupation of Gaza, who'd say that Christians retaliating against random atheists would be a proper response to the hypothetical incident of an atheist killing Christians at a concert.

No form of activism, advocacy, or politics is safe from being appropriated. Bigots will cosplay as liberals, conservatives, communists, atheists, Christians, Muslims, Jews, straight, queer, critical race theorists, and colorblind advocates, to name a few, if it enables them to advance their activism, advocacy, and goals.

Bigots will cosplay their hatred as anything that they think will work.

References

Du Bois, W. E. B. (1897, August). Strivings of the Negro People. *Atlantic*. Retrieved September 6, 2024, from https://www.theatlantic.com/magazine/archive/1897/08/strivings-of-the-negro-people/305446/

Lamis, A. P. (1990). *The two-party south* (2nd expanded edition). Oxford University Press.

Merriam-Webster. (n.d.). dog whistle. In *Merriam-Webster.com dictionary*. Retrieved November 19, 2024, from https://www.merriam-webster.com/dictionary/dog%20whistle

Mitchell, N. E. (2023, December 28). *Bigotry masquerading as philosophy was a 2023 low point*. MSNBC. Retrieved September 6, 2024, from https://www.msnbc.com/opinion/msnbc-opinion/hamas-israel-anti-semitism-islamophobia-rcna131486

Morris, T. (2017). *Dark ideas: How neo-nazi and violent jihadi ideologues shaped modern terrorism*. Lexington Books.

NBC News. (2015, January 13). *David Duke: From klansman to politician: Flashback: NBC News* [Video]. YouTube. Retrieved September 6, 2024, from https://www.youtube.com/watch?v=NIfW_98hi0o

Perlstein, R. (2012, November 13). Exclusive: Lee Atwater's infamous 1981 interview on the southern strategy. *Nation*. Retrieved September 6, 2024, from https://www.thenation.com/article/archive/exclusive-lee-atwaters-infamous-1981-interview-southern-strategy/

BIGOTRY PRESENTS ITSELF AS PHILOSOPHY

Bigotry appropriates the language and presentation of philosophy to make itself more accessible to the educated. It redefines or invents new terms and makes deceptive connections to pass itself off as intellectual diversity and one perspective among many to shield itself from actual philosophical scrutiny.

The ideological goal of bigotry is to convince people that it is a valid position to take, accepting that human beings are naturally divided into superior and inferior groups. This extends to knowledge produced by different groups. To achieve this end, bigotry presents itself as philosophy to give itself an air of intellectual rigor, to present itself as just another form of intellectual diversity that is only asking the "hard questions," and to protect itself from rebuke. This lesson has many historical and contemporary manifestations.

As mentioned in the introduction, Manning Marable (Hoffmann, 2022, 8:22) described how the bigotry of Jim Crow ranged from the profound viciousness of race riots and lynchings to the pettiness of separate water fountains and swimming pools. Many essays have been written about the profound forms of racism and other types of bigotry, but Marable demands that we remember how the petty forms are meant to tear the victim apart emotionally and intellectually because they target the soul. My father told me a story from his childhood that illustrates that point. He was born in

Washington, DC, after the Second World War and moved to Baton Rouge, Louisiana, when he was still a boy. One day, he went to get ice cream, and the woman working the counter simply ignored him and went about her other duties, refusing to take his order. My father told me that he stood there, confused and upset, until an older Black woman walked up and escorted him to the side of the stand where the colored window was. The woman at the counter could have served the child, who didn't know better, or explained that he was in the wrong place, but she chose to be petty and silent, causing emotional harm as well. What Marable and my father described are examples of the everyday petty cruelty of Jim Crow, but it also represents something more; it is a philosophical commitment to what the social sciences describe as "othering." There is another word for it: *dehumanization.*

Stanton (1996) described the third stage of his original genocidal process—dehumanization:

> Denial of the humanity of others is the step that permits killing with impunity. The universal human abhorrence of murder of members of one's own group is overcome by treating the victims as less than human. In incitements to genocide the target groups are called disgusting animal names—Nazi propaganda called Jews "rats" or "vermin"; Rwandan Hutu hate radio referred to Tutsis as "cockroaches." The targeted group is often likened to a "disease", "microbes", "infections" or a "cancer" in the body politic. Bodies of genocide victims are often mutilated to express this denial of humanity. Such atrocities then become the justification for revenge killings, because they are evidence that the killers must be monsters, not human beings themselves. (p. 3)

In lesson 4, I wrote that racial, sexual, gender, and religious slurs are just words; bigoted meanings make them slurs. Plainly stated, *nigger* is just a word. *Cracker* is just a word. *Cripple* is just a word. *Tranny* is just a word. *Retard* is just a word. *Whore* is just a word. What classifications of people are symbolized when slurs are spoken is what matters. To use a bigoted slur is an act of dehumanization, which is a philosophical endeavor.

One of the most famous manifestations of how bigotry presents itself as philosophy was book burning in Nazi Germany. Among the texts thrown onto the fires were the works of Karl Marx, Sigmund Freud, and Walter Benjamin, because they were contaminated with depraved Jewish ideas, according to the Nazis (Ball, 2014, p. 87). Writer Phillip Ball points out that Albert Einstein's books were burned also. This sticks out, even among antisemitism, because Einstein's area was physics. Ball (2014) wrote:

> But how could a scientific theory be objectionable? How could one even develop a pseudo-moralistic position on a notion that was objectively right or wrong? Besides, hadn't Einstein's relativity been proven? What did it even mean to say that science could be subverted by the "Jewish spirit?" (p. 87)

The Nazis were so philosophically committed to antisemitism that antisemitic physicists like Phillip Lenard and Johannes Stark devised a distinction between Aryan physics and Jewish physics to justify dismissing the work of Jewish academics they loathed (Ball, 2014). Ball described the Aryan physics thesis as the Aryan preference "to pursue an experimental physics rooted in tangible reality," while Jewish physics "wove webs of abstruse theory disconnected from experience" (pp. 95–96).

Ultimately, like all forms of bigotry, the antisemitic Aryan physics was really a means to an end. Ball (2014) wrote, "While the Aryan physicists were incapable of mounting a credible assault on Einstein's relativity in scientific terms, *Deutsche Physik* offered a new line of attack: relativity threatened to undermine the very essence of the Germanic world view" (pp. 96–97). It was easier for German physicists who detested Einstein for his fame out of jealousy to dismiss his work on philosophical grounds. In Nazi Germany, all one had to do to dismiss knowledge that was inconvenient for, or challenged, the preferred narrative was to brand it as "Jewish" because of some insane philosophical belief that race is real and some races are inferior and degenerate. This tactic of dismissing knowledge or an argument because of who created it, rather than on the merits, is known as the genetic fallacy (Crouch, 1993), and it is a favorite of bigots attempting to present their bigotry as philosophy today.

Another historical manifestation is found in the majority opinion for *Plessy v. Ferguson*. As every schoolchild in America knows, the *Plessy* decision ruled that segregation was constitutional and gave Jim Crow the sanction of the federal government—until 1965. How the Supreme Court justified its decision has faded from pop cultural memory, and as a result, most Americans do not realize that the Court admitted it disregarded the Constitution in its own ruling because of the majority's philosophical commitment to bigotry. The majority wrote:

> The object of the amendment was undoubtedly to enforce the absolute equality of the two races before the law, but, in the nature of things, it could not have been intended to abolish distinctions based upon color, or to enforce social, as distinguished from political, equality, or a commingling of the two races upon terms unsatisfactory to either. Laws permitting, and even requiring, their separation in places where they are liable to be brought into contact do not necessarily imply the inferiority of either race to the other, and have been generally, if not universally, recognized as within the competency of the state legislatures in the exercise of their police power. (*Plessy v. Ferguson*, 1896, p. 544)

Here, the Court acknowledges that the Fourteenth Amendment forbids segregation by law but that the Constitution is superseded by "the nature of things," or natural law, which means according to nature. This passage is tantamount to a confession that the Supreme Court had no legal reason to justify segregation and that they were invoking a claim that "segregation is natural" as justification for their ruling. Of course, this falls apart, as most appeals to nature inevitably do when one thinks through them. Something that is naturally occurring doesn't need a law to enforce it. However, the ruling in *Plessy* depended on the same philosophical leap that advocates for Aryan physics in Nazi Germany would latch on to later: that race is real and that some races are inferior and degenerate. The Nazis simply were willing to state this in the open, while the majority in the *Plessy* decision attempted to gaslight everyone about what segregation meant on paper and in practice.

A contemporary manifestation of bigotry trying to present itself as philosophy is seen in how bigotry will latch onto concepts that are designed to rebuke bigotry, using them to justify bigoted rhetoric and actions. An example of this is how some have used intersectionality to engage in rationing sympathy and empathy. Philosopher Olúfẹ́mi Táíwò (2022), quoting Jaya Rajamani, wrote on X, formerly twitter:

> from a comrade: "Not to be controversial but I think white women and all middle class and even rich women and anyone with a uterus is going to suffer . . . Weird that we're means testing sympathy instead of trying to build solidarity between everyone this will affect." (Táíwò, 2022)

In this sense, "means testing" refers to the position that asserts sympathy should be given to those who check off the required amount of marginalized identity boxes, while those who have too much privilege are deemed undeserving of such consideration. To be clear, intersectionality is designed to expose bigotry. It is a profound distortion of this framework to use it to ignore suffering because it is happening to a group that is considered privileged in society. Ignoring suffering because of *who* is experiencing it, such as ignoring the plight of White women and middle and upper-class women who cannot get an abortion or ignoring the crisis of masculinity (Illing, 2023; Reeves, 2024; Reeves & Smith, 2022) because men are a privileged group in society, is what bigots do as part of their efforts to dehumanize (Stanton, 1996) those they find inferior, threatening, or degenerate.

Ultimately, bigotry seeks to present itself as another form of intellectual diversity. Sometimes called viewpoint diversity, this can be understood as representing different perspectives and opinions within national conversations. Concerns about intellectual diversity are often raised with respect to public intellectuals and what ideas are being taught in elementary, secondary, and college classrooms. As an academic, I value intellectual diversity, and I have been the beneficiary of intellectually diverse environments for the decades I spent as a student. Bigotry is not a form of intellectual diversity. I do not use bigotry as a euphemism for any political ideology or social leanings here. *Liberalism*, *progressivism*, *centrism*, *leftism*, and *conservatism* are not synonyms of *bigotry*. Despite what the culture war would have people believe, occupying certain positions on the political spectrum does not automatically make one a bigot. Being an ardent opponent of gun control and an ardent supporter of the right to same-sex marriage and interracial marriage is not a contradiction. Millions of Americans simultaneously hold both these positions. Millions of traditionally masculine men reject toxically masculine ideas.

As stated in lesson 2:

> Bigotry is the opposite of intellectual, reasoned thought because it makes claims about the world without evidence and encourages irrational behavior. In the absence of evidence, bigotry embraces stereotypes as proof of its claims and will distort or ignore any contradictory information challenging those claims.

Because of this, bigotry does not qualify as intellectual diversity because it is not grounded in anything that reasonable and rational people would consider to be intellectual. At best, it is a series of gross generalizations based on insufficient proof. At worst, it is the attempted justification for the most brutal and depraved behavior people can devise. Largely, a major reason that bigotry does not qualify as intellectual diversity is that it is obsessed with what is nothing more than a figment of the bigoted imagination. French philosopher Jean-Paul Sartre (1948/1995) wrote about antisemites blaming all their personal failures on Jews, to the point that they inserted Jews into situations where there is no proof they were even present: "If the Jew did not exist, the anti-Semite would invent him" (p. 13). We see this with some sexist men who blame feminism for their inability to find a romantic partner, rather than admit that their own sexism is operating as something of a repellant to women, who see their sexism as potentially dangerous.

Bigotry is, as Arendt (1963/2006) described, the hatred that drove Adolph Eichmann; it is banal. This is why bigotry tries to present itself as *simply asking the questions that people are afraid to ask*, even though they all amount to: *Are some groups of humans superior to others?* Banality lacks any sort of depth, so what it lacks, it attempts to imitate. This imitation of intellectual depth is not limited to philosophy. As we shall see in lessons 9 and 10, bigotry tries to present itself as social concern and as both social and hard science because people know that asking the openly bigoted question or making the openly bigoted claim will get them branded as bigots, which, ironically, is a label that all but the most galling advocates actively avoid.

References

Arendt, H. (2006). *Eichmann in Jerusalem: A report on the banality of evil.* *Penguin.* (Original work published 1963). https://play.google.com/store/books/details?id=yGoxZEdw36oC

Ball, P. (2014). *Serving the Reich: The struggle for the soul of physics under Hitler* [eBook edition]. University of Chicago Press. https://www.proquest.com/docview/2134287036/F460BAC2710748E0PQ/2?accountid=14556&sourcetype=Books

Crouch, M. A. (1993). A "limited" defense of the genetic fallacy. *Metaphilosophy, 24*(3), 227–240. Retrieved from https://www.jstor.org/stable/24439006

Hoffman, D. (2022, November 12). *A firsthand account of the Jim Crow South from historian who lived it* [Video]. YouTube. Retrieved September 6, 2024, from https://youtu.be/nPBttI52sPw?si=d_1FO1QoIs4XZ8kL

Illing, S. (2023, August 7). *The new crisis of masculinity: What's the matter with men—and how do we fix it?* Vox. Retrieved September 6, 2024, from https://www.vox.com/the-gray-area/23813985/christine-emba-masculinity-the-gray-area

Plessy v. Ferguson, 163 U.S. 537 (1896). Oyez. Retrieved September 6, 2024, from https://www.oyez.org/cases/1850-1900/163us537

Reeves, R. (2024). *Of boys and men: Why the modern male is struggling, why it matters, and what to do about it.* Brookings Institution Press.

Reeves, R., and E. Smith. (2022, October 12). *Boys left behind: Education gender gaps across the US.* Brookings Institute. Retrieved September 6, 2024, from https://www.brookings.edu/articles/boys-left-behind-education-gender-gaps-across-the-us/#:~:text=In%201970%2C%20just%2012,now%20going%20the%20other%20way

Sartre, J. (1995). *Anti-Semite and Jew: An exploration of the etiology of hate.* Schocken Books. (Original work published in 1948).

Stanton, G. (1996). *The 8 stages of genocide* (working paper). Genocide Watch. Retrieved September 6, 2024, from http://www.genocide-watch.com/images/8StagesBriefingpaper.pdf

Táíwò, O. [@OlufemiOTaiwo]. (2022, June 25). "From a comrade: 'Not to be controversial but I think white women and all middle class and even rich women and anyone with a uterus is going to suffer.'" [Post] *X.* https://x.com/OlufemiOTaiwo/status/1540851131806621696

BIGOTRY PRESENTS ITSELF AS A CONCERN

Only the most committed bigots will announce themselves as bigots. Typically, bigotry presents itself as being concerned with protecting "community," "family," and "culture." This is done to give social moderates intellectual cover in supporting bigotry.

Of all the lessons presented in this book, this is the most complicated. It is critically important to state at the outset that concern, itself, is not a form of bigotry. Concern about the state of affairs in society is a good thing, which society depends on to survive. The absence of concern is nihilism at best and a lack of empathy at worst. All positive social change that has ever happened in the history of humanity was born of concern, but bigotry attempts to present its ideology as concern as well. It masks its goal of convincing society that some human beings are naturally superior to others and that the superior have no obligation to respect the rights of the inferior or to treat them as human beings, presenting it as positive social change. Of the three tactics that bigotry uses to present itself as anything other than hatred, concern is the most common tactic deployed in popular culture.

It is also vital to distinguish fear from bigotry in instances of concern on an interpersonal level. By fear, I do not mean fear of difference or fear of marginalized people gaining a voice and representation in society, because those are both driven by bigotry. Here, I mean fear of bigots and the harm they can inflict as a reason some people are reluctant to support their friends and family in being open with their sexuality, gender identity, or interracial relationships. A great deal of this fear is attached to a particular aspect of identity that is often ignored in popular culture conversations about intersectionality—generational identity (Winch, 2014). For example, there are millions of older people who lived through eras when open, often violent hostility to gay couples, mixed-race couples, and gender-nonconforming people was the norm. It is understandable that these older generations sometimes react out of concern for those they love when they oppose their loved ones engaging in such relationships or living their lives in the open; this reality is a testament to the lasting impact that bigotry has on the individual and society. The difference between the fearful response and the bigoted response is that the frightened person eventually moves past their fear to respect the decision of their loved one to live life on their own terms. The bigot does not, because the acceptance of difference is ultimately a moral action, and bigotry warps any sense of morality.

In the expansion of his original eight stages of genocide, Stanton made an observation that is important to understanding how bigotry presents itself as concern under his explanation of *dehumanization*:

> The majority group is taught to regard the other group as less than human, and even alien to their society. They are indoctrinated to believe that "We are better off without them." The powerless group can become so depersonalized that they are actually given numbers rather than names, as Jews were in the death camps. (Genocide Watch, n.d., para. 8)

This depersonalization can take on many forms, some of which have been discussed regarding slurs in lesson 8. However, the invocation of slurs in national debates is not a common occurrence because it unambiguously exposes the intention of bigots. This is where presenting bigotry as concern comes into play. The manifestation of bigotry presenting itself as concern can take on many forms, but the most common form that often goes undetected by ordinary people are conversations that reduce people to problems.

In his seminal work, *The Souls of Black Folks*, W. E. B. Du Bois (1903) speaks to this form of dehumanization:

> Between me and the other world there is ever an unasked question: unasked by some through feelings of delicacy; by others through the difficulty of rightly framing it. All, nevertheless, flutter round it. They approach me in a half-hesitant sort of way, eye me curiously or compassionately, and then, instead of saying directly, How does it feel to be a problem? they say, I know an excellent colored man in my town; or, I fought at Mechanicsville; or, Do not these Southern outrages make your blood boil? At these I smile, or am interested, or reduce the boiling to a simmer, as the occasion may require. To the real question, *How* does it feel to be a problem? I answer seldom a word. (pp. 1–2)

One of the particular forms of hell that marginalized people can experience in society is to be reduced to a problem in a national debate. It is important to note that these "debates" often revolve around what rights the problem group is entitled to and what rights they can be denied. Sometimes the word *problem* is replaced with *debate*, as in the "transgender debate," or it is replaced with "question," which has its own catastrophic history. Yet, the process remains the same. Humans are stripped of their humanity and complexity and reduced to a problem that others discuss. The issues the problem group faces are seen only through the gaze of others, and so-called solutions reflect this. A historical example of this in the United States is the "Indian problem," which drove the brutalization of Indigenous people for centuries.

When the topic of reducing people to a problem to be solved, a debate to be resolved, or a question to be answered is raised, the most well-documented manifestation is the "Jewish question" in

Nazi Germany. This era is also instructive for discerning how bigotry presents itself as concern. Historian Peter Hayes (2017) wrote:

> In sum: Nazi ideology was a witches' brew of self-pity, entitlement, and aggression. It was also a form of magical thinking that promised to end all of Germans' postwar sufferings, the products of defeat and deceit, by banishing their supposed ultimate cause, Jews and their agents. Yet, the centrality of the so-called Jewish problem was much more important and obvious to Hitler than to the average German voter. (p. 65)

Hayes (2017) asserted that Hitler came to prominence in response to the Great Depression and that antisemitism "could gain mass support only in tandem with a crisis that antisemites could exploit" (p. 65). It is important to remember that bigotry often spikes in times of great upheaval and crisis because people are looking for scapegoats and targets for their misplaced anger. It was not happenstance that the COVID-19 pandemic of 2020 also saw a spike in anti–Asian-American and Pacific Islander hate (Darling-Hammond et al., 2020).

The contemporary manifestations of bigotry presenting itself as a concern are the tactics of distorting the issue and misplacing the blame. We see this with the criticism of feminism offered by some members of the loose network of male commentators, commonly called the "manosphere." At the heart of their critiques is the assertion that feminism is attacking the concept of manhood and is at the heart of the crisis of masculinity. Certainly, the masculinity crisis is real (Illing, 2023; Reeves, 2024). Men have fallen behind women in educational attainment (Reeves & Smith, 2022). Men have higher rates of suicide (CDC, 2024). These are real concerns that society must address with the seriousness it deserves, but to blame feminism and women, as the more misogynistic members of the manosphere do, is an act of misplaced blame. It is driven by a similar brew of self-pity, entitlement, aggression, and magical thinking that Hayes (2017) credited for motivating the Nazis. It is a distortion of the real issue, which is a complex mix of structural shifts in every aspect of economics, culture, and politics with which society as a whole must grapple, rather than being the result of feminist machinations (Reeves, 2024). As with any crisis, bigots—in this case, misogynists—seek a scapegoat for a real issue that they have no real interest in solving.

One of the classic manifestations of bigotry presenting itself as concerns is "defending the family." The most common threat invoked by bigots, in this case, is queer people. The bigoted claim states that queer people are trying to destroy the family by normalizing things such as same-sex marriage and same-sex parenting. Of course, the irony is that the bigots attacking queer families are, by their actions, not defending families. The same sort of mental gymnastics were visible with attacks on the Black Lives Matter movement in 2020 and 2021. The assertion that the movement was anti-family was based on a single sentence:

> We disrupt the Western-prescribed nuclear family structure requirement by supporting each other as extended families and "villages" that collectively care for one another, especially our children, to the degree that mothers, parents, and children are comfortable. (Kertscher & Sherman, 2020, para. 6)

The attacks from critics of Black Lives Matter imply that extended families and other family arrangements, such as found families, do not qualify as families or are threats to the nuclear family, even though a nuclear family is included in extended families, while not conflicting with the idea of the found family. Of course, the point of invoking the defense of the family is not the actual defense of families. It is to attack family structures of groups that bigots simply hate, and to achieve this goal, bigots accuse the targeted group of doing what they wish to do.

Another very telling aspect of bigotry that presents itself as concern is its tendency to dismiss the concerns of any group it considers inferior or unworthy. Rather than acknowledge that the complaints of groups they consider to be "the other," or to be threatening, have merit, bigots accuse these groups of embracing a victimhood mentality so they can intellectualize their dismissal of things about which they simply do not care. Evidence of this was the negative responses to the first and second waves of Black Lives Matter protests in 2015 and 2020. The demands of the Black Lives Matter movement for police reform were dismissed as being grounded in emotion rather than fact when the data on police killings of Black people showed that Black people are not the majority of people killed by police (Ward et al., 2024).

The people demeaning protestors as embracing victimhood simply ignored that events like the murder of Michael Brown, Sandra Bland, and George Floyd were being interpreted by a Black culture that has been the subject of police brutality and murders for generations (Taylor, 2013). This is because bigots do not give the groups they hate the same context of history they reserve for themselves, which allows them to dismiss any concern with historical grounding they find to be threatening to their own expressed bigoted concerns (Mitchell, 2021). Another manifestation of this particular form of bigotry has been how people with disabilities have been left out of the national conversations about how to end the mandated COVID-19 mitigation measures, despite the increased chance of death and long COVID-19 faced by members of the community, about which I go into greater detail in the next lesson.

Sometimes bigotry manifests as concern for marginalized groups through a proxy issue. An example of this is evident in the debates within African American communities about sagging pants and wearing certain hairstyles associated with "ghetto culture." The argument goes that if Black people would stop sagging their pants and giving their children Afro-centric–sounding names, then the situation would improve in Black ghettoes. The technical name for this sort of politics is *respectability politics*. This particular instance is an example of classism that dismisses the real structural causes and impacts of poverty on a community, so they advance the classic respectability politics' claim that White culture would accept Black people if they only acted in ways that refute anti-Black claims about Black culture (Jefferson, 2023). We also see this in queer communities, in women's spaces, and in every combination of marginalized identities possible (Strolovitch & Crowder, 2018), with the idea that if marginalized groups followed traditional social mores—which is often defined from the perspective of racists, anti-queer bigots, classists, and misogynists—then the dominant society would accept them and grant them equal rights (p. 340). This form of bigotry presenting itself as concern is damaging in many ways, most notably that it creates a national debate where the inferiority or degeneracy of a marginalized group has been internalized by those outside of that community and members of the marginalized community itself. Toni Morrison (Portland State University, 2014) warned of this possibility in her famous comment on how racism is a distraction—attempting to disprove bigoted claims is a pointless endeavor because bigots will always move the goalposts.

In Toni Morrison's (Portland State University, 2014) words, "There will always be one more thing" (p. 11).

References

Darling-Hammond, S., E. K. Michaels, A. M. Allen, D. H. Chae, M. D. Thomas, T. T. Nguyen, M. Mujahid, & R. C. Johnson. (2020). After "the China virus" went viral: Racially charged Coronavirus coverage and trends in bias against Asian Americans. *Health Education & Behavior*, 47(6), 870–879. https://doi:10.1177/1090198120957949

Du Bois, W. E. B. (1903). *The souls of black folk: Essays and sketches.* A. C. McClurg and Company. Retrieved September 6, 2024, from https://play.google.com/store/books/details?id=7psUAAAAYAAJ

Genocide Watch (n.d.). *The ten stages of genocide by Dr. Gregory H. Stanton.* Retrieved September 6, 2024, from https://www.genocidewatch.com/tenstages

Hayes, P. (2017). *Why? Explaining the Holocaust.* W. W. Norton & Company.

Illing, S. (2023, August 7). *The new crisis of masculinity: What's the matter with men—and how do we fix it?* Vox. Retrieved September 6, 2024, from https://www.vox.com/the-gray-area/23813985/christine-emba -masculinity-the-gray-area

Jefferson, H. (2023). The politics of respectability and Black Americans' punitive attitudes. *American Political Science Review* 117(4), 1448–1464. https://doi.org/10.1017/S0003055422001289

Kertscher, T., and A. Sherman. (2020, August 28). *Ask PolitiFact: Does Black Lives Matter aim to destroy the nuclear family?* Politifact. Retrieved September 6, 2024, from https://www.politifact.com/article/2020/aug /28/ask-politifact-does-black-lives-matter-aim-destroy/

Mitchell, N. E. (2021, July 19). *Black childhood's end: Reflections on the anniversary of the lynching of George Floyd, the conviction of Derek Chauvin, and the source of Black rage at police killings.* The North Star with Shaun King. Retrieved September 3, 2024, from https://www.thenorthstar .com/p/black-childhoods-end-reflections/

Portland State University. (2014, May 6). *Morrison, Toni; St. John, Primus; Callahan, John; Callahan, Susan; and Baker, Lloyd, "Black Studies Center Public Dialogue, Part 2" (1975). Special Collections: Oregon Public Speakers.* 90. PDXScholar. Retrieved September 6, 2024, from https:// pdxscholar.library.pdx.edu/orspeakers/90/

Reeves, R. (2024). *Of boys and men: Why the modern male is struggling, why it matters, and what to do about it.* Brookings Institution Press.

Reeves, R., and E. Smith. (2022, October 12). *Boys left behind: Education gender gaps across the US.* Brookings Institute. Retrieved September 6, 2024, from https://www.brookings.edu/articles/boys-left-behind -education-gender-gaps-across-the-us/#:~:text=In%201970%2C %20just%2012,now%20going%20the%20other%20way

Strolovitch, D. Z., and C. Y. Crowder. (2018). Respectability, anti-respectability, and intersectionally responsible representation. *PS: Political Science & Politics* 51(2), 340–344. https://doi.org/10.1017/ S1049096517002487

Taylor, C. (2013). Introduction: African Americans, police brutality, and the U.S. criminal justice system. *The Journal of African American History*, 98(2), 200–204. https://doi.org/10.5323/jafriamerhist.98.2.0200

U.S. Centers for Disease Control and Prevention. (2024, October 29). *Suicide data and statistics.* Retrieved November 25, 2024, from https://

web.archive.org/web/20241125222949/https://www.cdc.gov/suicide/facts/data.html

Ward, J. A., J. Cepeda, D. B. Jackson, O. Johnson Jr., D. W. Webster, and C. K. Crifasi. (2024). National burden of injury and deaths from shootings by police in the United States, 2015–2020. *American Journal of Public Health* 114(4), 387–397. https://doi.org/10.2105/AJPH.2023.307560

Winch, A. (2014). Feminism, generation and intersectionality: Generational differences within feminism are also opportunities for dialogue. *Soundings* 58, 8–20. https://muse.jhu.edu/pub/248/article/565754

BIGOTRY PRESENTS ITSELF AS SCIENCE

Bigotry is invested in presenting its assertions as the result of scientific inquiry and fact because if all its conclusions are justified, then they are worthy of being taught in schools and considered in critical deliberations about pressing social issues. Having achieved the status of "fact," its policy goals morph from bigoted ramblings into potential actions in areas such as "public health measures" and "criminal justice reforms."

Of all the costumes that bigotry seeks to wear, science is the most coveted. This is because the pursuit of answers to any pressing social issue inevitably leads to social and hard scientific inquiry. Bigots often engage in the imitation of empiricism, where they rely on cherrypicked, decontextualized, and often fabricated data to justify bigoted conclusions that, in turn, can become part of the decision-making process if people do not recognize them for what they are. Of all the forms of weaponized ideas (Morris, 2017), bigotry presenting itself as science is the most dangerous.

Americans like to believe that bigotry is a product of ignorance because it provides an easy solution. If we simply educate people enough, they will become immune to bigotry. As stated in lesson 2, many of the greatest architects of bigotry have been highly educated men and women; education and thinking are not necessarily interchangeable. Phillip Ball (2014) wrote that the history of Nazi

Germany "explodes the comforting myth that science offers insulation against profound irrationality and extremism" (p. 88). Being an academic does not mean that a person is immune to bigotry and will not try to use their knowledge to justify bigotry. I wish this were false, but history tells us this is simply the case.

The most profound manifestation of bigotry presenting itself as science was eugenics and the impact of the 1927 Supreme Court case *Buck v. Bell*. The justices deliberated whether the state of Virginia was violating sexual assault survivor Carrie Buck's constitutional right to due process and equal rights guaranteed by the Fourteenth Amendment by seeking to sterilize her because she was mentally disabled (Lombardo, 2003, 2008). Broadly defined, eugenics was the medical and social movement that claimed that selective breeding would improve the human species (Lombardo, 2003, 2008; Washington, 2008). In an 8–1 decision, written by Justice Oliver Wendell Holmes, the Court ruled that Virginia's sterilization law, which allowed the state to sterilize mentally disabled people and people with epilepsy, did not violate the Fourteenth Amendment. Legal scholar Paul Lombardo (2003) asserted, "The law explicitly adopted eugenic theory, affirming the proposition that tendencies to crime, poverty, mental illness, and moral failings are inherited in predictable patterns" (p. 14). The ruling had an international impact, most infamously in Nazi Germany with the 1933 Law for the Prevention of Hereditarily Diseased Offspring, and over four hundred thousand sterilizations performed in the name of eugenics eventually morphed into the medical experimentations of the concentration camps (Lombardo, 2008, p. xii). The Nuremberg trials would later brand the eugenics-inspired experiments as crimes against humanity, and Lombardo notes that the Nazi doctors cited *Buck v. Bell* in their defense (Lombardo, 2008, pp. xii–xiii).

Eugenics was a truly intersectional manifestation of bigotry because it targeted multiple groups simultaneously. Education scholar Anne Winfield (2010) wrote:

Human beings, hundreds of thousands of them, were victims of the eugenics movement in the United States, either through forcible sterilization, anti-miscegenation laws, immigration restriction, or the sorting, testing, and tracking policies implemented in schools across the country during the early decades of the twentieth century and since. The programs and policies of the eugenics movement, rooted as they were in streams of intellectual history long preceding the twentieth century, were evident across the globe and were ultimately responsible for the Holocaust and other genocidal events. In America, victims fell into roughly three areas: poor, non-Aryan, and socially deviant. Those targeted by eugenicists included both urban and rural residents who were often deemed mentally "unfit" and labeled with the dubious term *feebleminded*. They ranged from unwed mothers and young boys who masturbated, to anyone whose poverty, isolation, language, or habits rendered them unacceptable by "polite" society. (p. 144)

This is why the victims of eugenics sterilization programs were truly diverse, ranging from poor White women, like the plaintiff in *Buck v. Bell*, Carrie Buck, to noted civil rights icon Fannie Lou Hammer, who was sterilized in Mississippi in 1961 without her knowledge (Washington, 2008). Its reach was also expansive. Noted scholar and civil rights activist Angela Davis (1983) pointed out that it was revealed in the 1970s that over 35 percent of reproductive-age women in Puerto Rico and 24 percent of reproductive-age Indigenous women in the United States had been sterilized under the U.S. government's long-lasting sterilization programs (pp. 231–235). It is important to note that no Supreme Court has ever overturned *Buck v. Bell*.

The dark legacy of eugenics reared its head during the COVID-19 pandemic. It is critical to note that disabled people have historically been subject to the most intense forms of bigotry presenting itself as science. Carrie Buck was sterilized in 1927 because she, her mother, and her daughter were declared mentally disabled under Virginia law (Lombardo, 2003, 2008). Disabled people were the explicit targets of the Nazi sterilization laws in the 1930s and 1940s. Throughout the course of the governmental and public response to the COVID-19 pandemic, which, as of the writing of this book, is still ongoing, commentators and government officials pointed out that the groups most suspectable to serious illness and death were the elderly and people with medical constitutions such as diabetes, obesity, cancer, being immunocompromised, and other disabilities (CDC, 2024). This, unto itself, was not bigotry, but the dismissal of the concerns of these populations in the national conversations about COVID-19 by some was, and remains, a manifestation of ableism in the style of eugenics. The pervasive ableism of the pandemic obscured what Mbembe (2003) called necropolitics, or the politics of who is exposed to harm and death and who is not, at play and contributed to practices like health-care rationing, the constricting of access to resources, supplies, and accommodations, and continuing to be left out of conversations about vaccination rates and long COVID (Lund & Ayers, 2022).

Contemporarily, there is no greater proof of the reach bigotry has when it presents itself as science than the enduring belief that race is a biologically valid category. Although the eugenicists did not invent the concept of race, they did a great deal to convince people that race is a biological fact. It is, according to the American Association of Biological Anthropologists, not (Fuentes et al., 2019). There are many definitions of race, but I find the following thought exercise to accurately describe how the idea functions: Consider Europe, Africa, and Asia. The idea of race would have us believe that all the cultures that inhabit those continents in a patchwork of states are all the same because of their skin color. The idea is absurd on its face, but people remain convinced that this fictitious idea invented by medieval Europeans is a scientific fact. Of course, this does not mean that race is not real in the cultural and social sense because it has been imposed upon the entire human population, and societies are organized around this most insane category (Fuentes et al., 2019). Still, the billions of people around the globe who believe that race is a biological fact are maintaining and engaging in the most successful manifestation of bigotry, presenting itself as science.

One of the favorite topics of bigots is maintaining the eugenic claim that certain races are genetically prone to criminal behavior. In America, the claim is that because the majority of people arrested for homicide and robbery are Black, this is proof of inherent Black criminality. Yet the racists who make this claim ignore that White people, according to the 2022 data from FBI Crime Data Explorer (2024) for persons arrested, make up the vast majority of people arrested for arson, rape, vandalism, drug abuse violations, and motor vehicle theft. What does this data tell us about the genetic disposition of White people in America? Absolutely nothing, because committing crimes is not a genetic trait that can be passed down in families. If the White supremacists who assert a genetic link between race and crime truly held the courage of their convictions, they would assert that White people are genetically predisposed to drug addiction, property crime, theft, and sexual predation. They do not, because they do not actually believe the assertion they are making. Furthermore, according to the same FBI data (FBI Crime Data Explorer, 2024), only 2.14 percent of the total population were arrested for any crime in 2022. Such small numbers do not support the idea that any group are genetically predisposed to crime. This is the same appeal to eugenics that is made when the reaction to a mass shooting is the assumption that the shooter is a White male and the argument that White males are "predisposed" to be mass shooters.

Another contemporary example of bigotry trying to present itself as science is the attack on what commentators have termed "gender theory." What gender theory refers to is the social science consensus position that gender and biological sex are different concepts. In short, biological sex is determined by chromosomes and includes the development of primary sex characteristics, such as the vagina and penis, and secondary sex characteristics, such as facial hair and the development of breasts. People can be male, female, or intersex, and it is important to note that the upper estimate of the global number of intersex people is around 1.7% of the total human population, according to the Office of the United Nations High Commissioner for Human Rights (2025). Gender is the cultural significance and roles assigned to people based on their sex. In academic language, gender is a social construct in the same way that race is, meaning it is not innate (Pinar et al., 1995). Like most social science assertions, the idea that gender is a social construct can be disproven. All one has to do to prove that gender is innate or natural is to provide evidence that gender does not vary from culture to culture, does not vary across time, and does not have to be taught to the young, as anything innate comes to people as naturally as breathing. Bigots actively seek to avoid proving their assertion concerning gender, which is why they pretend that the anthropological data isn't there and deliberately use sex and gender interchangeably. Their goal is to create proof through what is little more than ham-fisted wordplay, in order to attack anyone they consider to be gender-nonconforming, which often includes cisgender men and women who reject sexism.

In the end, bigotry seeks to present itself as rational thought because it counters the stereotype of the bigot as an uneducated, unwashed fool who spouts nonsense from a mouth full of yellowing teeth that reeks of decay. The truth is that the most effective and dangerous advocates of bigotry present themselves as David Duke did. They are calm and seemingly reasonable men and women with a simple difference of opinions about the equality of different groups of human beings. It takes a keen mind with special attention to detail to notice the leaps of logic and misuse of data the scientific bigot uses.

References

Ball, P. (2014). *Serving the Reich: The struggle for the soul of physics under Hitler* [eBook edition]. University of Chicago Press. https://www.proquest.com/docview/2134287036/F460BAC2710748E0PQ/2?accountid=14556&sourcetype=Books

Davis, A. (1983). *Women, race, and class*. Vintage Books. https://play.google.com/store/books/details?id=74QzFiv1w10C

Federal Bureau of Investigation. (2024, January 1). *Crime data explorer: Persons arrested 2022*. Retrieved September 6, 2024, from https://cde.ucr.cjis.gov/LATEST/webapp/#

Fuentes, A., R. R. Ackermann, S. Athreya, D. Bolnick, T. Lasisi, S. Lee, S. McLean, and R. Nelson. (2019). AAPA statement on race and racism. *American Journal of Physical Anthropology* 169(3), 400–402. https://doi.org/10.1002/ajpa.23882

Lombardo, P. A. (2003). Facing Carrie Buck. *The Hastings Center Report* 33(2), 14–17. https://doi.org/10.2307/3528148

Lombardo, P. A. (2008). *Three generations, no imbeciles: Eugenics, the Supreme Court, and Buck v. Bell*. Johns Hopkins University Press.

Lund, E. M., and K. B. Ayers. (2022). Ever-changing but always constant: "Waves" of disability discrimination during the COVID-19 pandemic in the United States. *Disability and Health Journal* 15(4), 101374. https://doi.org/10.1016/j.dhjo.2022.101374

Mbembe, A. (2003). Necropolitics. *Public Culture*, 15(1), 11–40. https://doi.org/10.1215/08992363-15-1-11

Morris, T. (2017). *Dark ideas: How neo-nazi and violent jihadi ideologues shaped modern terrorism*. Lexington Books.

Office of the United Nations High Commissioner for Human Rights. (n.d.). *Intersex people*. Retrieved February 5, 2025, from https://www.ohchr.org/en/sexual-orientation-and-gender-identity/intersex-people

Pinar, W., W. Reynolds, T. Slattery, and P. Taubman. (1995). *Understanding curriculum: An introduction to the study of historical and contemporary curriculum discourses* (Vol. 17). Peter Lang.

U.S. Centers for Disease Control and Prevention. (2024, July 30). *Underlying conditions and the higher risk for severe COVID-19*. Retrieved December 1, 2024, from https://web.archive.org/web/20241205044423/https://www.cdc.gov/covid/hcp/clinical-care/underlying-conditions.html

Washington, H. (2008). *Medical apartheid: The dark history of medical experimentation on Black Americans from colonial times to the present*. Vintage Books. Retrieved September 6, 2024, from https://play.google.com/store/books/details?id=apGhwRt6A7QC

Winfield, A. G. (2010). Eugenic ideology and historical osmosis. In E. Malewski (ed.), *Curriculum studies handbook—The next moment* (pp. 142–157). Routledge.

HOW DOES BIGOTRY TEACH PEOPLE TO ACT POLITICALLY?

Like it or not, the common adage that "Everything is politics" is true for the same reason that Martin Luther King Jr. articulated when he asserted that we all exist in "an inescapable network of mutuality" (King, 1963, para. 4). Politics is bigger than which political party is currently in power. Merriam-Webster (n.d.-a) offers five different definitions for the word *politics*. When I refer to politics here, I mean the fifth definition: "a) the total complex of relations between people living in society; b) relations or conduct in a particular area of experience especially as seen or dealt with from a political point of view."

Part a of the definition refers to community, state, and nation. The difficult truth is that we all live in interconnected communities of various sizes. Some may point out that many communities are disconnected from each other by space and conditions like poverty and racial segregation. While I understand this point, I disagree. The detachment of communities is one of the more enduring myths that many countries, including the United States, have allowed to stand. Let's consider the great American cultural divide of red, conservative America versus blue, liberal America. That divide is driven by disagreement over the direction of culture rather than geography. Red states have blue and purple sections and vice versa. In my own native Louisiana, New Orleans is a blue dot in a red ocean, but if either New Orleans or the state of Louisiana fails, the other suffers. Because we all live in a community, every aspect of our lives is impacted by how problems are framed and managed. This is why everything is politics.

Part b of the definition refers to the individual. Everything—identity, morality, climate change, salaries, taxes, art, and the routes public transit takes—is political because all these things are experienced by people to various degrees. This is critical to remember when discussing the impact of bigotry on the individual and, by extension, the community. To be subject to bigotry is to be a victim of bigotry, and to be a victim, one must have a direct experience or have seen the impact of a direct experience. I like to think of experiencing bigotry in terms of a terrorist bombing; the scale of damage radiates from the center of the explosion, with those closest experiencing the most direct harm, while those on the periphery perhaps not experiencing the harm directly to their bodies but having been subjected to it, regardless. We see this metaphor play out in how a hate crime impacts the direct victim, everyone who loves the victim, and the community where the victim resides. Bigotry is a kitchen table issue because it impacts every aspect of a person's life, including the household budget. After all, identity is not a theory. It is lived (Yep, 2016).

Carol Hanisch described the lived experience of navigating bigotry from a feminist perspective in her groundbreaking 1969 essay, "The Personal Is Political":

> We call it "the pro-woman line." What it says basically is that women are really neat people. The bad things that are said about us as women are either myths (women are stupid), tactics women use to struggle individually (women are bitches), or are actually things that we want to carry into the new society and want men to share too (women are sensitive, emotional). Women as oppressed people act out of necessity (act dumb in the presence of men), not out of choice. Women have developed great shuffling techniques for their own survival (look pretty and giggle to get or keep a job or man) which should be used when necessary until such time as the power of unity can take its place. Women are smart not to struggle

alone (as are blacks and workers). It is no worse to be in the home than in the rat race of the job world. They are both bad. Women, like blacks, workers, must stop blaming ourselves for our "failures." (para. 8)

Hanisch's understanding of the lived experience of navigating bigotry was echoed in the Combahee River Collective's concept of "identity politics," which demanded that lived experiences in society shape the politics of individuals and the community rather than abstract political theory (Combahee River Collective, 1977, para. 10).

Now, it is important to state that, despite "identity politics" being a favorite scapegoat for all of America's current cultural divisions, every form of politics are identity politics (Ford, 2005; Yglesias, 2015). What feminists, queer people, people with disabilities, Jewish people, Muslims, and different communities of color have done is no different than what the much-discussed White working class in "forgotten America" has done for generations. They have developed and advocated for a politics rooted in their own experiences, which can also be described as a politics based on identity.

You, the reader, may wonder where I am going with this discussion of identity politics. Bronner (2018) wrote:

> The bigot believes that his identity, his upbringing in a particular community, gives him special insights and so the ability to judge others. There is no possibility of transgressing what Helmuth Plessner termed "the boundaries of community." Those who do not listen to the inner voice of identity—or, better, *his* inner voice—are traitors by definition. Reaffirming the bigot's identity calls on him to view reality from the standpoint of his faith, his ethnicity, or his nation. (p. 99)

Simply stated, bigotry is a form of identity politics because it is a form of identity in the same fashion as one identifies with a religion or a political party. I do not mean to equate believing in a god or gods to being a bigot because that would be a false equivalence and intellectually dishonest, considering that some of our most celebrated voices against bigotry, like Martin Luther King Jr. and Malcolm X, were firmly rooted in theology. What I mean is that bigotry is, beneath all the slurs and sputtering rage, a firm belief in a rather brutal and demented moral and political ordering of the world. When we understand bigotry as a form of identity and identity politics, then how it teaches people to act politically for the goal of winning the culture war becomes clear.

The term *culture war* has many meanings, as varied as the writers who publish on the subject. At its core, it represents very real cultural clashes over the vision of America's society, touching every aspect of American life and unfolding across the country. From 1600 Pennsylvania Avenue to the back roads of any number of dying towns in "flyover country," "Who do we want to be?" is not a question that only elected officials get to debate; it belongs to the people. As such, everyone gets to participate in the massive project of swaying national opinion. There is another term for moving the national opinion: *moving the Overton Window.*

The Overton Window is a model for understanding how ideas move from the fringe to becoming politically acceptable. In short, the ideas within the Window are the ideas society considers acceptable, and those outside the Window are considered unacceptable, or fringe. Most politicians avoid fringe ideas and determine their support for certain issues by what is within the window of acceptability. What is important to remember is that the Overton Window is not fixed. It can be shifted by convincing the public to shift their opinions (Mackinac Center, 2019). Bearing this in mind, winning the culture war looks like setting the parameters of the Overton Window so that your particular idea is in the center, or at least in the window of acceptability. A twenty-first-century example of this happened with same-sex marriage. In May 2008, only 40 percent of Americans supported it, but this shifted to 58 percent in July 2015, after the Supreme Court declared that same-sex marriage was constitutional. In May 2024, that support was 69 percent (Gallup, 2025). But just like shifting the Overton Window can push against bigotry and guarantee the rights of those who should have never been denied in the first place, it can also enshrine bigotry (Dan, 2022; Miller-Idriss, 2022; Sciarretti, 2022). Bigots know this, and their political goal is to shift the Overton Window of acceptable ideas in their favor.

Shifting the Overton Window takes more than arguments on the internet. It necessitates the act of convincing people that your way of seeing *their* world is correct. This means that it requires learning how to engage in activism and advocacy. Another word for this is *praxis*, which Merriam-Webster (n.d.-b) defines as, "Action, practice" and the "practical application of a theory." Black activist, advocate, and intellectual Fred Hampton described the importance of praxis in a 1969 speech given at the Olivet Baptist Church in Chicago. Hampton said:

> I don't care how much theory you got, if it don't have any practice applied to it, then that theory happens to be irrelevant. Right? Any theory you get, practice it. And when you practice it you make some mistakes. When you make a mistake, you correct that theory, and then it will be corrected theory that will be able to be applied and used in any situation. That's what we've got to be able to do. (Hampton, 1969/2020, para. 50)

Of course, Hampton is correct. Politics is not chemistry. No equation is guaranteed to yield the desired result. This is because the X factor in all cultures, with which the humanities and social sciences constantly wrestle, is people. Humans are dynamic. Moods, social circumstances, and environments all change. Sometimes this change is slow, while other times it happens at breakneck speed. Praxis can also be understood as evangelism in the traditional religious sense, which is really a methodology and tactic of convincing individuals, communities, and entire cultures that the way you see an issue and how it should be addressed is correct. Unfortunately, bigots can be master-level practitioners of the arts of public persuasion, and they have developed their own tactics to achieve their goal of convincing the culture to give them the power to solve both real and imagined issues facing the country. This is the subject of the fourth part of this book.

Part IV of *On Bigotry* contains the following lessons:

- Lesson 11: Bigotry does not give up easily.

- Lesson 12: Bigots will take advantage of members of their targeted groups who advocate for their own inferiority.

- Lesson 13: Bigotry does not compromise.

- Lesson 14: Bigotry demands action from bigots.

- Lesson 15: Bigotry loves moral panics.

- Lesson 16: Bigots want you to think they are unintelligent.

- Lesson 17: Bigotry loves false moral equivalence.

- Lesson 18: Bigots always claim that they are the real victims.

- Lesson 19: Bigotry gaslights everyone.

- Lesson 20: Bigotry cannot be disproven.

Of all the sections of this book, Part IV is the most overtly political in the common sense of the word, as it will draw on the American culture war to provide examples for each of its lessons. Still, I feel it is important at the outset of this final section to illuminate the intellectual sleight of hand that all forms of bigotry try to pull: convincing the average citizen that bigotry is simply another form of intellectual diversity within the Overton Window. All bigoted activism and advocacy seek to convince people to reduce millions of living, breathing, and feeling human beings to abstract political symbols and targets for their anger and resentment. Once that happens, there are no limits to the horrors that people will justify inflicting on men, women, and, as we saw with the family separations at the United States border with Mexico in 2018, children (SPLC, 2022). This sleight of hand is immoral and irrational, and it has been and continues to be devastatingly effective.

References

Bronner, S. E. (2018). From modernity to bigotry. In J. Morelock (ed.), *Critical theory and authoritarian populism* (pp. 85–105). University of Westminster Press.

Combahee River Collective. (1977). *The Combahee River Collective Statement*. Library of Congress Web Archive. Retrieved September 7, 2024, from https://www.loc.gov/item/lcwaN0028151/

Dan, P. (2022, May). *The consequences of populism: The inevitable resurgence of antisemitism* [Conference Paper]. ASN 2022 Convention, New York City, United States. https://www.researchgate.net/publication/360504548_The_consequences_of_populism_The_inevitable_resurgence_of_antisemitism

Ford, R. T. (2005). Political identity as identity politics. *Unbound*, 1(53), 53–57. https://journals.law.harvard.edu/legalleft/previous-issues/vol-i-2005/

Gallup. (2025). *LGBTQ+ rights*. Retrieved February 5, 2025, from https://news.gallup.com/poll/1651/gay-lesbian-rights.aspx

Hampton, F. (2020). *Power anywhere where there's people* [Speech Transcript]. The Hampton Institute. Retrieved September 6, 2024, from https://www.hamptonthink.org/read/power-anywhere-where-theres-people-fred-hampton. (Original work published 1969).

Hanisch, C. (1969, February). *The personal is political*. Carolhanisch.org. Retrieved September 6, 2024, from https://www.carolhanisch.org/CHwritings/PIP.html

King Jr., M. L. (1963, April 16). *Letter from a Birmingham jail*. Africa Studies Center at the University of Pennsylvania. Retrieved September 6, 2024, from https://www.africa.upenn.edu/Articles_Gen/Letter_Birmingham.html

Mackinac Center for Public Policy. (2019). *The Overton Window*. Retrieved September 6, 2024, from https://www.mackinac.org/OvertonWindow

Merriam-Webster. (n.d.-a). Politics. In *Merriam-Webster.com dictionary*. Retrieved November 19, 2024, from https://www.merriam-webster.com/dictionary/politics

Merriam-Webster. (n.d.-b). Praxis. In *Merriam-Webster.com dictionary*. Retrieved November 19, 2024, from https://www.merriam-webster.com/dictionary/praxis

Miller-Idriss, C. (2022). *Hate in the homeland: The new global far right*. Princeton University Press.

Sciarretti, K. (2022). *The rise of white supremacy in the twenty-first century* [Master's thesis, University of New Haven]. University of New Haven Digital Archive. https://digitalcommons.newhaven.edu/nationalsecurity-mas/1/

Southern Poverty Law Center. (2022, March 23). *Family separation: A timeline*. Retrieved November 16, 2024, from https://www.splcenter.org/news/2022/03/23/family-separation-timeline

Yep, G. A. (2016). Toward thick(er) intersectionalities: Theorizing, researching, and activating the complexities of communication and identities. In K. Sorrells and S. Sekimoto (eds.), *Globalizing intercultural communication: A reader* (pp. 86–94). Sage.

Yglesias, M. (2015, June 5). *All politics is identity politics*. Vox. Retrieved September 6, 2024, from https://www.vox.com/2015/1/29/7945119/all-politics-is-identity-politics

LESSON 11
BIGOTRY DOES NOT GIVE UP EASILY

Bigotry thinks in decades, not election cycles. Defeats are simply setbacks. It will lay low, reflect on how it was defeated, and evolve to counter future opposition until the conditions are ripe to make inroads into popular culture.

One of the more dangerous myths about bigotry, in general, is that it is fragile and only produces fragile individuals and movements. While it cannot be disputed that bigots are an emotionally and intellectually fragile bunch who are forever seeking out a scapegoat for all their personal failings, this is not true for bigotry as an ideology. If any form of bigotry was fragile, then they would simply be brief flashes in American culture. History tells us that bigotry is an intergenerational problem that responds to external opposition and defeat by evolving, and it exists in a constant state of reflection and revision to achieve its goals. In this sense, bigotry is an antifragile, meaning adaptive, ideology (Taleb, 2012).

Across the political spectrum, a cultural reality with which citizens wrestle is America's cycles of social progress and regress. Both sides of the political spectrum blame each other for regression in race, gender, and sexual-orientation relations and for the larger unraveling of America's social fabric. The answer to the question of why social progress regarding issues like sexism and homophobia ebbs and flows is obvious: the regression is proof of bigotry's influence on American attitudes.

Simply put, the cycle of progress and regress is proof that anti-bigotry and bigotry are still battling each other for cultural supremacy. This clash has taken on many forms in the United States and has always existed, although it has often gone unrecognized. For example, while it is true that White supremacy is baked into the foundations of the country, the same is also true of the resistance to White supremacy (West, 2019, as cited in Mitchell, 2024b). This means that American culture is built on that fundamental clash, which is the source of the cycle of progress and regress in terms of race. The same is true for gender, sexual orientation, religion, disability, and poverty, to name just a few ways that people identify. When we remember that bigotry is an active social and political force in America, and an antifragile ideology that responds to external resistance by refining its methods and evolving rather than surrendering, recent shifts in society become intelligible, and the history is laid bare.

Regarding race, there have been two moments in the twenty-first century that millions of Americans held up as a moment of hope for the country finally turning the page on its history of state-sponsored racist depravity. The first was the election of the first Black president, Barack Obama, in 2008, which many pundits and politicians hailed as the birth of a "post-racial America." Most recently, pundits and activists declared that America was in a moment of "racial reckoning," meaning a moment when the culture confronted the legacy of endemic racism, following the lynching of George Floyd.

Contrary to what some public intellectuals and academics assert, the election of the first Black president was a historic moment that demanded people reassess how much progress in race relations had occurred since the implosion of Jim Crow in 1968. The reaction to the George Floyd video triggered a similar reaction to that of the images of Emmett Till in 1955, in that it galvanized millions of Americans to demand that the country confront racism in every sector of American life. Unfortunately, both the birth of a post-racial America and America's racial reckoning were beautiful moments of wishful thinking.

It is not my intention to imply that wishing and working for such moments are trivial pursuits. I believe that if America does not become a post-racial society, which necessitates a reckoning with the very concept of race and the horror it has inflicted upon humanity, this country will continue to destabilize until the damage is irreparable. Still, these goals were never going to materialize without major resistance because bigotry, specifically White supremacy in this case, is still scratching at the edges of the Overton Window and trying to seep back into the realm of acceptable social and political thought.

The main reason that the post-racial America heralded by the election of Barack Obama, and the racial reckoning of 2020 never really materialized, was because of White backlash. White backlash is a form of identity politics in which White people react negatively to any social and political gains by non-White communities. Anyone with a passing knowledge of Black American history can find evidence of White backlash. Jim Crow was the White backlash to Black emancipation from slavery and gains in political power during Reconstruction (Cineas, 2024). The defeat of the "Great White Hope," Jim Jefferies, by the first Black heavyweight boxing champion of the world, Jack Johnson, on July 4, 1910, caused nationwide anti-Black race riots (Alderman et al., 2018). We still live in the shadow of ongoing White racist America's long resistance to desegregation that was launched in the wake of *Brown v. Board of Education* in 1954 (Mitchell, 2024a). This resistance has been successful in rolling back some of the gains of the civil rights movement, such as gutting the Voting Rights Act of 1965 through the *Shelby v. Holder* decision in 2013, among other setbacks (Mitchell, 2024a.

It is important to state that not all White people are part of White backlash to communities of color gaining rights and power in the United States. As stated in lesson 4, no group is inherently bigoted. It is important to remember this fact because White allyship was also a motivation for White backlash. White bigots saw Obama get millions of White votes in 2008, and they saw millions of White people protesting alongside Black Lives Matter in the name of racial justice. While it is currently en vogue to dismiss the White people and White-dominated institutions that hung "Black Lives Matter" signs in their front lawns and windows, White bigots saw this as a profound betrayal that intensified their backlash. Because bigotry is strong, White supremacy included resistance by communities of color and White allies in their reflection and recalibration efforts, which gave birth to the anti–Critical Race Theory movement, anti-woke movement, and the current anti-diversity movement. White supremacy took a beating in 2020, but it did not give up, and as of the writing of this book in the autumn of 2024, the anti-diversity movement has moved firmly into the Overton Window.

We are also currently witnessing a resurgence in anti-LGBTQ+ bigotry. According to data from the ACLU (2024), 533 anti-LGBTQ+ legislative bills were filed in the United States in 2024 by the time this lesson was written. The Public Religion Research Institute (PRRI) stated in its 2024 report:

> Asked about their support for or opposition to policies that protect LGBTQ Americans from discrimination in housing, employment, and public accommodation, more than three-quarters of U.S. adults (76%) favor the enactment of such policies. This represents a five-percentage-point increase compared with when the question was first asked in 2015, although support for such nondiscrimination protections dropped from a high of 80% of Americans in 2022. (p. 12)

Some will assert that a 4 percent drop is nothing worth worrying about, especially when the 2023 support remains higher than it was in 2015, at 71 percent (PRRI, 2024, p. 13), but this drop also follows the very public resurgence in anti-LGBTQ+ rhetoric and laws in American life. It is also worth pointing out the numbers by party affiliation. The PRRI data showed that "support for non-discrimination protections for LGBTQ people" among Democrats was 78 percent in 2015 and 89 percent in 2023 (PRRI, 2024, p. 13). For Republicans, support was 61 percent in 2015 and 59 percent in 2023 (PRRI, 2024, p. 13). Republicans are the only group in which support was less in 2023 than it was in 2015, when same-sex marriage was declared a constitutional right by the Supreme Court. Still, 59 percent shows that a majority of Republicans support non-discrimination protections. What the decline suggests is that anti-queer bigots are targeting the culture and making small gains with Republicans. We can see the evidence of this shift with the increased number of states that have laws that either censor or heavily restrict LGBTQ+-related topics in the school curriculum through "Don't Say Gay" laws (Movement Advancement Project, 2024). The anti-LGBTQ+ movement has become so animated that it has turned into a moral panic, which will be discussed later in this section of the book.

Another example of resurgent anti-LGBTQ+ bigotry and a perfect encapsulation of how bigotry wrecks the ability of a person to think—a topic covered in lesson 2—are the false claims by anti-transgender activists that Olympic female boxers from Algeria and Taiwan were transgender women despite their birth records listing them as born female (Puleo, 2024). We also are witnessing the popularity of misogynistic content emanating from the more bigoted corners of the manosphere and the world of podcasting. An example of this popularity is how manosphere terminology, like *alphas* and *betas* to describe dominant versus submissive men has become common in popular, and political, culture, along with threats of sexual violence becoming something of a go-to response for men toward women who act in ways they don't approve of or who simply reject them (Jane, 2018). The question we must ask ourselves is, What does all this resurgence in bigotry tell us about bigotry itself?

It tells us that, contrary to the hopes of many, bigotry is still active in the cultural landscape and making gains in pushing back the progress they see as threatening. It is easy for those opposed to bigotry and bigots to dismiss them as buffoons hiding behind keyboards, endlessly complaining about a world that passes them by. The world would be easier if this were true, but it is not. Bigots are calculating, dedicated, and worst of all, patient. For them, this is a long war rather than a skirmish, and they know, based on history, such as with the rise of Jim Crow and the Nazis, progress today does not mean progress tomorrow.

War never ends if you don't surrender, and bigots have no intention of surrendering. So, for those of us who embrace anti-bigotry, we must redefine success in such a way that it does not depend on the concept of bigots giving up.

That is just wishful thinking.

References

Alderman, D. H., J. Inwood, & J. A. Tyner. (2018). Jack Johnson versus Jim Crow: Race, reputation, and the politics of black villainy: The fight of the century. *Southeastern Geographer* 58(3), 227–249. https://www.jstor.org/stable/26510077

American Civil Liberties Union. (2024, December 6). *2024 Legislative Session: The ACLU is tracking 533 anti-LGBTQ bills*. Retrieved February 2, 2025, from https://www.aclu.org/legislative-attacks-on-lgbtq-rights-2024

Cineas, F. (2024, June 3). *The "racial reckoning" of 2020 set off an entirely new kind of backlash*. Vox. Retrieved September 7, 2024, from https://www.vox.com/policy/351106/backlash-politics-2020-george-floyd-race

Jane, E. A. (2018). Systemic misogyny exposed: Translating rapeglish from the manosphere with a random rape threat generator. *International Journal of Cultural Studies* 21(6), 661–680. https://doi.org/10.1177/1367877917734042

Mitchell, N. E. (2024a, May 17). *The joy of the Brown v. Board decision and the 70 years of resistance that's followed*. MSNBC. Retrieved September 7, 2024, from https://www.msnbc.com/opinion/msnbc-opinion/brown-v-board-supreme-court-anniversary-segregation-rcna152023

Mitchell, N. E. (2024b, February 19). *Want to learn how to respond to fascism? Study Black history.* MSNBC. Retrieved September 7, 2024, from https://www.msnbc.com/opinion/msnbc-opinion/study-black-history -to-resist-fascism-rcna138668

Movement Advancement Project. (2024). *LGBTQ Curricular Laws.* Retrieved September 7, 2024, from https://www.lgbtmap.org/equality -maps/curricular_laws

Public Religion Research Institute. (2024, March 12). *Views on LGBTQ rights in all 50 states: Findings from PRRI's 2023 American values atlas.* Retrieved September 7, 2024, from https://www.prri.org/research/ views-on-lgbtq-rights-in-all-50-states/#page-section-2

Puleo, M. (2024, August 3). Questions and answers: The Olympic women's boxing gender controversy. *Athletic.* Retrieved September 7, 2024, from https://www.nytimes.com/athletic/5678780/2024/08/04/ olympic-boxing-gender-controversy/

Taleb, N. (2012). *Antifragile: Things that gain from disorder.* Random House.

BIGOTS WILL TAKE ADVANTAGE OF MEMBERS OF THEIR TARGETED GROUPS WHO ADVOCATE FOR THEIR OWN INFERIORITY

Bigots will let members of their targeted groups advocate for their ideas, only to betray them later. There's no such thing as trust falling into an abyss.

Merriam-Webster (n.d.-c) defines a *useful idiot* as "a naive or credulous person who can be manipulated or exploited to advance a cause or political agenda." The common understanding of the concept is a person who advocates for policies and cultural movements that will inevitably harm them. For this lesson, I define the useful idiot, concerning bigotry, as "a person or movement that advocates for the inferiority of their own community." This act damns the useful idiot to a self-loathing feedback loop, as they avoid the reality that they are also advocating for their own inferiority. Bigots embrace people who advocate for their own inferiority because they provide the bigots intellectual cover from charges of bigotry. The retort is simple: "How can I be a bigot when members of X community agree with me?" It is nothing more than the classic depiction of the White racist claiming they cannot be racist because some of their best friends are Black. Inevitably, the bigot turns on these people when they are of no more use to the bigot's cause because no amount of loyalty erases that the bigot still hates them.

Before we discuss the three manifestations of the act of intellectual self-mutilation that is advocating for the inferiority of one's own community, which I will use interchangeably with "useful idiot," it is necessary to describe what this advocacy is *not*. Like all forms of bigotry, it does not fit neatly into America's political spectrum. Therefore, it is intellectually dishonest to ascribe any of this to conservatism or liberalism. As I stated in the introduction, no group is immune to bigotry.

It is critical that opponents of bigotry remember that experiencing bigotry can be traumatic for some individuals, and it is always an act of abuse, committed by the perpetrator. Most people are aware of the three responses to trauma: fight, flight, and freeze. Therapist Pete Walker (2003) added a fourth response, relevant to understanding the impact of bigotry on the individual—fawning.

According to Walker, the fawning response develops when the victim of abuse cannot fight back or run away because that triggers greater abuse from the abuser. Instead, the victim of the abuse seeks to appease and ingratiate themselves to the abuser by becoming "useful" and supportive (Walker, 2003, para. 5). The ultimate goal of fawning is the same as the other three trauma responses—to secure some measure of physical and mental safety and avoid further harm (Mathew, 2024; Walker, 2003). Walker described fawning in the context of child abuse, but it also applies to victims of bigotry. Some people think of fawning as something chosen freely (Wallace et al., 2023). This view ignores that fawning is an act of self-preservation for those who cannot escape the endemic abuse of the environment in which they find themselves (Wallace et al., 2023).

Here is an example of what fawning looks like: A Black student named Morris attends a majority White, highly respected private school where he is one of a handful of non-White students on campus. Some of the White students say "nigger" when they are rapping the lyrics of the latest hip-hop record. Morris has been taught, as many Black people are taught by their parents, to respond to any

White person saying "nigger" around them with immediate confrontation, including violence if necessary. If he were to follow this cultural norm, Morris would get into a lot of fights and risk being expelled from the school his parents have paid a lot of money for him to attend. He complains to the teachers, and nothing is done. In the end, Morris chooses to ignore his White classmates when they sing rap songs, and still say "nigger," because he is trapped in an environment where he cannot fight everyone, due to the White students' larger numbers, and he cannot flee because his parents won't send him to another school. So, he swallows his anger and does what he must to survive the situation.

Let's look at another example. Mandy is walking from a club to meet her friends three blocks down the street, at a restaurant for a late dinner. As she walks, she passes a group of young men. She hopes they don't notice her. They do. As she passes by, one of the men remarks how good she looks tonight and tells her to smile. The other men laugh and join in on the catcalling. Mandy speeds up her walk but flashes the men a slight smile to ingratiate herself with them. Shortly after, she arrives at the restaurant. In her heart, Mandy wanted to tell these men to piss off for their disrespect, but she is aware that if she does, that might escalate the situation. What if the men feel emasculated because of the rejection, get angry, and decide the only way they can feel like men again is to attack her? Mandy knows that being beaten up is not the worst thing they can do to her. So, she swallows her anger and does what she must to survive the situation.

Fawning can take on many forms (Woolard, 2023). As I write these words, a queer person somewhere is pretending to be straight or cisgender because they live in an environment where being openly queer or gender-nonconforming is dangerous. An Asian student with an ethnic name allows her classmates and teachers to call her by an "American name" like Jenny because they complain about how hard it is to say her given name. And yet, they never struggle with saying European names like Michelangelo or Tchaikovsky. A

White ally agrees with a non-White activist's claim that they are inherently racist, fearing that any attempt to defend themselves will be perceived as an act of fragility, and consequently, an admission of guilt in an activist space. The reality of fawning exposes the cruelty of attributing all acts where a person does not react to a bigoted provocation with outrage as respectability politics, which is when a member of an oppressed minority community advocates that oppressed people emulate the culture and habits of their oppressor (Jefferson, 2023). It is easy to attribute the fawning response to self-loathing behavior and call people who fawn "useful idiots," or "Uncle Tom," rather than confront the fact that fawning is evidence that bigotry as a force in society is alive and well.

As I stated earlier, useful idiots typically manifest in one of three ways. The best term that describes the first manifestation is the "pick-me," and it is an extreme form of fawning. The difference between the general fawning response and the pick-me mentality is that the former is an act of individual survival, while the latter requires a person to accept the inferiority of their community as a social and political fact. Conceptually, Danielle Procope Bell (2023) described the pick-me mentality as a manifestation of "tactical patriarchal femininity" that appeals to financially stable Black men who want a woman who will assume a submissive role in exchange for financial security (p. 1705). Procope Bell (2023) argued that the motivation for adopting this mentality is a combination of a fear of being single for a long period of time, being subject to the particular form of misogyny directed at Black women by a society called *misogynoir*, and the threat of poverty (p. 1706). As Procope Bell pointed out, there is a sizeable presence of online creators who churn out content for men in the Black manosphere, and Black women who find this sort of relationship appealing and generate money for the creators. Procope Bell wrote, "Pick-Me Black women are masters of self-objectification and alter themselves according to the stated preferences of Black manosphere men" (p. 1706). The concept that Procope Bell described can be applied outside the Black community.

It is critical that people opposed to bigotry remember that the pick-me mentality is a response to bigotry, where the individual is driven to find lasting safety in an intolerant and hostile society. In their mind, the choice is between the cruelty of impoverishment in the brutal realities of the current American economy or finding economic security in the confines of a possibly oppressive social relationship (Procope Bell, 2023). In short, supplication is the point, and the pick-me mentality betrays a degree of pessimism toward the prospect of society overcoming ingrained bigotry.

The second manifestation of a useful idiot is the "grifter." According to Merriam-Webster (n.d.-a), the definition of *grift* is "to obtain (money or property) illicitly (as in a confidence game)." When applied to bigotry, a grifter can be thought of as a merchant of hatred who earns a living or merely gains social or political clout from stirring up bigotry and from supplying bigots with talking points (Cane, 2024). If we apply this to members of groups targeted by bigots who advocate for their own inferiority, the grift takes on the role of sanitizing bigoted talking points about the grifter's own community. Why does the grifter do this? Because the lure of clout and money is too great and bigots are always looking for members of the communities they hate to repeat their arguments.

The third manifestation of the useful idiot is the "committed, internalized bigot." It is important to note that both the pick-me mentality and the grifter mentality are manifestations of internalized bigotry by extension, but they may lack true bigoted conviction. The hallmark of a committed internalized bigot is that they genuinely hate members of their own group, in a manner similar to the hatred of bigots from other groups. So, a Black pick-me and a grifter may engage in antiblackness as a means for attaining security or money for their endeavors, but a Black committed internalized bigot believes that Black people are inferior as an article of faith. I understand how this may be confusing for you, the reader, because the notion of a person being a bigot against their own group seems illogical.

Often, when people discuss subjects such as racism, sexism, and other forms of bigotry, what they are really discussing is how groups externalize or outwardly direct hatred. The classic example of this is White people hating Black people and vice versa. Internalized bigotry, logically and in the same vein as Huber et al.'s (2006, p. 184) definition of internalized racism, takes place when an individual consciously or unconsciously accepts their own inferiority and that hate is directed by a member of the group toward the group itself. A classic example of this is colorism within the African American community, where Black people further divide themselves along skin tone, hair texture, and other physical markers in favor of those with lighter skin and straighter hair. The lines between those who embrace the pick-me mentality, the grifter mentality, and the committed internalized bigot are not neat; they can also coexist within an individual, and most critically for the opponents of bigotry, within movements.

A lesser-known but still active example of this level of useful idiocy is with the cisgender members of the LGBTQ+ community who want to kick transgender people out of the larger community. The reason for this is a belief that transgender people are causing harm to the public's perception of the queer community, which threatens the stability of queer rights as a whole (Brydum, 2015; Murphy, 2015). The entire argument rests on the faulty assumption that transphobic bigots are singular in their hatred, which does not extend to LGB folks. While there are undoubtedly those sorts of bigots active in society, it is also true that many transphobic bigots view the entire queer community as degenerates and as a threat to society. This is why the anti-transgender moral panic, discussed in lesson 15, quickly morphed into a larger anti-queer moral panic, complete with accusations of grooming (Block, 2022; Romano, 2022). The anti-transgender LGB movement is an example of internalized bigotry that presents itself as concern and a self-inferiority advocacy movement that anti-queer bigots embraced until they were no longer useful.

A historical example of useful idiocy is the sad case of George Schuyler. Largely forgotten today, Schuyler was one of the most impactful Black writers in pre–civil rights movement America. His lasting work, *Black No More*, is one of the great satires of America that still has much to say about race relations and the idea of race, almost a century after its original publication in 1931. Throughout his life, Schuyler shifted from being a prominent civil rights advocate who collaborated with Roy Wilkins to investigate discrimination against Black workers on the Mississippi flood project during the Great Depression, to a man who, by 1961, defended Portuguese colonial rule in Africa (West, 1977), opposed the Civil Rights Act of 1964 (Leak, 2001), and most notoriously, denounced Martin Luther King Jr. as a "Typhoid Mary, infecting the mentally disturbed with the perversion of Christian doctrine, and grabbing fat lecture fees from the shallow-pated," in response to King receiving the Nobel Prize in 1964 (Leak, 2001, p. 105).

Henry Louis Gates wrote about Schuyler in 1992, "As Toni Morrison wrote recently in 'Playing in the Dark,' a collection of essays, 'The trauma of racism is for the . . . victim, the severe fragmentation of the self.' Nowhere is this trauma more clearly revealed than in the writings of George Schuyler" (para. 27). If Schuyler's shift does not make sense to you, the reader, consider that you are trying to view his actions as if they were rational, but you cannot rationalize irrational behavior. Sometimes trauma experienced long enough harms the mind until the individual engages in an activity that defies explanation. Schuyler's opposition to the Civil Rights Act of 1964, because it violated "individual liberty and preference" (Leak, 2001, p. 103) made no sense then and makes no sense today, but that is true for everyone who argues for the inferiority of their own community. Bigotry can break people in shocking and inexplicable ways, and a civil rights legend presenting his internalized bigotry against himself as philosophy remains shocking. George Schuyler died in 1977, seldom remembered by a Black culture to which he had become hostile, and discarded by a White, reactionary culture that once used him as "proof" of Black dissension over the civil rights movement once he was no longer useful.

Another prominent manifestation of useful idiocy is the "trans-exclusionary radical feminist" movement, commonly known as TERFs (Merriam-Webster, n.d.-b). In short, TERFs believe that transgender women are a threat to cisgender women and that transgender men have been brainwashed into thinking they can simply choose not to be women (Burns, 2019). So, TERFs oppose all transgender rights, and to achieve this end, they have aligned themselves with the larger antifeminist movement on the right wing, although TERF membership straddles the entire political spectrum and includes both queer and straight advocates. Video essayist Natalie Wynn (Contrapoints, 2023) asserted TERFs are not "the final boss" or the great devil of the anti-transgender movement (1:48:00). She asserted:

> The devil is patriarchy. It's the right-wing men who will be the ones to put Gender Critical theory into brutal practice. . . . TERFs are the real handmaidens. They're useful idiots who put a concerned female face on the patriarchal violence against trans people that will ultimately be enacted by right-wing men. (Contrapoints, 2023, 01:48:09)

As stated in lessons 1 and 2, bigotry destroys a person's ability to think along with any sense of morality. The TERF movement is a stark example of how that intellectual catastrophe extends to political advocacy. In their bigotry, TERFs have politically intertwined themselves with advocates for a hard return to American patriarchy who have no real interest in women's liberation as a whole, to the extent that they blame feminism for the current crisis of masculinity. Meanwhile, the anti-transgender movement uses TERFs as proof that their goals are not sexist because TERFs are cisgender women who call themselves feminists.

The harsh truth of anti-trans laws is that for many of them to function as safeguards for cisgender women, the laws must also apply to cisgender women in the sense that cisgender women must conform to a sexist notion of what it means to be feminine. An example occurred in Utah, in 2024 (Alfonseca, 2024). On social media, former state school board member Natalie Cline accused a teenage basketball player of being trans, although she was cisgender. Cline claimed that the basketball player's physical build caused her to question the player's sex and stated in a later social media post, after she deleted her accusation:

> We most certainly recognize that there is great variety within females when it comes to physical characteristics, and of course, we are accepting of these differences and want all girls to feel welcome in school sports. Sadly, our good faith efforts to be accepting of differences has, at times, been taken advantage of causing a loss of trust, which leads to suspicion about girls who are more buff than most. (Alfonseca, 2024, para. 7)

The spate of anti-transgender laws and the moral panic that has energized them incentivize a form of vigilantism where cisgender people claim to be able to spot a transgender woman. However, this is all based on misogynistic ideas of what femininity looks like. As a result, cisgender women who are too muscular or simply do not look "feminine enough" are subject to anti-trans and misogynistic bigotry. TERFs have become enablers of the most classical form of misogyny—scrutinizing women's bodies under a male gaze.

Regardless of the form it takes, advocating for the inferiority of one's own community requires a great deal of willful ignorance and self-delusion. Bigots are not shy about their desires to harm the targets of their hatred, so for a member of the target group to be a useful idiot, they must ignore all their clear pronouncements while pretending they do not hear the dog whistles. In the end, the pick-me, the grifter, and the committed internalized bigot must delude themselves into thinking they are somehow exempt from what the bigots say about the community to which they belong. The Black useful idiot must believe that every other Black person is inferior except for them. The TERF must convince themselves that the misogynists will not subject them to misogyny. The queer anti-transgender useful idiot must convince themselves that straight anti-transgender bigots do not lump all gender non-conforming and non-heterosexual people together. All the aforementioned groups do this with all evidence to the contrary staring them in the face, while having the audacity to be surprised when the inevitable day comes that the bigoted movements for which they advocated, turn on them and discard them. Everyone who advocates for their own inferiority is destined to become a modern-day George Schuylers—politically, socially, and culturally homeless. In the end, the usefulness is always temporary.

A political pop cultural metaphor (Krugman, 2024) perfectly captures the fate of a useful idiot:

HEADLINE: A person who voted for the Leopards Eating Faces Party is shocked when the leopard eats their face.

References

Alfonseca, K. (2024, February 9). *Utah official falsely suggests teen student is transgender, now faces calls to resign.* ABC News. Retrieved September 7, 2024, from https://abcnews.go.com/US/utah-school-board-official-falsely-suggested-teen-girl/story?id=107100300

Block, M. (2022, May 11). *Accusations of "grooming" are the latest political attack—with homophobic origins* [Radio broadcast transcript]. National Public Radio. Retrieved September 7, 2024, from https://www.npr.org/2022/05/11/1096623939/accusations-grooming-political-attack-homophobic-origins

Brydum, S. (2015, November 6). LGBT groups respond to petition asking to "Drop the T." *Advocate.* Retrieved September 7, 2024, from https://www.advocate.com/transgender/2015/11/06/lgbt-groups-respond-petition-asking-drop-t

Burns, K. (2019, September 5). *The rise of anti-trans "radical" feminists, explained.* Vox. Retrieved December 1, 2024, from https://www.vox .com/identities/2019/9/5/20840101/terfs-radical-feminists-gender -critical

Cane, C. (2024). *The grift: The downward spiral of Black republicans from the party of Lincoln to the cult of Trump.* One Street Books.

Contrapoints. (2023, April 17). *The witch trials of J.K. Rowling | ContraPoints* [Video]. YouTube. Retrieved September 7, 2024, from https://www.youtube.com/watch?v=EmT0i0xG6zg

Gates, H. (1992, September 20). A fragmented man: George Schuyler and the claims of race. *New York Times.* Retrieved September 7, 2024, from https://www.nytimes.com/1992/09/20/books/university-presses -a-fragmented-man-george-schuyler-and-the-claims-of.html

Huber, L. P., R. N. Johnson, & R. Kohli (2006). Naming racism: A conceptual look at internalized racism in US schools. *Chicano-Latino Law Review* 26, 183–206. https://heinonline.org/HOL/P?h=hein.journals/ chiclat26&i=187

Jefferson, H. (2023). The politics of respectability and Black Americans' punitive attitudes. *American Political Science Review* 117(4), 1448– 1464. https://doi.org/10.1017/S0003055422001289

Krugman, P. (2024, October 31). Leopards are telling you that they will eat your face. *New York Times.* Retrieved November 24, 2024, from https://www.nytimes.com/2024/10/31/opinion/trump-musk-mike -johnson.html

Leak, J. (ed.). (2001). *Rac(e)ing to the right: Selected essays of George S. Schuyler.* University of Tennessee Press.

Mathew, L. (2024). Racism is life-threatening and continues the cycle of racial trauma: What can clinicians do to interrupt this cycle? *Clinical Social Work Journal* 52, 265–273. https://doi.org/10.1007/s10615-023 -00913-y

Merriam-Webster. (n.d.-a). Grift. In *Merriam-Webster.com dictionary.* Retrieved November 19, 2024, from https://www.merriam-webster .com/dictionary/grift#:~:text=%3A%20to%20obtain%20(money%20 or%20property,grifter%20noun

Merriam-Webster. (n.d.-b). TERF. In *Merriam-Webster.com dictionary.* Retrieved November 19, 2024, from https://www.merriam-webster .com/dictionary/TERF

Merriam-Webster. (n.d.-c). Useful idiot. In *Merriam-Webster.com diction-ary*. Retrieved November 19, 2024, from https://www.merriam-web-ster.com/dictionary/useful%20idiot

Murphy, T. (2015, November 11). Change.org petition wants to take the T out of LGBT. *New York Magazine*. Retrieved September 7, 2024, from https://nymag.com/intelligencer/2015/11/can-you-take-the-t-out-of-lgbt.html

Procope Bell, D. (2023). "Pick-Me" Black women: Tactical patriarchal femininity in the Black manosphere. *Feminist Media Studies* 24(8), 1704–1722. https://doi.org/10.1080/14680777.2023.2262163

Romano, A. (2022, April 21). *The right's moral panic over "grooming" invokes age-old homophobia: "Groomer" accusations against liberals and the LGBTQ community are recycled Satanic Panic.* Vox. Retrieved September 7, 2024, from https://www.vox.com/culture/23025505/leftist-groomers-homophobia-satanic-panic-explained

Walker, P. (2003, January/February). Codependency, trauma, and the fawn response. *Pete-Walker.com*. Retrieved September 7, 2024, from http://www.pete-walker.com/codependencyFawnResponse.htm

Wallace, D., C. P. Moore, and K. Roller. (2023). Black girls are taught to survive: Historical trauma and the strong Black woman's embodiment. *International Body Psychotherapy Journal* 22(1), 16–30. https://tinyurl.com/cfhn25hc

West, H. (1977, September 8). George S. Schuyler, 87, satirist on race affairs. *Washington Post*. Retrieved September 7, 2024, from https://www.washingtonpost.com/archive/local/1977/09/09/george-s-schuyler-87-satirist-on-race-affairs/18b39526-3b13-4161-88b9-9464acf4c51f/

Woolard, A. (2023, July 5). *What is "fawning"? How is it related to trauma and the "fight or flight" response?* The Conversation. Retrieved September-ber 7, 2024, from https://theconversation.com/what-is-fawning-how-is-it-related-to-trauma-and-the-fight-or-flight-response-205024

LESSON 13
BIGOTRY DOES NOT COMPROMISE

There is no compromise with bigotry because the ideas of "I am a human being" and "some human beings are more human than others" are irreconcilable. What's the civil rights compromise between TERFs or racists and transgender folks or people of color? Any step toward bigotry is simply bigotry.

The American political system is structurally built around the concept of compromise. The framers of the Constitution deliberately created a style of government that can only function assuming one party does not have an overwhelming majority and the factions sit down and hammer out an agreement with which they can all accept. As a concept for good government and personal relationships with friends and family, compromise is a virtue, but it has limits. Novelist Robert Jones Jr. said, "We can disagree and still love each other unless your disagreement is rooted in my oppression and denial of my humanity and right to exist" (Williams-Jent, 2021, para. 4). He is correct, of course. Some topics do not allow for compromise, and in rejection of the classic American platitude of coexistence, people cannot simply agree to disagree.

Bigotry is one of these topics. A question that I pose to you, the reader, is what civil or human rights do you currently enjoy that you would surrender to appease a bigot who thinks you are threatening, degenerate, or subhuman? The answer is none, and this is why bigots go to great lengths to present their ideology as just another form of intellectual diversity. For bigots, the point of the compromise is to get people to open legal and cultural doors that cannot be easily closed. As stated in lesson 3, once we decide that it is acceptable for certain classes of people to have more rights than others, the only debate is over who gets full rights and who gets to be oppressed.

It is essential to point out that a tense debate over complex topics does not automatically qualify it as a bigoted discourse that invites compromise with bigots. Serious public issues demand candor and a willingness to critique both the best-laid plans and the best of intentions. It is easy to tell the difference between a tense debate over complex topics and a debate where bigots are seeking to get well-meaning people to compromise. In a bigoted conversation, the topic fundamentally rests on denying a group of people their civil and human rights, subjecting them to harm, or reducing the group to a problem to be solved rather than acknowledging them as human beings. Tense debates over complex topics do not do any of this.

We see this lesson manifest in how elementary and secondary education have been swallowed into the depths of the culture war debates over how to teach about the history of bigotry, how to teach about identity, and how the compromises with bigots have placed teachers in a truly untenable position. Teachers face ethical decisions every day that range from the mundane, such as allowing a student to turn in a late assignment, to the nightmare scenarios of how to respond in an active shooter situation (Mitchell, 2023, para. 1). In recent years, America's unyielding culture war has forced teachers and teacher preparation programs to confront a profound ethical dilemma born from compromises with bigots: What do you do when the state commands you to do something unethical? This is the situation teachers have been subjected to, at the hands of elected officials who pander to the twin moral maelstroms of the anti–Critical Race Theory and anti–gender ideology movements.

So, what are the compromises with bigots reflected in the so-called anti-CRT and anti–transgender education laws? Regarding the anti-CRT laws, the compromise was made with bigots who view Black history as a form of anti-White indoctrination. Regarding anti–transgender education laws, the compromise was made with people who view transgender and gender-nonconforming youth as suffering from a mental health crisis and the victims of a mass grooming conspiracy. For the bigots, these laws are incremental victories where they did not get everything that they wanted this time with the goal of coming back for the rest. More importantly, it shifted the Overton Window in their favor, where the possibility of such laws has entered the realm of normal politics.

Multiple states have passed laws and introduced bills that impose restrictive measures on educational content and practices. For example, Florida's STOP WOKE Act requires educators to teach a distorted version of America's racial history (Fawcett & Hartocollis, 2023). Another example is Arizona's governor vetoed 2023 Senate Bill 1001, which forbids school employees and independent contractors from using a student's chosen pronouns if they differ from the under 18 years of age student's biological sex, unless the district has parental permission. This bill also permits school employees and contractors to refuse to use an individual's chosen pronouns if doing so contradicts their religious or moral sentiments (Snyder & Wong, 2023). The STOP WOKE Act is an example of what philosopher Carter G. Woodson famously described as miseducation, or teaching lies and distortions as if they were facts, in his famous 1933 text *The Miseducation of the Negro*. Subjecting gender-nonconforming students, meaning children, to harassment and disrespect from teachers, meaning adults, is a normalization of state-sanctioned violence (Movement Advancement Project & GLSEN, 2017). Of course, the violence is not physical, but not all violence is physical. Often, verbal violence can hit a person with the force of a physical blow and is capable of leaving mental scars. Some writers and public intellectuals will dismiss the notion that violence can be anything other than physical. My response to them is if that is the case, then explain verbal abuse and its documented negative impact on both physical and mental health (Office on Women's Health, 2024), especially in gender-nonconforming youth (Norris & Orchowski, 2020). That is what the so-called anti-gender ideology laws that force teachers to ignore students' chosen names and pronouns seek to do—use teachers to abuse other people's children.

Teachers are forbidden from miseducating students and inflicting harm on them, but in the wake of the anti–Critical Race Theory, the gallingly bigoted anti-trans movements, and ambitious politicians who feel they can become senators and presidents by embracing both of those movements, teachers have been placed in an ethical bind. The National Education Association code of ethics (NEA, 2020) states in Principle 1, rules 3, 4, and 5 that teachers: "shall not deliberately suppress or distort subject matter relevant to the student's progress, shall make reasonable effort to protect the student from conditions harmful to learning or to health and safety, and shall not intentionally expose the student to embarrassment or disparagement." All these ethical principles are found in one form or another in every state's (including Florida's) code of teacher conduct (Florida Department of Education, 2024). However, ethics only matter if you hold yourself accountable to them. The authors and advocates of these laws lack ethics, and by extension morals, so they are only accountable for their rage and bigotry. This is evidenced by their determination to deny Black students access to AP African American studies courses in Florida (Fawcett & Hartocollis, 2023; Mazzei & Hartocollis, 2023) and to subject gender-nonconforming students to state-mandated harm (Movement Advancement Project & GLSEN, 2017).

Both miseducation and mandated abuse laws are increasingly placing teachers in an ethical nightmare, because noncompliance can result in being fired and having one's teaching license revoked, possibly permanently in that state. Ethically speaking, the question is,

"How should you respond when the state wants you to miseducate children or inflict harm on children as a goal of policy?" This ethical dilemma is a difficult one because there are multiple complications. This conversation looks entirely different for a teacher fresh out of college or graduate school who is still young, single, and childless versus a seasoned teacher with children of their own, who depends upon meager salaries, and often second jobs, to make ends meet.

The ethical dilemma is not just financial.

The reward of being a teacher is the opportunity to become a positive part of someone's story. We all remember the teachers who cared for us and changed our lives for the better. However, the cost of being a teacher includes becoming a part of someone's story in a less-favorable way. We also remember, with anger and hurt, the teachers who shamed us. It is fair to say that teachers who comply with laws that force them to teach historical lies and distortions as if they were facts, and subject children to state-sanctioned bullying that turns the school into a hostile environment, will be remembered as mouthpieces of ideologies obsessed with fighting the culture war, and more egregiously, they will be accomplices in the abuse of other peoples' children for the crime of being nonbinary or transgender. Simply put, teachers are being forced to be everything that they have been trained *not* to be.

This situation only exists because the twin disasters of the anti-CRT and anti–gender ideology movements have enough political capital to force legislation through while bearing no further thought to what they are forcing teachers to do. For them, to quote Adam Serwer, cruelty is the point (2018). As a curriculum theorist, these laws make me feel many emotions, but shock has rarely been one because I do not find bigotry or its penchant for corrupting everything it touches to be shocking. I expect cruelty from people who believe that cruelty is a virtue. Bigots are nothing if not predictable.

Still, it is important to point out an often-ignored fact in these debates: teachers did not ask to be put in these situations, and many parents did not demand this cruel service of them. This is only happening because ordinary people decided to compromise with bigots. America expects teachers to act in many roles, which is a fair expectation because students are not empty vessels. They are human beings with all the complexities inherent to humanity. A teacher may have to act as a mentor, counselor, disciplinarian, emotional support person, and educator in the course of a single class. This is the job, and millions of teachers perform their jobs admirably. Deceiver and abuser on behalf of the state should not be part of the job description.

In this case, compromise with bigots has opened the door to increasingly draconian laws of a similar vein because once mandating that Black students be taught lies about their own history and forcing teachers to become persecutors of students of all genders because any anti-transgender law will be applied to cisgender people, the only thing to discuss is scope. One compromise leads to another and another and another, until the bigots have gotten all the power they initially sought. This is when the actions begin.

References

Fawcett, E., and A. Hartocollis. (2023, January 21). Florida gives reasons for rejecting A.P. African American Studies class. *New York Times*. Retrieved September 7, 2024, from https://www.nytimes.com/2023/01/21/us/florida-ap-african-american-studies.html

Florida Department of Education. (2024). *Principles of professional conduct for the education profession in Florida*. Retrieved September 7, 2024, from https://www.fldoe.org/teaching/professional-practices/code-of-ethics-principles-of-professio.stml

Mazzei, P., and A. Hartocollis. (2023, January 19). Florida rejects A.P. African American studies class. *New York Times*. Retrieved September 7, 2024, from https://www.nytimes.com/2023/01/19/us/desantis-florida-ap-african-american-studies.html

Mitchell, N. E. (2023, September 12). *Anti-trans measures force teachers to choose between the law and ethics*. MSNBC. Retrieved September 8,

2024, https://www.msnbc.com/opinion/msnbc-opinion/-transgender-notification-policy-california-school-district-rcna103962

Movement Advancement Project & GLSEN. (2017). *Separation and stigma: Transgender youth and school facilities*. Retrieved September 7, 2024, from https://www.lgbtmap.org/policy-and-issue-analysis/transgender-youth-school

National Education Association. (2020, September 14). *Code of ethics for educators*. Retrieved September 7, 2024, from https://www.nea.org/resource-library/code-ethics-educators

Norris, A. L., and L. M. Orchowski. (2020). Peer victimization of sexual minority and transgender youth: A cross-sectional study of high school students. *Psychology of Violence* 10(2), 201–211. https://doi.org/10.1037/vio0000260

Office on Women's Health. (2024, December 6). *Emotional and verbal abuse*. Retrieved February 2, 2025, from https://www.womenshealth.gov/relationships-and-safety/other-types/emotional-and-verbal-abuse#:~:text=What%20are%20the%20effects%20of,pain%2C%20depression%2C%20or%20anxiety

Serwer, S. (2018, October 3). The cruelty is the point. *Atlantic Magazine*. Retrieved September 7, 2024, from https://www.theatlantic.com/ideas/archive/2018/10/the-cruelty-is-the-point/572104/

Snyder, I., and K. Wong. (2023, May 23). SB 1001: Arizona's "pronoun bill" vetoed by Gov. Katie Hobbs: What you should know. *Fox 10 Phoenix*. Retrieved November 16, 2024, from https://www.fox-10phoenix.com/news/arizona-bill-would-require-teachers-get-parents-permission-to-use-students-preferred-pronoun

Williams-Jent, R. (2021, February 25). *Robert Jones Jr. cultivates community with "Son of Baldwin," "The Prophets."* Watermark. Retrieved September 7, 2024, from https://watermarkonline.com/2021/02/25/robert-jones-jr-cultivates-community-with-son-of-baldwin-the-prophets/

Woodson, C. (2005). *The miseducation of the Negro*. Dover Publications. (Original work published 1933).

BIGOTRY DEMANDS ACTION FROM BIGOTS

Bigotry is not idle, and it does not encourage idleness. Bigotry is missionary in its zeal and commands its believers to be cruel to those it deems a threat. This is done to keep the targets of bigotry in a constant state of terror.

This lesson focuses on other forms of action aside from physical violence, which was discussed in lesson 7. This distinction is vital because there are many forms of action bigots employ that are firmly within the normal range of political activity, such as protesting, advocating for elected officials, and other visible forms of sloganeering. One of these forms of action is "vice signaling," which is critical to understanding how bigotry demands action from bigots (Berlatsky, 2020; Táíwò, 2022). A simple example of this is the neo-Nazis wearing bigoted shirts in public. They know it will offend the people whom they hate while appealing to people by whom they want to be accepted.

Invoking the work of historian David Perry, Berlatsky (2020) described this concept as "a public display of immorality, intended to create a community based on cruelty and disregard for others, which is proud of it at the same time" (para. 3). Táíwò (2022) asserted that "people vice signal by behaving in a way that they expect out-group members to find injurious or vicious," while garnering favor in the group to which they are affirming loyalty (p. 299). Berlatsky and

Táíwò both agree that the point of vice signaling is to confirm membership in a community by actively seeking to inflict some manner of emotional harm on groups seen as the other. For all forms of bigotry, this is a classic tactic of political engagement and organizing.

If you want to figure out what a bigot will do to confirm their bigotry to the world, it is a safe bet to pick the cruelest thing you can imagine. But more than that, cruelty has a political utility that is intrinsic to the world and systems that bigots create, if given the opportunity. It bonds bigots together. Adam Serwer (2018) wrote about looking at lynching photos:

> Their names have mostly been lost to time. But these grinning men were someone's brother, son, husband, father. They were human beings, people who took immense pleasure in the utter cruelty of torturing others to death—and were so proud of doing so that they posed for photographs with their handiwork, jostling to ensure they caught the eye of the lens, so that the world would know they'd been there. Their cruelty made them feel good, it made them feel proud, it made them feel happy. And it made them feel closer to one another. (para. 3)

Vice signaling is cruel by design because that is the point. In Serwer's (2021) view, cruelty can take on many forms, such as the cruelty of the backlash, the cruelty of teaching historical lies as if they were true, the cruelty of lying about the current crisis society faces, and how it got here, and the demand that the victims of bigotry and societal injustice soften their condemnation in the name of civility that has never been extended to them. All vice signaling is performative cruelty. I do not use the word *performative* in a dismissive sense. Rather, I mean that it is performative because a person must act it out in the world. Vice signaling can range from a racial slur and a belittling joke to imposing laws that harm people like the anti-poor bigoted laws that criminalize unhoused people for being forced to sleep outdoors (Santa Cruz, 2024).

An example of vice signaling is asserting that "all lives matter" in response to the Black Lives Matter movement. Now, it is important to point out that "all lives matter" is a pillar of social justice philosophy (Kammer, 1991/2004), so the words themselves are not the issue, but rather how they were used during the height of the BLM protests, making them vice signaling. On its face, there is no conflict between saying that all lives matter and that Black lives matter, as all lives would be inclusive of Black lives. However, bigots appropriated the social justice plank, semantically bleached it so it lost all its original meaning, and then weaponized the phrase to try to silence and undermine the BLM movement (Goodman et al., 2023; Stollznow, 2021). The assertion from the All Lives Matter crowd was that there was something intrinsically wrong with Black people advocating for their rights against cruel and unusual punishment by the police. This was and remains an attempt by anti-Black bigots to cosplay their disdain for Black people protesting as an intellectual appeal to humanity (Stollznow, 2021). The opponents of Black Lives Matter used the slogan "all lives matter" to cause emotional injury to members of BLM while affirming their own racial-conservative credentials. In this sense, "all lives matter" is a textbook example of vice signaling.

Another example of vice signaling is the refusal to use an individual's chosen pronouns. First and foremost, it is profoundly disrespectful because it causes harm to gender-nonconforming people, and it violates federal civil rights law against harassment in the workplace (Sexual and Gender Minority Research Office, 2024). This performative cruelty is, of course, the point. Like with "all lives matter," the refusal is justified with an attempt to cosplay simple anti-queer bigotry as philosophy, specifically that they only refer to people based on their biological sex rather than their gender. This example veers into the classic bigoted tendency to claim knowledge that one does not have because in doing so, we assume that we know the sex of everyone we see over the course of our day. Truth be told, we do not actually know the sex of strangers with any certainty. This is irrelevant to the point of the vice signaling, however, which is to make gender-nonconforming people feel ostracized, mocked, and threatened while confirming one's membership to the anti-queer movement.

While the focus of this lesson is not violence, the subject cannot be avoided when it comes to vice signaling. There are forms of non-physical violence, such as stochastic terrorism, where bigoted rhetoric increases the likelihood that a bigot will engage in physical violence (Nelson, 2022). Some assert that stochastic terrorism can only occur when a political leader or major public figure, such as a president or media figure with a large audience, engages in such rhetoric. I respectfully disagree with this emphasis because an idea can only be realized if people spread it. I assert that stochastic terrorism requires the work of ordinary bigots on the local level in the same manner that oppression does. The "great leaders" can say whatever they wish, but they need middlemen and -women to sell it on the grassroots level. In this sense, stochastic terrorism happens on the local level, too.

Vice signaling among bigots is often a vehicle for stochastic terrorism, which can lead to acts of physical violence. I shall refer to this phenomenon as the vice signaling–stochastic terrorism–physical violence pipeline.

One of the most glaring manifestations of the vice signaling–stochastic terrorism–physical violence pipeline happened at the Unite the Right Rally held in Charlottesville, Virginia, on August 11 and 12, 2017. The infamous "Tiki Torch Parade" is an example of stochastic terrorism. White non-Jewish men marched through the University of Virginia campus chanting, "Jews will not replace us!" (Gabbatt, 2017) while carrying torches designed to invoke the image of Nazis marching in Nuremberg, Germany. It was also designed to terrorize Jewish people and anyone else whom the marchers considered a threat. While it was not actual physical violence at that moment, terror does not require physical action to achieve its actual goal of inflicting physical harm on the individual. Some may dismiss the idea that words and marching can have a physical impact on the individual. My response to this is to ask if they think that fearing for your life is pure emotion with no impact on the body. Is a panic attack not a physical response to a danger that may not be physical? Those who dismiss that words and protests can cause physical harm pretend that fear cannot be real because they simply lack the resolve or possess an awareness of how they appear to outsiders. Invoking fear in the target is one of the points of all forms of terrorism, including stochastic terrorism.

If the rally at Charlottesville ended with the antisemitic march through campus, it would have been the sort of thing that simply became part of living memory for that community, where locals talk about when the bigots came to town with some tiki torches. But that is not where things ended. To describe the events that happened as a rally, a protest, or even a riot is intellectual dishonesty in pursuit of mitigating the horror of August 12. The best descriptor for what happened was a race riot in the long tradition of American race riots. A White supremacist mob attacked counter-protestors and found themselves fighting in the streets against anti-Fascists who had arrived in Charlottesville after the antisemitic march (Stockman, 2017). Like most race riots, it included a lynching. Some may dispute calling the murder of Heather Heyer (Burke & Sotomayor, 2018) a lynching because she was White, and she was not hanged. My response to this is that White people have been murdered by White supremacists throughout history for the crime of resisting White supremacy, as Viola Liuzzo was, during the civil rights movement in 1965 (National Park Service, 2022). Also, lynchings, by definition, do not require a hanging. They are simply defined as being "put to death (as by hanging) by mob action without legal approval or permission" (Merriam-Webster, n.d.-b). Liuzzo was shot while driving (National Park Service, 2022). Heyer was hit by a car. Both were killed because vice signaling turned into stochastic terrorism, which morphed into physical violence.

Another example of the vice signaling–stochastic terrorism–physical violence pipeline is catcalling. Merriam-Webster (n.d.-a) defines *catcalling* as "the act of shouting a loud, sexually suggestive, threatening, or harassing call or remark at someone publicly." This action is typically directed at both cisgender and gender-nonconforming women, by men. As a manifestation of vice signaling, the reason men engage in this behavior is that they are signaling their misogyny to each other, to confirm their masculinity while engaging in performative cruelty to women. As a manifestation of stochastic terrorism, catcalling is designed to be an explicit or implicit threat, where the catcaller is actually daring the victim to respond with anger, because an angry response may be interpreted as justification for violent action by the catcaller, which is the point at which the stochastic terrorism inspires physical violence (RAINN, 2024; Rascoe, 2023). Catcallers may claim they are "giving compliments," but that is just an attempt to cosplay their bigotry as philosophy. The goal is to terrorize women in the public space while affirming their own commitment to misogyny.

If bigotry rendered people into isolationists who avoided interacting with a society they find deplorable, then bigotry would not be much of a topic of discussion outside of social science, human science, and humanities academia. However, bigotry demands evangelization and the visible confirmation of being a member of the congregation. This is why the second assertion of the idea of anti-bigotry that I am describing in this book is that given enough time and opportunity, a bigot will unambiguously confirm their bigotry toward groups they deem inferior, threatening, or degenerate in word, action, or both. The iron law of bigotry is that a bigot will inevitably out themselves because they are driven to be cruel and to display that cruelty to the entire world.

References

Berlatsky, N. (2020, May 7). As Bethany Mandel's "grandma killer" tweet proves, vice-signaling is the right's newest and most toxic trend. *Independent*. Retrieved September 8, 2024, from https://www.independent.co.uk/voices/bethany-mandel-grandma-killer-tweet-coronavirus-lockdown-protest-a9504391.html

Burke, M., and M. Sotomayor. (2018, December 7). *James Alex Fields found guilty of killing Heather Heyer during violent Charlottesville White nationalist rally*. NBC News. Retrieved September 8, 2024, https://www.nbcnews.com/news/crime-courts/james-alex-fields-found-guilty-killing-heather-heyer-during-violent-n945186

Gabbatt, A. (2017, August 16). "Jews will not replace us": Vice film lays bare horror of neo-Nazis in America. *Guardian*. Retrieved September 8, 2024, https://www.theguardian.com/us-news/2017/aug/16/charlottesville-neo-nazis-vice-news-hbo

Goodman, S., V. Tafi, and A. Coyle. (2023). Alternative "Lives Matter" formulations in online discussions about Black Lives Matter: Use, support and resistance. *Discourse & Society* 34(3), 291–316. https://doi.org/10.1177/09579265221118016

Kammer, F. (2004). *Doing faithjustice: An introduction to Catholic social thought* (revised edition). Paulist Press. (Original work published in 1991).

Merriam-Webster. (n.d.-a). Catcalling. In *Merriam-Webster.com dictionary*. Retrieved December 1, 2024, https://www.merriam-webster.com/dictionary/catcalling

Merriam-Webster. (n.d.-b). Lynching. In *Merriam-Webster.com dictionary*. Retrieved December 1, 2024, https://www.merriam-webster.com/dictionary/lynching

National Park Service. (2022, July 13). *Viola Liuzzo*. Retrieved September 8, 2024, https://www.nps.gov/semo/learn/historyculture/viola-liuzzo.htm

Nelson, B. (2022, November 5). How stochastic terrorism uses disgust to incite violence. *Scientific American*. Retrieved September 8, 2024, https://www.scientificamerican.com/article/how-stochastic-terrorism-uses-disgust-to-incite-violence/

Rape, Abuse & Incest National Network. (2024). *Street harassment.* Retrieved September 8, 2024, https://www.rainn.org/articles/street -harassment

Rascoe, A. (Host). (2023, October 29). The Sunday Story: This is what it feels like to be catcalled [Audio podcast transcript]. In *Up first.* National Public Radio. Retrieved September 8, 2024, https://www.npr .org/transcripts/1198908962

Santa Cruz, N. (2024, June 29). *U.S. Supreme Court ruling will allow more aggressive homeless encampment removals.* Pro Publica. Retrieved September 8, 2024, https://www.propublica.org/article/us-supreme-court -grants-pass-homelessness

Serwer, A. (2018, October 3). The cruelty is the point. *Atlantic Magazine.* Retrieved September 8, 2024, https://www.theatlantic.com/ideas/ archive/2018/10/the-cruelty-is-the-point/572104/

Serwer, A. (2021). *The cruelty is the point: The past, present, and future of Trump's America.* One World.

Sexual and Gender Minority Research Office. (2024, January). *The importance of gender pronouns and their use in workplace communications.* Retrieved September 8, 2024, https://web.archive.org/web/20240911133812/ https://dpcpsi.nih.gov/sgmro/gender-pronouns-resource

Stockman, F. (2017, August 14). Who were the counterprotesters in Charlottesville? *New York Times.* Retrieved November 16, 2024, from https://www.nytimes.com/2017/08/14/us/who-were-the -counterprotesters-in-charlottesville.html

Stollznow, K. (2021, January 13). *Why is it so offensive to say "all lives matter"?* The Conversation. Retrieved September 8, 2024, https://thecon- versation.com/why-is-it-so-offensive-to-say-all-lives-matter-153188

Táíwò, O. (2022). Vice signaling. *Journal of Ethics and Social Philosophy* 22(3), 295–316. https://doi.org/10.26556/jesp.v22i3.1192

BIGOTRY LOVES MORAL PANICS

Dehumanization can take on many forms that we recognize as bigoted, such as likening people to vermin. One of the more common forms of this reduces people to a problem that must be solved with resolve and decisive action. This is done to foster a moral panic in which bigoted solutions have a greater chance of being considered.

In 1972, Stanley Cohen introduced the modern concept of moral panic in his classic work, *Folk Devils and Moral Panics*. Cohen described the cycle of a moral panic in five broad phases: First, the cycle of moral panic begins with a social condition or practice, individual, or community identified as a threat to the culture and its values. Second, the subject of moral panic is stripped of all nuance and turned into a dehumanized or threatening stereotype by the media, one that must be confronted by society. Third, the moral discourse regarding the threat begins in the pop culture debate among politicians, pundits, and other experts on how to best solve this issue that, in reality, they do not understand. Dissenting voices are reacted to with a startling amount of hostility. Fourth, "solutions" and "responses" are created, which can take many forms. Finally, the issue that once roiled the entire culture loses its prominence and recedes. This recession does not necessarily mean that the issue vanishes. Sometimes it returns to the fringe of society, and other times it becomes a permanent part of the cultural discourse (Cohen, 1972/2011, pp. 34–35). Regardless of whether it fades into memory or permanently alters the cultural landscape, a moral panic is a flashpoint in a society where many things once thought impossible become possible or inevitable.

Moral panic is one of the few concepts that most Americans learn about in high school history class. There are many examples of moral panics throughout history. Every witch hunt and subsequent witch trial was a moral panic. Most famously, in the United States, was the red scare of the 1950s, where much of the citizenry was convinced that a multitude of communists were actively infiltrating every American institution in a nefarious attempt to add the United States to the Soviet Empire. The legacy of the red scare still haunts the American cultural landscape as we see with the claims that colleges and racial justice movements are overrun by Marxists long after the USSR imploded.

Eric Goode and Nachman Ben-Yehuda (1994) wrote about the nature of moral panic:

> The moral panic, then, is characterized by the feeling, held by a substantial number of the members of a given society, that evil-doers pose a threat to the society and to the moral order as a consequence of their behavior and, therefore, "something should be done" about them and their behavior. (p. 31)

Understanding what "something" can look like is critical to understanding why moral panics impact society in the varied ways they often do. Something can look like increased hostility from the culture, a reassertion of the power of institutions against the subject of the panic, new laws, and the harsher enforcement of those laws (Goode & Ben-Yehuda, 1994). A moral panic often hits society on multiple fronts, which can have the impact of overwhelming the opposition. Combatting bigotry in popular culture is a difficult and time-consuming endeavor on its own. Adding the urgency of advocating against laws and policies that are being driven by bigotry, energized by a moral panic in their favor, is exhausting emotionally, intellectually, and often physically.

Goode and Ben-Yehuda (1994) list five criteria for moral panic (pp. 33–41): First, there must be an elevated amount of concern about the dangers the threat poses to society, swirling in popular culture. Second, there must be widespread hostility toward the threat, meaning they must be *seen* as a real danger to society that takes on an "us versus them" dynamic. Third, there must be widespread agreement that the threat is real, even though it may be and often is imagined. Fourth, moral panics are grounded in "disproportionality," meaning there must be a widespread belief that the threat inflicts a greater harm and is more ubiquitous than it factually is. Lastly, moral panics are volatile events, meaning they erupt from the grassroots, although they can bubble under the surface of society or even be cyclically triggered by external events. In this sense, a moral panic functions like a panic attack in an individual—a short and intense heightened state of fear, hostility, and catastrophizing-driven problem identification and creation.

As a concept, moral panic is often invoked to discuss intense moments of social clash. For bigots, it is an opportunity because they know that people in a state of panic are easy to appeal to, convince, and lead. The most insidious part of moral panic is that when people are caught in the throes of it, they often suspend their moral and intellectual discernment to convince themselves that wrong is right, and "necessary evil" begins to expand. It is easy for moral panic to become the normal state of affairs where "the deviant" are subject to increasing brutality at the hands of the public and the state, and this is seen as *normal* and *good* (Cohen, 1972/2011; Goode & Ben-Yehuda, 1994). A reality that makes bigotry and the moral panics they embrace so challenging to confront is that a critical mass of bigots and members of their moral panics are convinced they are doing the right thing.

Currently, the most virulent manifestation of a bigoted moral panic is the anti-queer-driven attack on K–12 education (Block,

2022; Mitchell, 2023; Romano, 2022). What began as bigots going after transgender students and teachers for asserting their civil rights in the face of social and legal discrimination, such as banning the staff from using a student's chosen pronouns, quickly spread to an attack on queer teachers for existing and schools for trying to create welcoming environments for queer students and non-queer students from queer families. The bigoted claim was that queer teachers were trying to indoctrinate students into queer lifestyles and groom them for sexual abuse (Block, 2022; Romano, 2022). The grooming libel is a tried-and-tested tactic to attack queer people that has been historically effective (Block, 2022; Romano, 2022). Like all moral panics, the facts were distorted to fit the groomer narrative. For the panic movement, hanging pride flags, or a teacher having a picture of their spouse who may be the same sex as they are, is tantamount to grooming. This is only because bigoted movements never play by the rules that apply to their targets. They do not extend this concern to heterosexual teachers having the same pictures of their spouses.

This moral panic prompted multiple states to pass "Don't say gay" laws, which forbid instruction on the topic of sexuality and gender identity before a certain age, which varied by state. It is important to note that the Florida law was heavily altered after litigation in federal court, so this analysis deals with the law as designed initially rather than what exists now (Mazzei, 2024). Some may claim that this law is simply a curriculum law that is not part of a moral panic. This claim ignores Florida governor Ron DeSantis's former press secretary, Christina Pushaw, tweeting (on what is now X) that, "The bill that liberals inaccurately call 'Don't Say Gay' would be more accurately described as an Anti-Grooming Bill," and, "If you're against the Anti-Grooming Bill, you are probably a groomer or at least you don't denounce the grooming of 4–8 year-old children. Silence is complicity. This is how it works, Democrats, and I didn't make the rules" (Romano, 2022, para. 2). This should not be surprising, because moral panics attract politicians looking to make a name for themselves by brandishing their image as defending public morality from evildoers (Cohen, 1972/2011, pp. 34–35).

Of course, like all moral panics tend to do if they get any sort of political power, the laws were written in a manner that they can be interpreted in entirely contradictory ways because they are written from a bigoted perspective that inherently rests on the deranged claims rooted in nothing but a desire to cosplay cruelty as something other than what it is. In the case of the "Don't Say Gay" laws, it was presented that teaching students about sexuality, sexual orientation, and how gender works is a form of grooming. An example of how the law can be interpreted in contradictory ways is how a ban on teaching about sexual orientation or gender identity would have to be extended to any instruction to impart those things. A plain text reading of a "Don't Say Gay Law" would forbid any instruction that depicts marriage, mother-father status, parent-child status, or any gendering of a character of a historical figure because they all convey instruction on sexuality, sexual orientation, and gender identity. This highlights another key aspect of the moral panic—it doesn't apply its own logic to itself. This is because there is no logic to a moral panic. If there were, then it would not be a panic.

For those who practice anti-bigotry, it is important to be mindful of moral panics because they can spread quickly and convert the unlikeliest of people. Moral panics can reach from the halls of power to intimate relationships. They can subject people to the horrific spectacle of watching someone you know become someone you knew, as the person you care about becomes a bigot you barely recognize. In *On Tyranny: Twenty Lessons from the Twentieth Century*, Timothy Snyder (2017) discusses Eugène Ionesco's absurdist play, *Rhinoceros*, about how fascism spreads. In the play, individuals who fall victim to propaganda turn into rhinoceroses. Snyder points out that Ionesco bases this play on life in Romania when the virulently antisemitic Iron Guard came to power (p. 69). He quoted Ionesco at length:

> University professors, students, intellectuals were turning Nazi, becoming Iron Guards, one after the other. At the beginning, certainly they were not Nazis. About fifteen of us would get together to talk and to try to find arguments opposing theirs. It was not easy. . . . From time to time, one of our friends said: "I don't agree with them, to be sure, but on certain points, nevertheless, I must admit, for example, the Jews . . . ," etc. And this was a symptom. Three weeks later, this person would become a Nazi. He was caught in the mechanism, he accepted everything, he became a rhinoceros. Towards the end, only three or four of us were still resisting. (Snyder, 2017, pp. 69–70)

Snyder also reminds us to listen for dangerous words. He wrote, "The most intelligent of the Nazis, the legal theorist Carl Schmitt, explained in clear language the essence of fascist governance. The way to destroy all rules, he explained, was to focus on the idea of the *exception*" (Snyder, 2017, p. 100). This logic can and should be applied to moral panics, as well. It is essential to pay attention to how people talk about the subjects of moral panics and how once ordinary-sounding phrases like "gender ideology," and "we must act," can take on new, menacing tones. Words are often the first sign that moral panic is taking root, that bigotry is spreading, and that people are allowing themselves to become moral monsters.

References

Block, M. (2022, May 11). *Accusations of "grooming" are the latest political attack—with homophobic origins* [Radio broadcast transcript]. National Public Radio. Retrieved September 7, 2024, from https://www.npr.org/2022/05/11/1096623939/accusations-grooming-political-attack-homophobic-origins

Cohen, S. (2011). *Folk devils and moral panics.* Routledge. (Original work published 1972). https://play.google.com/store/books/details?id=FA6tAgAAQBAJ

Goode, E., and N. Ben-Yehuda. (1994). *Moral panics: The social construction of deviance*. Blackwell Publishers.

Mazzei, P. (2024, March 11). Legal settlement clarifies reach of Florida's "Don't Say Gay" law. *New York Times*. Retrieved September 8, 2024, https://www.nytimes.com/2024/03/11/us/florida-dont-say-gay-law -settlement.html

Mitchell, N. E. (2023, September 12). *Anti-trans measures force teachers to choose between the law and ethics*. MSNBC. Retrieved September 8, 2024, https://www.msnbc.com/opinion/msnbc-opinion/-transgender -notification-policy-california-school-district-rcna103962

Romano, A. (2022, April 21). *The right's moral panic over "grooming" invokes age-old homophobia: "Groomer" accusations against liberals and the LGBTQ community are recycled Satanic Panic*. Vox. Retrieved September 8, 2024, https://www.vox.com/culture/23025505/leftist -groomers-homophobia-satanic-panic-explained

Snyder, T. (2017). *On tyranny: Twenty lessons from the twentieth century*. Crown.

BIGOTS WANT YOU TO THINK THEY ARE UNINTELLIGENT

The common perception of a bigot is an uneducated, impoverished person who clings to bigotry to feel good about themselves. While these bigots do exist, these are not the men and women who write bigoted policies and bigoted laws. That is the work of educated advocates who use prevailing stereotypes about bigots as being unintelligent to hide their work from scrutiny until the time is right for them to act.

Sun Tzu wrote in *The Art of War*:

So the Master said, Know your enemy and know yourself, and fight a hundred battles without danger. Know yourself but not your enemy, and win one battle but lose another. Know neither your enemy nor yourself, and there is sure to be danger in every battle. (Tzu, 2021, p. 44)

This is one of the more famous quotes that people invoke in all sorts of settings, and it is interpreted in many ways. One way to think of this quote is to never underestimate your opponent, because you will not be able to appreciate their capabilities. There is a strategic opportunity that arises here—letting your opponent underestimate you. This is, of course, a common tactic in all manner of conflicts throughout history, and it has proven to be highly effective. Regarding bigotry, bigots utilize this tactic in an often-unexpected manner.

While it cannot be said of all bigots, many of them have no issue with people thinking they are unintelligent brutes. Their reason for this is simple—the prevailing stereotypes of bigots allow them to hone their craft, plot, strategize, and organize out of sight from the popular culture, until the time is right to reveal their plans.

As a Southerner, I am intimately acquainted with America's stereotype of a bigot. In the mind of America, "racist" conjures an image of a sweaty "redneck" (itself a racial and class-based slur) wearing a "Make America Great Again" hat. They live in rural America, in dire poverty, possibly in a trailer park that flies a confederate, Blue Lives Matter, or the Revolutionary War–era "Don't Tread on Me" Gadsden flag, depending on the current state of affairs. They drive a pickup truck, complete with bumper stickers and a gun rack. Their spoken English drips with a Southern or Appalachian accent. Most importantly, the stereotypical racist is not only unintelligent; they are distrustful of any information that contradicts their beliefs. Do these kinds of racists exist? Of course. But this is not representative of all racists. The stereotype of the unintelligent bigot doesn't stop with racists. Incels have become the go-to stereotype of a misogynist, while the stereotype of the anti-queer bigot is a raging buffoon who can't stand seeing two men hold hands. Again, do these people exist? Absolutely. Are they representative of all bigots? No.

I know it's comfortable for many people to dismiss bigots simply as hillbillies, frothing-at-the-mouth proto-fascists, or some bros sitting at the computer creating memes. But this is an act of self-deception and a dangerous assumption. In his full-throated criticism of *White Rural Rage: The Threat to American Democracy*, scholar and essayist Tyler Austin Harper (2024) called out this tendency. He wrote:

> Instead of reckoning with the ugly fact that a threat to our democracy is emerging from right-wing extremists in suburban and urban areas, the authors of *White Rural Rage* contorted studies and called unambiguously metro areas "rural" so that they could tell an all-too-familiar story about scary hillbillies. Perhaps this was easier

than confronting the truth: that the call is coming from inside the house. It is not primarily the rural poor, but often successful, white metropolitan men who imperil our republic. (Harper, 2024, para. 9)

Concerning the work of opposing bigotry, Harper's (2024) warning was that assuming all bigots are rural, uneducated, "good ol' boys" is self-defeating because it blinds people to where the danger is germinating. While we should not ignore the stereotypical bigots, as they are the foot soldiers of bigotry, we cannot ignore the bigotry brewing in the suburbs and the higher-priced zip codes. Furthermore, the stereotypes of bigots blind people to the bigotry that brews within marginalized communities, as bigotry is not limited only to those with privilege or white skin. As stated in the introduction, no community is immune to bigotry. Concerning the larger point of this lesson, the call is indeed coming from inside the proverbial house, and anti-bigots cannot ignore the voice on the other end of the line who makes bigoted movements successful—the bigoted advocate.

The bigoted advocates are educated critically in the humanities, the social sciences, public policy, and law. They are experienced organizers in issues-based and political advocacy, and they are the veterans of many campaigns. They understand the political arts of rhetoric, campaigning, and outreach. They understand how the system works. As discussed in lesson 11, the bigoted advocate thinks in decades, not election cycles, and they are determined. It is critical to note that bigoted advocates are the people who write bigoted laws. This is not to say that people without post-secondary education cannot create a law. Still, the drafting of a law that will pass muster in court and be implemented is a detailed task that often requires specialized training and education. What sets aside the bigoted advocates from the ordinary bigots is that they have this training. They are, bluntly stated, the people who create institutional and systemic bigotry. They are also the little Eichmanns who make the bigoted policies work, normalizing them in society. They are the district attorney who refuses to investigate hate crimes. They are the teacher who punishes the poor students from the ghetto, the reservation, and the trailer park more harshly than the wealthy students from the suburbs.

I do not wish to gloss over the fact that the bigoted advocate and policymaker is educated. As discussed in lesson 2, education and thinking are not necessarily interchangeable concepts, and the greatest architects of bigotry have often been educated men and women. This point was eloquently made in Lisa Delpit's (1995/2006) seminal work, *Other People's Children: Cultural Conflict in the Classroom*. She included a letter from a principal who survived the Holocaust, to the faculty:

> Dear Teacher:
>
> I am the survivor of a concentration camp. My eyes saw what no person should witness:
>
> - Gas chambers built by learned engineers.
>
> - Children poisoned by educated physicians.
>
> - Infants killed by trained nurses.
>
> Women and babies shot and burned by high school and college graduates. So I am suspicious of education. My request is: Help your students become human. Your efforts must never produce learned monsters, skilled psychopaths, educated Eichmanns. Reading, writing and arithmetic are important only if they make our children more humane. (Delpit, 1995/2006, pp. xx–xxi)

This letter was a warning to everyone about who the architects of the practical horror of bigotry are. Society is full of historical and contemporary examples of this.

A historical example is the legal influence that Jim Crow had on Nazi Germany. In lesson 10, I asserted that while race is a scientific fiction, it has had a material impact on people. One of the most consequential examples of this is race being used as a legal category. Race was the original organizing reality of American society and politics (Mills, 1997/2014), with the distinction between free states and slave states along with the 3/5th compromise and later Jim Crow. It is important to note that the Nazis themselves were students of American Jim Crow legislation. In *Hitler's American Model*, James Whitman (2018) explained that when the Nazis wanted to write the antisemitic Nuremberg laws, they looked to the United States. Whitman (2018) wrote,

> In the early 1930s, as the Nazis were crafting the program of racial persecution enshrined in the Nuremberg Laws, they took a great interest not only in the way Henry Ford built cars for the masses, not only in the way Hollywood built its own mass market, not only in FDR's style of government, not only in American eugenics, and not only in American westward expansion, but also in the lessons to be garnered from the techniques of American racist legislation and jurisprudence. (p. 10)

On June 5, 1934, state secretary with the Reich Ministry of Justice and later president of the People's Court, Roland Freisler, who attended the infamous Wannsee conference where the Holocaust was planned, stated:

> This jurisprudence would suit us perfectly, with a single exception. Over there they have in mind, practically speaking, only coloreds and half-coloreds, which includes mestizos and mulattoes; but the Jews, who are also of interest to us, are not reckoned among the coloreds. (Whitman, 2018, p. 1)

It is impossible for us to dismiss men like Freisler and the earlier architects of Jim Crow as unintelligent, as many of these men were university-educated lawyers. In 1865, Greek and Latin were standard parts of the university curriculum, and the Klan was founded by college-educated men; it is not happenstance that "Ku Klux" was taken from the Greek word *kuklos*, which translates to "circle" in English (Baudouin, 2011, p. 9).

Contemporarily, all one needs to do is look at any of the laws seeking to inflict harm on certain communities, through specific rules that presumably apply to everyone, but practically only apply to distinct groups. A classic example is found in school policies that prevent students from wearing their hair in styles such as box braids, dreadlocks, and afros (NAACP Legal Defense and Educational Fund, 2024). It was clear to the casual observer that these laws targeted Black students for wearing their hair in styles that preserved the natural texture while not punishing them for perming their hair. The argument was that these styles were not professional. In a practical sense, the schools were telling Black students that the way their hair grew from their scalps was unprofessional. Such miseducation (Woodson, 1933/2005) being enshrined in school policy is the work of educated bigots who understand the hidden curriculum (Apple, 2019), and how school rules teach students how they are seen by institutions and society. In lesson 15, I mentioned that some states have laws that ban staff from using a student's chosen pronouns. The data shows that such bullying has a negative impact on the mental health outcomes of gender-nonconforming youth. Can it be a coincidence these laws are passed, even though they target a community in a way that is documented to cause mental harm? Some make this claim, but I respectfully disagree. I assert that this is the work of educated bigoted advocates, seeking to use the law to inflict harm on a large scale because imposing such cruelty is the point of bigoted laws.

Oppression requires intelligence to pull off because it is a deliberate act. No form of oppression happens by accident. To construct a system of genocide on one extreme, or a system of marginalization on the other, engineering culture to support any form of oppression requires knowledge of the law, the social sciences, the humanities, the arts, and the hard sciences. It takes a keen intellect to construct a system of education that actively seeks to miseducate people into thinking they are inferior, or to justify genocide, as we saw with

Jim Crow education for Black students (Watkins, 1993, 2001), the education of women to be subservient to men for generations, and the Nazis teaching an entire generation of German children that genocide was necessary to "solve the Jewish question." It is critical that anti-bigots resist the hubris-generating adoption of the stereotype of the unintelligent bigot and respect their intellectual acumen. If anti-bigots do this, they can respond to bigotry in real time rather than having to devise a response that gives bigots time to shift the Overton Window in their favor.

References

Apple, M. W. (2019). *Ideology and curriculum* (4th edition). Routledge.

Baudouin, R. (ed.). (2011). *Ku Klux Klan: A history of racism and violence* (6th edition). Southern Poverty Law Center.

Delpit, L. (2006). *Other people's children: Cultural conflict in the classroom.* The New Press. (Original work published in 1995). https://www.google.com/books/edition/Other_People_s_Children/H9lYESPjKjAC?hl=en&gbpv=0

Harper, T. (2024, April 4). An utterly misleading book about rural America. *The Atlantic.* Retrieved September 8, 2024, from https://www.theatlantic.com/ideas/archive/2024/04/white-rural-rage-criticism/677967/

Mills, C. (2014). *The racial contract.* Cornell University Press. (Original work published 1997). https://play.google.com/store/books/details?id=GnmuAwAAQBAJ

NAACP Legal Defense and Educational Fund. (2024). *The Crown Act: Creating a respectful and open world for natural hair.* Retrieved September 8, 2024, from https://www.naacpldf.org/crown-act/

Tzu, S. (2021). *The art of war.* Translated, edited, and introduced by Peter Harris. Vintage Books. https://www.proquest.com/docview/2604693202/6B0DEF848A29431APQ/1?accountid=14556&sourcetype=Books

Watkins, W. H. (1993). Black curriculum orientations: A preliminary inquiry. *Harvard Educational Review* 63(3), 321–339. https://doi.org/10.17763/haer.63.3.26k2433r77v631k2

Watkins, W. H. (2001). *The White architects of Black education: Ideology and power in America, 1865–1954*. Teachers College Press.

Whitman, J. (2018). *Hitler's American model: The United States and the making of Nazi race law*. Princeton University Press. https://play.google.com/store/books/details?id=pQZpDQAAQBAJ

Woodson, C. (2005). *The miseducation of the Negro*. Dover Publications (Original work published 1933).

BIGOTRY LOVES FALSE MORAL EQUIVALENCE

When bigotry can no longer present itself as anything other than what it is, it will begin to falsely compare itself to things that are not bigotry to muddy the waters about what bigotry is, how it manifests, and how it spreads.

Merriam-Webster's (n.d.-a) dictionary defines *equivalence*, in a rhetorical sense, as "the relation holding between two statements if they are either both true or both false so that to affirm one and to deny the other would result in a contradiction." In short, for two statements to be equivalent, they must both be true. An example of an equivalent statement would be, "If you live in New Orleans, then you live in Louisiana." While this may upset some of my friends in New Orleans, saying that you live in New Orleans is the equivalent of saying that you live in Louisiana. False equivalence is a logical fallacy, which attempts to claim that two statements are equivalent because they have some characteristics in common even though they differ in others, such as impact, scale, complexity, detail, and the possibility of an outcome (PBS, 2024). The most common example of this might be "apples and oranges."

We often see false equivalence in political rhetoric, especially when elections draw near. A very common expression is "Candidate A and Candidate B are the same!" Now, this may indeed be true when looking at their platforms and voting records, but if there are stark differences, then to say that they are the same is a false equivalence. An example would be that "Candidate A supports the right to an abortion while Candidate B supports a national abortion ban." The candidates are not the same, so to claim that they are is a false equivalence.

Bigots love false equivalences of any variety, but they especially love false moral equivalence because it muddies the waters of the debate and protects them from rebuke. It also provides the intellectual grounding to engage in gaslighting, which will be discussed in lesson 19. It is critical to understand moral false equivalence because while bigotry is an economic and political ideology, it is fundamentally a code of morality. Simply stated, moral false equivalence is when people compare different actions, dismiss the details, and say they have the same moral significance. Howard Brody (1997) explored this topic around the hotly debated subject of physician-assisted suicide. He wrote:

> A succinct summary of the validity of the moral equivalence hypothesis was provided a decade ago by Raanan Gillon. He distinguished two arguments: that there is a necessary moral *equivalence* between killing and letting die, and that there is no necessary moral *difference* between killing and letting die. Both, he states, are false; there are a few circumstances in which letting a patient die would be morally equivalent to killing the patient, but there are many more cases in which, due to the specific circumstances, the two acts would be quite morally distinct. (Brody, 1997, p. 943)

Details matter a great deal in determining whether there is moral equivalence or not. In the case of the difference between letting someone die and killing them, a key question is whether or not the patient has a do-not-resuscitate order. In this situation, letting them die is not the moral equivalent of killing them because the patient has stipulated that no efforts should be made to save their life. This is wholly different from a situation in which a doctor could save a patient and chooses not to do so. In this case, the doctor's decision not to save a life is the moral equivalent of killing them.

Another example of false moral equivalence is claiming that Corrie Ten Boom lying to protect the Jewish people she was hiding from the Nazis, during the German occupation of the Netherlands, is no different from a person committing perjury on the stand to protect a guilty friend from being convicted. While both involve lying to authorities, Ten Boom was trying to save people from genocide while the individual committed perjury to protect a guilty friend. Bigots hope people will ignore the differences and say that the apples and the oranges are the same.

What does false moral equivalence look like, then, relative to bigotry? In discussing identity politics and race, David Ingram (2004) rejected the notion that "genuine politics" is conducted by individuals who intentionally separate themselves into simultaneous interest organizations and groups (p. 54). He wrote:

> I intend to rebut this charge. To do so, I argue against two standard assumptions. The first assumption is that identity politics entails rules of fairness that apply to all groups in the same way. If it's wrong for white people to affirm their interests as white people, then (following this assumption) it's wrong for blacks to affirm their interests as blacks; conversely, if it's okay for blacks to affirm their interests as blacks, it's okay for whites to do the same. (Ingram, 2004, pp. 54–55)

Ingram (2004) argued that this assumption is false because of the social and cultural marginalization or power dynamics (p. 55). He wrote:

> Affirming "black pride" is not equivalent to affirming "white pride," since the former—unlike the latter—is a defensive strategy aimed at rectifying a negative stereotype. In general, racial categories that have an illegitimate origin can come to serve legitimate political purposes when affirmed in a positive way by subaltern groups. The

> same does not apply when racial categories are affirmed by dominant racial groups, for affirmations of white pride—however thinly cloaked as affirmations of ethnic pride—serve to mask and perpetuate white privilege. (Ingram, 2004, p. 55)

As stated earlier, false equivalence ignores glaring differences. Regarding bigotry, that difference is often marginalization rather than being the norm. This does not mean that bigotry is excusable when it comes from marginalized communities. An example of this is non-White people directing racial slurs and epithets at White people. Another example of this is internal racial policing that denies individuals the right to create their own identities (Ingram, 2004, p. 54), like Black people calling other Black people "Oreos" and "Uncle Toms" for taking positions that are seen as deviant from the Black cultural norm, and colorism, because they seek to impose a racial classification system on other people. Considering power dynamics in society means that the details and context matter; two things bigots earnestly dismiss because they are inconvenient. Regarding false moral equivalence, moral foundations matter because semantics are utilized to create equivalence where none exists.

A classic example of false moral equivalence is Black power versus White power. Black power emerged as a concept during the civil rights movement and gained popularity in the 1970s, with the emergence of groups like the Black Panther Party. Fred Hampton articulated the philosophy behind Black power for the Black Panther Party, in a 1969 speech:

> We say all power to all people.
> *All power to all people.*
> We say white power to white people.
> *White power to white people.*
> Brown power to brown people.
> *Brown power to brown people.*
> Yellow power to yellow people.
> *Yellow power to yellow people.*

Black power to black people.
Black power to black people.
X power to those we left out.
X power to those we left out. (Abdelfatah et al., 2021. Italics were added to note the crowd's response.)

Historically, Black power is a statement of empowerment rather than hatred of any non-Black people. It was a statement of resistance in a society that actively sought to teach Black people to hate themselves. On the other hand, White power, or White pride, is a White supremacist slogan that bigots adopted to perpetuate White supremacy.

Another false moral equivalence on full display every summer is pride versus straight pride (Crowley et al., 2024). Pride Month is a celebration of queer life in all its complexity. Some of the more common forms of celebration are festivals that range from gatherings in exhibition halls, complete with information booths, to street parties and parades. The argument for straight pride can be boiled down to "heterosexual relationships should be celebrated, too." The false equivalence in this is that heterosexual relationships have been celebrated in America for the entire span of American history. Except for interracial marriages, the right to a heterosexual marriage has never been denied. The nuclear family, often held up as the cornerstone of society, is routinely depicted as heterosexual.

In contrast, queer people and families have only recently started to emerge as a community from the margins of society. Sodomy laws that banned all forms of same-sex sexual activity only became unconstitutional in 2003, with the Supreme Court decision in *Lawrence v. Texas*. Same-sex marriage only became a federal right in 2015, with the Supreme Court decision in *Obergefell v. Hodges*. It became illegal to fire queer people for being queer with the Supreme Court decision in *Bostock v. Clayton County* in 2020. Many states still do not grant the same parental rights to same-sex couples as they do to heterosexual couples (Movement Advancement Project, 2023). The reality on the ground is that the queer community just started having their civil rights affirmed and are still not listed in the *Civil Rights Act of 1964*, which would extend all rights that heterosexual people enjoy to queer people. The difference between pride and straight pride is that pride is still a marginalized community, celebrating their existence and victories while also acknowledging how much time and fortune, and how many lives it took to secure these rights. Straight pride is simply vice signaling to anti-queer bigots, born of the anger that bigots feel seeing the targets of their bigotry celebrating themselves.

The tenth lesson of Snyder's (2017) *On Tyranny* is:

> To abandon facts is to abandon freedom. If nothing is true, then no one can criticize power, because there is no basis upon which to do so. If nothing is true, then all is spectacle. The biggest wallet pays for the most blinding light. (p. 65)

Jason Stanley (2020) articulated a similar concern in his description of unreality. He wrote:

> When propaganda succeeds at twisting ideals against themselves and universities are undermined and condemned as sources of bias, reality itself is cast into doubt. We can't agree on truth. Fascist politics replaces reasoned debate with fear and anger. When it is successful, its audience is left with a destabilized sense of loss, and a well of mistrust and anger against those who it has been told are responsible for this loss. . . . Regular and repeated obvious lying is part of the process by which fascist politics destroys the information space. (p. 57)

It is important to point out that false moral equivalence does not obliterate facts so much as it distorts them through the stripping of nuance and the classic appeal to "all things being equal." When Synder and Stanley's assertions are applied to bigotry, the goal of false moral equivalence becomes clear. Bigotry cannot defend itself on its own merits, so it tries to eliminate the need for a defense. This is why bigots love this tactic—they know that all things are not equal, but they get to pretend that they are. False moral equivalence collapses the distinction between the marginalized and centered, between oppressor and oppressed, between perpetrator and victim. How can there be a crime if we are all guilty?

False moral equivalences attack truth, facts, and the importance of detail to discernment. It is another intellectual sleight of hand. Merriam-Webster's (n.d.-b) dictionary defines *skullduggery* as "underhanded or unscrupulous behavior" and "a devious device or trick." False moral equivalences are a particularly effective skullduggery because they can shut down debate and rebuke. If everything is bigotry, then nothing is bigotry because we are all victims. This is the theme that extends through this lesson and lessons 18 and 19.

References

Abdelfatah, R., R. Arablouei, J. York, J. Caine, L. Kaplan-Levenson, L. Wu, P. Shah, and V. Yvellez (Hosts). (2021, April 15). The Real Black Panthers [Audio podcast transcript]. In *Throughline*. National Public Radio. Retrieved September 8, 2024, from https://www.npr.org/transcripts/986561396

Brody, H. (1997). Physician-assisted suicide in the courts: Moral equivalence, double effect, and clinical practice. *Minnesota Law Review* 82(4), 939–964. https://heinonline.org/HOL/P?h=hein.journals/mnlr82&i=949

Crowley, K., C. Mulroy, and A. Forbes. (2024, June 13). Pride 2024: Why we don't have a month dedicated to heterosexuality. *USA Today*. Retrieved November 17, 2024, from https://www.usatoday.com/story/news/nation/2024/06/13/straight-pride-celebration-fallacy/74068516007/

Ingram, D. (2004). *Rights, democracy, and fulfillment in the era of identity politics: Principled compromises in a compromised world*. Rowman & Littlefield Publishers.

Merriam-Webster. (n.d.-a). Equivalence. In *Merriam-Webster.com dictionary*. Retrieved November 19, 2024, from https://www.merriam-webster.com/dictionary/equivalence

Merriam-Webster. (n.d.-b). Skullduggery. In *Merriam-Webster.com dictionary*. Retrieved November 19, 2024, from https://www.merriam-webster.com/dictionary/skulduggery

Movement Advancement Project. (2023). *Relationships at risk: Why we need to update state parentage laws to protect children and families*. Retrieved September 8, 2024, from https://www.mapresearch.org/2023-parentage-report

Public Broadcasting Service. (2024). False Equivalence: Why It's so Dangerous [Video]. In *Above the Noise*. KQED San Francisco. Retrieved November 17, 2024, from https://kcpt.pbslearningmedia.org/resource/above-the-noise-false-equivalence/above-the-noise-false-equivalence/

Snyder, T. (2017). *On tyranny: Twenty lessons from the twentieth century*. Crown.

Stanley, J. (2020). *How fascism works: The politics of us and them*. Random House.

LESSON 18
BIGOTS ALWAYS CLAIM THAT THEY ARE THE REAL VICTIMS

Only the most open bigots identify as such. Most bigots, when confronted with evidence of their bigotry, will claim that they are being persecuted.

Victim status is a real thing. A great deal of law revolves around the question of who is the perpetrator and who is the victim. Those who are acknowledged as being the victim of a transgression are commonly seen as being owed justice in the form of restitution from the perpetrator, or the satisfaction of the perpetrator being punished for their crime, in some way. Even the concept of self-defense rests on the question of who is the perpetrator and who is the victim. This is relevant on the individual, social, and global levels because self-defense implies the use of force. In this lesson, victim and victimhood refer to the collective group rather than the individual.

Concerning bigotry, there is a dark irony when the subject of victims comes up. Bigots of all stripes denounce how society has "become too soft" and people are "too easily offended." I am not saying that anyone who makes these assertions is a bigot, as that is not true, but bigots utilize this rhetoric as part of their efforts to present their bigotry as philosophy and concern. The irony lies in how bigots claim they are victims of the resistance to them, and that they are the targets of bigotry by their victims. While the former claim is consequential, the latter claim can take on deadly significance, as history tells us that genocides often begin with the perpetrators claiming self-defense. The Nazis claimed they were protecting Germany from Jewish plots to destroy it. Segregationists claimed Jim Crow was necessary to keep Black people from harming White people, especially White women. Anti-queer bigots are currently asserting that American society needs to protect its children from the LGBTQ+ community. Victim status is powerful, which is why we must always remember power dynamics in society when assessing any claim (Ingram, 2004; Stanley, 2020). Yet power dynamics are not the sole determination of victimhood. We must also consider the moral justifications of action and the penchant for bigots to make false moral equivalences.

The claims of victimhood among bigots are complicated because they feed on real feelings of fear and resentment among the more dominant groups in society. Therefore, what drives this fear and resentment? It is the factual and the perceived loss of privileged status. This is not a new phenomenon in society, nor is it a new topic within the social sciences. Jason Stanley (2020) reminded us that:

> There is a long history of social psychological research about the fact that increased representation of members of traditional minority groups is experienced by dominant groups as threatening in various ways. More recently, a growing body of social psychological evidence substantiates the phenomenon of dominant group feelings of victimization at the prospect of sharing power equally with members of minority groups. (p. 94)

This reaction is key to understanding some of the pathways into bigotry and the core of its advocacy. While the bigots who embrace the sheer hatred of other groups openly do exist, bigots often present their bigotry as concern about the loss of status. This appeal is frequently cloaked in the loss of tradition, purity, and culture. These feelings of social displacement can be, and often are, redirected into support for bigoted movements, especially on but by no means limited to, the far-right wing of the American political spectrum (Stanley, 2020).

It is unwise for opponents of bigotry to dismiss the feelings of fear and resentment that members of dominant groups have, because those feelings are the foundations of seeing marginalized communities as threats. In the same way that it is unreasonable to expect members of marginalized communities not to react when they feel threatened, the same consideration must be extended to members of dominant groups. Stanley's (2020) concept of how fascism creates a sense of victimhood provides critical insight into how these feelings operate. He wrote:

> Whether or not the anguish that accompanies loss of privileged status is similar to the sense of oppression that accompanies genuine marginalization, it is anguish nevertheless. . . . Rectifying unjust inequalities will always bring pain to those who benefited from such injustices. This pain will inevitably be experienced by some as oppression. (Stanley, 2020, p. 98)

This knowledge should not hinder efforts to combat bigotry and create an equitable society. This understanding of the world from the perspective of some members of dominant communities, however, should inform how anti-bigotry advocates against bigotry. This is why empathy is a fundamental trait for anti-bigots to possess.

Because bigotry believes in a natural hierarchy of human beings, it sells people a vision of a society where this hierarchy is normal. This normalization creates "expectations" in some people that society will meet this bigoted vision, and when it does not, bigots will claim victim status (Stanley, 2020, p. 101). The power dynamics at play here are a dominant group being upset at the factual or perceived loss of dominance, and the only means to soothe their anger is having their dominant status reestablished. There is a term for this sort of identity politics—the politics of resentment.

Jeremy Engels (2010) described the politics of resentment:

> The goal of this politics is to keep an audience weak and in need of leadership by keeping them perpetually hostile at their purported victimizers. The victimage ritual is hence guilty by design. By keeping the wound exposed and raw . . . many leaders in our contemporary democracy, ensure that their audiences remain angry, resentful, and weak and in need of their leadership. (p. 305)

The politics of resentment creates a culturally engaged rage-centered morality (Engels, 2010, p. 309). It is a form of identity politics where grievance becomes the core of a community's identity and promotes separatism (Yamamoto, 1999). Like bigotry itself, no community is immune to the politics of resentment, and bigots can provide the necessary tinder to spread widespread grievance. To justify this grievance and claim of victimhood, bigots often turn to false moral equivalence. There are multiple examples of this happening currently in American society.

In lesson 17, false moral equivalence was described as comparing different actions, dismissing key details, and claiming they have the same moral significance. One form of this is claiming harm when that harm is really the lessening of dominant or privileged status. This does not mean that harm is never inflicted on a dominant group, such as through an act of violence or harassment. While the loss of privilege is real, the perception of losing privilege as harm is perceived, and therefore, fictitious.

An example of false moral equivalence is bigots claiming that others are violating their right to freedom of speech when people deny them platforms or shout them down as they speak in public spaces. The common argument from bigots is that cancel culture, which I define as "the weaponization of the concept of moral turpitude to get people fired or to reduce their social capital," is rampant (Mitchell, 2022, para. 3). It cannot be disputed that people use the tactics of cancel culture to silence dissent across the political spectrum. This can be a harmful cultural practice because it stifles reasoned discussion and debate on critical topics. However, spouting bigotry does not fall into the category of critical topics. The claim that denouncing or canceling bigots causes harm because it violates free speech is an absurd argument to make because the right to rebuke someone is also an exercise in free speech.

Yes, you have the right to say whatever you want, and the government cannot censor you within reason, the notable exceptions being incitement to violence or making threats. That has nothing to do with your right to an audience. You have no right to be taken seriously and no right to be spared from rebuke. The audience has the right to boo. The critic has the right to critique you (Mitchell, 2022). You are not entitled to a platform (Mitchell, 2022, para. 18). The false moral equivalence that bigots make here is between reasoned discussion and debate on critical topics and bigoted rhetoric.

One of the more visible examples of false moral equivalence and a classic example of the politics of resentment is feminism versus the men's rights movement. The Anti-Defamation League's (ADL) Center on Extremism (2024) described the men's rights movement as:

> A part of the manosphere, a broad set of male supremacist, anti-feminist, misogynist and sometimes violent movements that exist largely online. MRAs embrace traditional masculinity as the ideal state of men in society and vehemently reject the principles and advancements of feminism. (para. 1)

The ADL points out that men's rights activists (MRAs) are largely concentrated on law and policy and generally do not pose a physical threat to women (ADL, 2024, para. 2). However, I suspect that feminists may disagree with the latter assertion.

The primary claims of the MRAs are:

- Men do not have unequal social and/or economic power representative of an oppressive patriarchy.

- Men are systematically disadvantaged at similar or greater rates and with similar or greater severity than women.

- Women use existing sexual harassment and child molestation laws to abuse men by restricting their freedoms.

- The expansion of sexual assault laws and policies designed to assist victims of sexual assault make it too easy for ill-intentioned women to ruin men's lives.

- Modern cultural efforts to address sexual assault, such as the MeToo movement, have made it impossible for men to "safely" approach women without risking a harassment or assault lawsuit. (ADL, 2024, para. 7)

In short, the MRAs' claim that men have been victims of feminism and that society must be liberated from this oppression.

While in lesson 9, I acknowledged that the crisis of masculinity is real (Illing, 2023; Reeves, 2024), I also stated that misogynists are seeking a scapegoat for a legitimate issue. The MRAs blame feminism for profound shifts in economics and society. Did feminism have a hand in causing some of these? Yes, but what does that mean in practical terms? To illustrate this, we must ask a different question. Did men lose privilege in society because of women challenging gender roles to gain their civil rights? Yes. Is this the source of the crisis of masculinity? No (Reeves, 2024).

We must consider power dynamics in assessing whether men have been the victims of feminism. The first assertion of the men's rights activists, according to the ADL (2024), is "Men do not have unequal social and/or economic power representative of an oppressive patriarchy." In plain speech, this claim means that because there are powerless men and poor men, the patriarchy does not exist. However, this ignores the details of how patriarchies function. In countries around the world that are uncontestably patriarchal, poor men and powerless men still exist. What can we draw from this observable fact? In a patriarchal system, not every man gets to be a patriarch. The anguish of the crisis of masculinity is real, and women can engage in acts of interpersonal sexism toward men that can be profoundly cruel. However, the politics of resentment embraced by the men's rights movement blames feminists for male oppression, despite women, as a political group, lacking the power and representation to impose a matriarchy, or female rule, on men. The false moral equivalence between the men's rights movement and feminism is that feminism fights for the liberation of both men and women while the men's rights movement fights for the preservation of male privilege, so that they may be elevated to being patriarchs.

Talking members of both dominant and marginalized groups off the bigoted ledge is the cultural and political project of the twenty-first century. People tend to fear change, especially when this change will directly impact them. For the opponents of bigotry, it is neither a sin, nor is it selling out to acknowledge this dynamic. At the same time, they cannot let this dynamic derail the goal of creating an inclusive, equitable, and equal society. False moral equivocating to claim victim status has a larger purpose, which is the subject of lesson 19—gaslighting.

References

The Anti-Defamation League. (2024, January 24). *Men's rights activists: What you need to know*. Retrieved September 8, 2024, from https://www.adl.org/resources/blog/mens-rights-activists-what-you-need-know

Engels, J. (2010). The politics of resentment and the tyranny of the minority: Rethinking victimage for resentful times. *Rhetoric Society Quarterly* 40(4), 303–325. https://www.jstor.org/stable/27862454

Illing, S. (2023, August 7). *The new crisis of masculinity: What's the matter with men—and how do we fix it?* Vox. Retrieved September 6, 2024, from https://www.vox.com/the-gray-area/23813985/christine-emba-masculinity-the-gray-area

Ingram, D. (2004). *Rights, democracy, and fulfillment in the era of identity politics: Principled compromises in a compromised world*. Rowman & Littlefield Publishers.

Mitchell, N. E. (2022, January 17). The villainy you teach. *The North Star with Shaun King*. Retrieved September 8, 2024, from https://www.thenorthstar.com/p/the-villainy-you-teach

Reeves, R. (2024). *Of boys and men: Why the modern male is struggling, why it matters, and what to do about it*. Brookings Institution Press.

Stanley, J. (2020). *How fascism works: The politics of us and them*. Random House.

Yamamoto, E. K. (1999). *Interracial justice: Conflict and reconciliation in post–civil rights America*. NYU Press.

BIGOTRY GASLIGHTS EVERYONE

Bigoted gaslighting takes on two forms. In the first form, bigots present intertwined values as being in conflict. In the second form, bigots try to make their victims question their own experiences as victims of bigotry. Both forms serve the same end: to silence the victims, which denies society critical knowledge about how bigotry manifests and of societies' own capabilities to defeat it.

Merriam-Webster's dictionary (n.d.-a) defines *gaslighting* as "to psychologically manipulate (a person) usually over an extended period of time so that the victim questions the validity of their own thoughts, perception of reality, or memories and experiences confusion, loss of confidence and self-esteem, and doubts concerning their own emotional or mental stability." It is the performance of denying what is objectively true to get a person to question what they know to be objectively true. This lesson seeks to highlight how bigotry attempts to gaslight entire cultures. They do this in two ways. First, bigots invoke false dichotomies, where they claim that certain values and solutions are contradictions to other values. Second, they try to get their targets to question their own experiences with bigotry.

I have long held the opinion that societies are capable of anything individuals are because society is a collective of individuals. This is one of the assumptions that informs my research into bigotry and runs throughout this book. Both the individual and society can experience profound trauma that sets them on new trajectories, as we have seen with war and natural disasters (Aydin, 2017). In the sense that individuals and societies can be traumatized, they can also be victims of gaslighting. An example of this is teaching children that the Civil War was fought over "states' rights," despite the citing of the preservation of slavery by multiple states of the Confederacy as the cause for secession. Another example is the last stage of the genocide process, which is denial (Stanton, 1996). The reason for bigoted gaslighting on a cultural level is to deny society knowledge about itself and what it is capable of.

An example of the first form of bigoted gaslighting is the current debate over equality versus equity. To be blunt, framing the debate this way is a compromise with bigotry because it sets equality and equity as contradictory concepts rather than being intertwined. The current basic advocacy definition of *equality* is treating everyone the same, while *equity* addresses everyone's particular circumstances (Minow, 2021). A useful metaphor that is often used to describe the two concepts is, "Equality is giving everyone a shoe, equity is giving everyone a shoe that fits" (Minow, 2021, p. 174). I enjoy this metaphor because of its implication: there is no equality without equity because wearing shoes that do not fit can hurt your feet.

Let's consider these two concepts from a disability perspective, applied to the simple notion of access to a building. A person with a disability that limits their physical mobility may have difficulty walking up the stairs to enter a building. In this case, how does society guarantee everyone equal access to the building? The answer is to improve access to the building by creating easily traversed ramps for those in wheelchairs, or those who cannot walk up the stairs easily, as well as elevators. Bigots have been somewhat successful in advancing an argument that people should reject equity in favor of equality. The irony is that while people may invoke this bigoted argument in service of their bigotry, its application is purely performative. I assert that no one, including the most devoted bigot, rejects equity, especially when they stand to benefit from it.

Two thought exercises around equity in everyday life expose the farce of bigots embracing equity versus equality. The first is triage in an emergency room. If the bigot had the courage of their convictions, they would demand that everyone be seen in the order that they arrived, as they do at the Department of Motor Vehicles. So, the woman in labor or the bigot themselves, as they have a stroke, would wait until the doctors treat the person with a nosebleed who arrived. The second is one to which I personally relate, as a native of the Gulf South—federal aid after a natural disaster. If the bigot actually believed that equity is a woke plot, then they would demand that the federal disaster aid be distributed evenly between a town that only experienced 10 percent damage to homes, and the town where they lived, which was entirely destroyed. But logically, the bigot would never do either of these. They would demand that people do not ignore them when they are in greatest need, experiencing the greatest hardships, or in the greatest danger. The bigot would demand to be helped first with the needed resources; they would demand equity.

The second form of bigoted gaslighting attacks the foundational knowledge about how bigotry operates—the lived experience of victims of bigotry. One of the foundational assertions of the often-demonized Critical Race Theory is the practice of "naming one's own reality" (Ladson-Billings, 1998, pp. 13–14), which shows that lived experience is evidence of how laws, policies, and cultural practices operate. A non-bigotry-related example of this is experiencing side effects from a medication. The side effect is an experience, and enough experiences inform doctors and researchers about how a medication functions in the real world. When applied to laws, policies, and cultural practices, how people experience these measures is relevant to assessing the impact of the law. An example of this would be to ask, "What impact did social distancing policies have on people during the COVID-19 pandemic in 2020?" This could be answered in many ways, such as with infection and death rates across the pandemic, but what about the isolation with which millions of people struggled? This sort of data is how people experience an event, law, policy, or phenomena. The loneliness was experienced, and those who experienced it have the authority to speak on it.

The same is true of bigotry. The primary reason we know that bigotry comes in so many forms, ranging from the petty to the genocidal, is because the victims of bigotry talk about what they have experienced. These stories become data for social scientists and knowledge for communities. There may be no better phrase that encapsulates this than the survivor of past oppression saying, "I've seen this before," to the young. The existence of this knowledge is a problem for bigots because it limits their ability to act. For example, it becomes more difficult for antisemites to dog-whistle to other antisemites because Jewish folks have a body of knowledge about antisemitism, passed down through generations, which has trained their ears to pick up on the most subtle antisemitic rhetoric. The same is true for any group subjected to bigotry. As a Black man, I learned early on that being called "articulate" can be a backhanded insult rooted in antiblackness, and how to tell the difference between the insult and the well-intended compliment. This knowledge also extends to recognizing when a conversation or debate is rooted in bigotry, as when people refer to any non-heterosexual orientation as "a lifestyle," as if it were the equivalent of choosing to craft brew beer or not. This body of knowledge serves to protect the targets of bigotry because it helps them recognize the signs and respond appropriately. It provides an intellectual space for "psychic self-preservation," meaning that the knowledge protects the victims of bigotry from being convinced that it is all in their head (Ladson-Billings, 1998, pp. 13–14).

This is why bigots actively seek to gaslight their targets: so they will question their own assessment of a situation. This is not the same as a person considering whether they overreacted or misread a situation, because that is the individual themselves engaging in reflection and discernment. Angelique Davis and Rose Ernst (2017) have defined *racial gaslighting* as "the political, social, economic and cultural process that perpetuates and normalizes a white supremacist reality through pathologizing those who resist" (p. 761). What pathologizing means here is to deem a person's reaction as "medically or psychologically abnormal (Merriam-Webster, n.d.-b)." Davis and Ernst (2017) have argued that racial gaslighting produces "racial spectacles" narratives, which are deployed to cover up the power of White supremacy (p. 763). An example of this was the attempt to dismiss the Black Lives Matter movement in 2014 and 2020 as made up of people who hate America and the police rather than a protest movement demanding the state respect their right, under the Eighth Amendment to the U.S. Constitution against cruel and unusual punishment, not to be killed by the police. Some opponents of Black Lives Matter would bring up Black-on-Black crime rates in response to BLM demands that police be held accountable (Mitchell, 2016). This argument is a textbook example of how pathologizing works, but it is also one that reveals the bigotry of the person who makes the argument. The implication is that Black people are more violent than other groups, and because of this, the police must have the power to engage in extrajudicial killings in very public settings to keep the community in line; the word for this is *lynching* (Mitchell, 2016, p. 5).

The racial narrative is created to hide the real cause of a problem, attributing it to something else that benefits White supremacy. Davis and Ernst's (2017) concept of racial gaslighting and the racial narrative—where a dominant group constructs a narrative that portrays marginalized communities' negative reactions to their oppression as irrational or threatening—helps us understand how bigotry gaslights individuals. Simply stated, bigots characterize the negative reaction as the product of "being over-sensitive" and the preservation of the knowledge of how bigotry can manifest as "embracing victimhood mentality."

Arguably, the most common form of this is the dismissal of anger by "tone-policing," in which the focus shifts to how people call out bigotry rather than the bigotry they are condemning. This doesn't include responding to bigotry with bigotry or crafting a message among political movements. The reason bigots engage in tone-policing is that it is a distraction from the bigotry that has just been exposed, and most crucially, it "minimizes" the victim of bigotry's experience (Davis & Ernst, 2017, p. 763). It is tantamount to the dismissal of evidence in a criminal case, and an act of the bigot attempting to claim victim status because they did not like the way they were spoken to while rebuked; it is an act of performative fragility. The result of this tone-policing is to convince the victims of bigotry to second-guess their reactions to bigotry, with the hope that they will remain silent.

Gaslighting is a form of abuse inflicted on both the individual and society. All stripes of bigotry actively engage in gaslighting because bigots are inherently abusers. To be clear, it is an act of abuse to subject people to bigotry and to indoctrinate the young into bigotry. It is an act of abuse to teach a White child to hate other children with darker skin and vice versa. It is an act of abuse to teach a boy to hate women, which includes his female family members, by extension. It is an act of abuse for communities of color to teach their children colorism. All bigotry is gaslighting people to convince other people to question objective reality—that there is no hierarchy of human beings. When we buy in to the false dichotomies that bigotry creates, it distorts our view of reality. When we allow the victims of bigotry to be gaslit into silence, we erase the evidence that bigotry causes harm. To reiterate a point from lesson 17, Snyder (2017) wrote, "If nothing is true, then no one can criticize power" (p. 65). When applied to bigotry, if we allow ourselves to be gaslit by bigots, then bigotry is merely one philosophy among many and not the source of a great deal of human suffering.

References

Aydin, C. (2017). How to forget the unforgettable? On collective trauma, cultural identity, and mnemotechnologies. *Identity*, 17(3), 125–137. https://doi.org/10.1080/15283488.2017.1340160

Davis, A. M., and R. Ernst. (2017). Racial gaslighting. *Politics, Groups, and Identities* 7(4), 761-774. https://doi.org/10.1080/21565503.2017.1403934

Ladson-Billings, G. (1998). Just what is critical race theory and what's it doing in a nice field like education? *Qualitative Studies in Education* 11(1), 7–24. https://doi.org/10.1080/095183998236863

Merriam-Webster. (n.d.-a). Gaslight. In *Merriam-Webster.com dictionary*. Retrieved November 19, 2024, from https://www.merriam-webster.com/dictionary/gaslight

Merriam-Webster. (n.d.-b). Pathologize. In *Merriam-Webster.com dictionary*. Retrieved November 19, 2024, from https://www.merriam-webster.com/dictionary/pathologize

Minow, M. (2021). Equality vs. equity. *American Journal of Law and Equality* 1, 167–193. https://doi.org/10.1162/ajle_a_00019

Mitchell, N. E. (2016). In defiance of hidden deaths: Black Lives Matter as a living philosophy. *Just South Quarterly, Fall 2016*. Retrieved November 19, 2024, from https://jsri.loyno.edu/sites/loyno.edu.jsri/files/Black%20Lives%20Matter%20A%20Living%20Philosophy.pdf

Snyder, T. (2017). *On tyranny: Twenty lessons from the twentieth century*. Crown.

Stanton, G. (1996). *The eight stages of genocide (working paper)*. Genocide Watch. Retrieved September 4, 2024, from http://www.genocide-watch.com/images/8StagesBriefingpaper.pdf

BIGOTRY CANNOT BE DISPROVEN

You can never disprove bigotry, because bigots will always fabricate one more reason to justify your inferiority.

In lesson 9, I referred to Toni Morrison's 1975 statement about the futility of disproving racism. Her complete statement was:

> It's important, therefore, to know who the real enemy is, and to know the function, the very serious function of racism, which is distraction. It keeps you from doing your work. It keeps you explaining over and over again your reason for being. Somebody says you have no language, so you spend 20 years proving that you do. Somebody says your head isn't shaped properly, so you have scientists working on the fact that it is. Somebody says that you have no art, so you dredge that up. Somebody says that you have no kingdoms, so you dredge that up. None of that is necessary. There will always be one more thing. (Portland State University, 2014, pp. 10–11)

When I first discovered these words, I felt liberated. As a younger man in college and early in my professional career, I had defended my existence to bigots, and by doing so, I had reduced myself to a topic of debate. This is one of the meanings of Morrison's words I learned the hard way. Our humanity is not up for debate, and we lose by engaging with bigots who claim otherwise.

To this end, for the opponents of bigotry, civility should be seen as a strategy (Mann, 2021) rather than the default position anyone should assume. Politicians, pundits, scholars, and religious leaders routinely call for civility and "turning down the temperature" on cultural and political debates in an America that is already clearly divided. I agree with this sentiment to a certain extent. As I argued in lesson 13, there are some topics where it is inappropriate for people to simply agree to disagree. There are also some topics where maintaining civility is difficult at best, but also counterproductive. I am not suggesting that anyone subject others to a tirade of profanities. After all, Merriam-Webster's (n.d.) dictionary defines *civility* as "civilized conduct especially courtesy, politeness," and "a polite act or expression." This definition is vague, so it is susceptible to interpretation. We must be careful how people define civility in a moment of social tension because that momentum can be used to silence warranted critique and rebuke. It is not an act of incivility to call a bigot a bigot if they are, in fact, engaging in or supporting bigoted activities and rhetoric. It is simply accurate categorization.

I want to ask a few questions of the readers who disagree with the assertion that people should always refuse to debate their humanity. For White readers, do you wish to engage in a debate about whether White people are inherently racist creatures who bring misery, death, and destruction everywhere they go? For male readers, do you wish to engage in a debate about whether men are inherently toxic, prone to violence, and intellectually inferior to women? For straight, cisgender readers, do you wish to engage in a debate about how you actively seek to groom young people into your "lifestyle" by merely existing? Some may say they do, but many more would rather have a root canal with no painkillers than be made to defend their humanity in this way. While the hypotheticals I have presented here are deliberately extreme, they are simply reworkings of the sorts of public debates to which marginalized communities are subjected regularly, by society.

Yet, while we must not fall for the trap of defending our humanity to those who are intellectually invested in building a society around our inferiority, those opposed to bigotry must continue to denounce bigotry with their whole chests. What does this look like? An example was during the civil rights movement, when marchers would wear placards that said, "I am a man," and the early queer liberation chant of, "We're queer, we're here!" Both of these statements rejected bigotry while also refusing to engage with the idea that their humanity was up for debate. This is the same philosophy that undergirds any protest. The old adage that "the truth speaks for itself" is incorrect. The truth must be announced, advocated for, and defended. The same is true for announcing justice and denouncing injustice. This is one of the meanings of Morrison's assertion that racism "keeps you from doing your work" (Portland State University, 2014, p. 10). For those opposed to bigotry, the work is actually denouncing bigotry in all its forms. Of all the tactics that bigotry employs in this section, its function as a distraction may be the most commonly utilized.

Debating whether or not queer people are inherently groomers is a distraction that saps energy from real debates over securing full civil rights for queer people. Debating whether or not women are inferior to men is a distraction that saps energy from real debates over issues like the gender pay gap and a woman's right to get an abortion. The issues that I have just mentioned are only a small sampling of the galaxies of issues that these communities navigate every day, from which bigots seek to distract them, by trying to lure them into pointless arguments over their own humanity. Debates over which group of humans is more human than others are one hundred percent a bad-faith argument, ended by the simple declaration that this human being is, factually, human. Morrison's appeal is clear: Never debate your own humanity. If you do, the bigots win, because their goal is simply to have the debate.

What does Morrison mean by "there will always be one more thing?" (Portland State University, 2014, p. 11). Simply put, committed bigots will never admit they are wrong. To preserve their bigotry, they will distort whatever facts they can find, and when they run out of facts to distort, they will invent increasingly deranged claims. Why? Many theories seek to answer this. My own hypothesis has been the main argument of this book—that bigotry is more than simply hating groups that are different from yours. It is an ideology that people use to orient how they see the world, construct their communities, and interact with human beings around them.

Natalie Wynn (Contrapoints, 2023) offered an explanation that she calls the *bigotry whirlpool*:

> The deeper you go in, the harder it is to leave. For the same reasons that it's hard to quit a cult or scam. To quote video essayist, Dan Olson—"One of the most insidious elements of a confidence scam is that the victims who invested the most are often the most passionate defenders because shame is a powerful force in the human psyche, and they can't bear the shame of admitting they were tricked." Reformed bigots have to face not only the shame of being dupes, but also the guilt of having devoted years of life to harming vulnerable people. (Contrapoints, 2023, 01:49:26)

In the end, bigotry is a hustle. It is difficult for people to admit that they have been hustled and that they once believed in utter nonsense. This is also why, as I will explain in the conclusion, it is critical that people who oppose bigotry embrace former bigots and welcome them into the community without reminding them constantly how they were once bigots. It is both cruel and counterproductive to the goal of resisting bigotry. Shaming bigots for their bigotry is acceptable behavior. Shaming former bigots for their past bigotry is not.

In a 1954 sermon delivered in Detroit, Martin Luther King Jr. said:

> But I'm here to say to you this morning that some things are right and some things are wrong. Eternally so, absolutely so. It's *wrong* to hate. It always has been wrong and it always will be wrong! It's wrong in America, it's wrong in Germany, it's wrong in Russia, it's wrong in China! It was wrong in two thousand B.C., and it's wrong in nineteen fifty-four A.D.! It always has been wrong, and it always will be wrong! (1954/n.d., para. 20)

This simple maxim that sits at the heart of all opposition to bigotry is that bigotry is simply wrong. Bigots are wrong because they hate, and most importantly, they know it. They know their entire ideology is an attempt to cosplay their petty, unthinking hatred as something other than what it is. Dr. King's words also provide justification as to why we should refuse to debate our humanity with bigots. Debating with someone you know is demonstrably wrong is simply a waste of time, and as Morrison said, a distraction.

Bigots are wrong about humanity. That is the beginning and the end of the debate.

References

Contrapoints. (2023, April 17). *The witch trials of J.K. Rowling | ContraPoints*. [Video]. YouTube. Retrieved September 7, 2024, from https://www.youtube.com/watch?v=EmT0i0xG6zg

King Jr., M. L. (n.d.). *Rediscovering lost values* [Speech Transcript]. The Martin Luther King, Jr. research and education institute at Stanford University. Retrieved September 8, 2024, from https://kinginstitute.stanford.edu/king-papers/documents/rediscovering-lost-values-0 (Original work published 1954).

Mann, R. (2021, December 15). Don't let them civilize you. *Something like the truth: By Robert Mann*. Retrieved November 17, 2024, from https://robertmann.substack.com/p/dont-let-them-civilize-you

Merriam-Webster. (n.d.). Civility. In *Merriam-Webster.com dictionary.* Retrieved November 19, 2024, from https://www.merriam-webster.com/dictionary/civility

Portland State University (2014, May 6). Toni Morrison, Primus St. John, John Callahan, Susan Callahan, Lloyd Baker. *Black Studies Center Public Dialogue, Part 2 (1975). Special Collections: Oregon Public Speakers.* 90. PDXScholar. Retrieved September 8, 2024, from https://pdxscholar.library.pdx.edu/orspeakers/90/

CONCLUSION

THE WORLD IS A PUNK BAR

I first saw the Nuremberg TV movie, about the military tribunal that tried the surviving Nazi leadership for war crimes in 2000, when I was eighteen years old. There is a scene where Captain Gustave Gilbert and Justice Robert H. Jackson, played marvelously by Matt Craven and Alec Baldwin respectively, discuss the nature of evil. Gilbert says to Jackson:

> I told you once that I was searching for the nature of evil. I think I've come close to defining it. A lack of empathy. It's the one characteristic that connects all the defendants. A genuine incapacity to feel with their fellow man. Evil, I think, is the absence of empathy. (Rintels & Simoneau, 2000)

In the twenty-five years since I first heard those lines, I have never encountered a more succinct and correct explanation of evil. In the research for the writing of this book, I discovered that the TV series is the origin of this famous quote attributed to Gilbert, even though it is not something he actually wrote in any of his books. It is, however, an accurate summation of his conclusions about the Nazi leadership. I extend this assertion, regardless of its direct or indirect origins, to all forms of bigotry because bigotry kills empathy in individuals and nations. In America's constant debates over the real impact of any form of bigotry on the culture and the lives of ordinary people, this simple truth is often left unspoken: bigotry is evil because it kills empathy. Gilbert was right. The one thread that connects the racist, homophobe, transphobe, sexist, religious bigot, ableist, and classist is that they lack the empathy required to recognize the humanity in those they have branded as "other."

As an undergraduate student at Louisiana State University, I read Christopher Browning's (1992/1998) classic text *Ordinary Men: Reserve Police Battalion 101 and the Final Solution in Poland,* and it planted an idea in my mind that I still carry with me. Supernatural creatures are not real. There are no such things as vampires, werewolves, zombies, or ghosts. There are no supernatural creatures hiding in closets or underneath beds, waiting to tear us to shreds. The greatest threat to humanity is doing monstrous things in the name of monstrous ideas. All bigotry renders men and women monstrous. In this sense, monsters are very real, and they are not born. Other monsters create them.

Bigotry is the great corruptor because it requires individuals, communities, and societies to morally, spiritually, and mentally debase themselves, their families, and their communities, to live up to its ideals. It is a vicious practice and ideology taught to children and enshrined into law. Bigotry is the product of the worst parts of human imagination, the ability to deny the humanity of other humans. People kill in the name of bigotry. People pauperize in the name of bigotry. People burn books, art, and histories in the name of bigotry. Bigotry creates cultures where violence is the norm, and rights, worship, ethics, morals, science, and even cities are rendered grotesque in service to this most insane idea.

A question I ask myself with some regularity is, "How do you confront something as big as bigotry?" In 2020, I gained valuable insight from the most unusual of places: X, formerly Twitter. In July 2020, writer Michael B. Taggert went viral for a thread about an incident at what he described as a "crustpunk bar" (Perry, 2020). According to Taggert, a man sat next to him and was immediately thrown out by the bartender, who then revealed that the man was a neo-Nazi. The bartender then said:

> You have to nip it in the bud immediately. These guys come in and it's always a nice, polite one. And you serve them because you don't want to cause a scene. And then they become a regular and after a while they bring a friend. And that dude is cool too. And then THEY bring friends and the friends bring friends and they stop being cool and then you realize, oh shit, this is a Nazi bar now. And it's too late because they're entrenched and if you try to kick them out, they cause a PROBLEM. So, you have to shut them down . . . you have to ignore their reasonable arguments because their end goal is to be terrible, awful people. (Perry, 2020)

This thread spoke to me on many levels, but especially as a Southerner, because this process is something I see happen all too often. Bars and clubs that were once tolerant places, that only cared about the color of your money, slowly get taken over by bigots, until one day, they become known as "that racist place." This process is not limited to bars. Institutions, towns, cities, and even branches of government are not immune to this slow transition.

I was fortunate enough in my youth to have found myself in an anti-bigotry subculture, which are numerous in the South, if you know where to look. I call it a subculture because that is how it functioned. We hung out in certain bars and clubs and lived in the same areas. We were hostile to bigots when they did have the temerity to show up, because we wanted no part of what we saw as the everyday, dominant culture of Louisiana. I overheard many White friends check some White bigot who mentioned something bigoted in the bar with a loud "Why do you think it's okay for you to say that to me? Get the fuck out of here!" only to see a person rapidly shuffle out the door with their head down. For a college professor who was once a young, self-described Afropunk, this subculture was a refuge where I never doubted my sanity, because this mix of people of all races, genders, sexual orientations, religions, and politics saw the same bigotry that I did and pushed back on it with a collective voice of "not in my bar."

The philosopher Karl Popper described the paradox of tolerance in *The Open Society and Its Enemies, The Spell of Plato*, volume 1:

> Unlimited tolerance must lead to the disappearance of tolerance. If we extend unlimited tolerance even to those who are intolerant, if we are not prepared to defend a tolerant society against the onslaught of the intolerant, then the tolerant will be destroyed, and tolerance with them. (1963, p. 265)

What Popper meant was that bigots use tolerance to gain power in society, and once in power, they make intolerance the law of the land. This quote is an accurate summation of bigotry's political project: to create societies where their bigotry is taught to individuals as the normal way to think about the world and its inhabitants. He argued that the only way to maintain a tolerant society was to refuse to tolerate bigots and bigotry. The paradox is that this contradicts the very idea of tolerance. This is the philosophy of anti-bigotry subcultures and communities.

I believe that Popper was correct in his assertion. The only way to preserve a society free from the domination of bigots is to treat bigotry as anathema to, and a perversion of, our cultural values. Yet I do not agree with him entirely. As an American, I have a firm commitment to free speech. As such, I cannot condone arresting people for words or making bigotry a crime, which Popper (1963) advocates for, because once that precedent is set, it will only be abused. Being intolerant of bigotry does not equate to permission to violate civil rights and civil liberties. All attempts to do so must be opposed as one would oppose bigotry itself.

You, the reader, may have noticed that in the course of this book, I have never invoked the liberal versus conservative or the Democratic versus Republican binaries. That omission is intentional. Any group can live together in harmony with another group, even when they disagree. This is true of our political spectrum as well.

There is nothing inherent to liberalism or conservatism that allows bigotry to thrive. Liberals can easily say that bigotry hinders progress while conservatives can say that bigotry undermines traditional American values of life, liberty, the pursuit of happiness, and individual freedom with an equal amount of ease.

Bigotry is a political ideology unto itself that must be carried into mainstream politics by individuals, which American history shows us has been the case across the various iterations of the political spectrum. As a country, we are obligated to enforce laws that prevent discrimination, because as Martin Luther King Jr. asserted, it is morally right, but also because it guarantees that the country maintains stability while thriving. Of all the notable characteristics of the Jim Crow South, the endemic transracial poverty and general poor quality of life were the most visible. Millions of non-White people were kept in poverty because of the color of their skin, while millions of White people were kept in awful poverty because they had been convinced that the bigotry they clung to would keep them warm and fed, even as they shivered and were racked by hunger pangs; the "public and psychological wage" of Whiteness (Du Bois, 1935/2007, p. 1036) mattered more than their paycheck. Karl Marx was incorrect. The true opiate of the people is not religion. It is bigotry.

But this book is not a work of political philosophy. The lessons I have unpacked are meant to expose what bigotry does to individuals and how it operates as an ideological force in American culture, so it is necessary to conclude this book by asking one more question in line with Popper's paradox: "What should we do to keep bigotry on the margins of society?" There are a few actions and a mindset that individuals can take to treat their world as if it were a punk bar.

First, it is important to acknowledge that while many people are drawn into bigotry later in life, it is far more common for the instruction in bigotry to begin when a person is young. Bigots go after children and teenagers because young people are impressionable, and they do not know any better. This is compounded by the fact that, often, their instructor in bigotry is a parent or another family member. This is why it is important for parents to teach their children that bigotry is *wrong*. Children must be taught that difference is normal and nothing to be afraid of because it gives them a resistance toward bigotry when they do encounter it. It also provides children who have been taught bigotry with a path back toward their humanity, through their peers.

Second, we must reject tolerance as a goal. Now, I know what you are thinking after reading the introduction to this section about punk bars and the paradox of tolerance: "What is he talking about? He just wrote a few paragraphs about the necessity of protecting tolerance." But this is where I think Popper is incorrect. I agree that we must marginalize bigotry and bigots in society, but I have an issue with the idea of tolerance.

Merriam-Webster's (n.d.-b) dictionary defines *tolerance* as the "capacity to endure pain or hardship; sympathy or indulgence for beliefs or practices differing from or conflicting with one's own." We have preached the virtue of tolerance in the United States for generations without really confronting the hidden curriculum (Apple, 2019) of what this means in reality. We have taught millions of people to endure difference, which is not as noble of a goal as we think it is. For example, imagine you are on a long plane ride, and there is a crying child on board. You tolerate the child crying but you don't like it; you don't accept it. That is the hidden curriculum of tolerance—putting up with something that bothers you for as long as you must. Tolerance is good for situations like a crying child or someone coughing in a theater. It is not good for dealing with bigotry, because in doing so, we are tolerating a danger that we should find morally repugnant.

Whenever I encounter anyone who says anything along the lines of, "I tolerate gay people," or "I tolerate Jews," my immediate response is, "Well, what is your issue with gay people or Jews?" The issue with tolerance is that it deals with behavior and not thought. It allows for a person to actively maintain their bigotry but hide it very well, out of concern for what is considered acceptable in polite society. It never lasts because tolerance has a limit. Eventually, the crying child will grate your nerves. You will become annoyed at the coughing person in the theater. The tolerance of groups of people often gives way to resentment. This is clear in America's historical ebbs and flows of bigotry being active in the cultural and political mainstream.

We should teach acceptance rather than tolerance. We should teach the young that human beings are diverse in many ways and that they are obligated to accept people as they are. Acceptance of difference leaves no room for bigotry in action or thought. It erases fear and resentment based on the silly assumptions of bigotry and replaces them with the knowledge that comes from encountering other people's humanity. Most importantly, acceptance interrupts the lessons that bigotry wishes to teach. Bigotry cannot thrive in a culture of acceptance, and it slinks back to the fringes of society, where it belongs.

Third, as I stated in lesson 20, we must embrace former bigots. It is critical to remember that no one is born a bigot. Racism, sexism, homophobia, antisemitism, ableism, and every other form of bigotry are taught. Anything that is learned can be unlearned, and because of this, people committed to anti-bigotry must embrace those who have walked away from bigotry. We must also give them grace to fully unlearn the bigotry they have been indoctrinated with for years, and in many cases, decades. To be certain, former bigots may make mistakes, but rather than call them out, it is critical to call them in, and there is a difference. To call out is a rebuke, whereas calling in, according to scholar and activist Loretta Ross, is seeking to repair relationships and educate (Zomorodi 2021). Opponents of bigotry must remember that they had to be educated, too.

Fourth, we must accept that identity is lived and that lived experience varies (Yep, 2016). We often treat identity as a monolithic experience rather than a spectrum, which is a mistake. It is important to be able to sit with the complexities of lived experience within a community because the variation is the truth of the community. Life is intersectional, and it cannot and should not be reduced to a single facet. For example, if a Black person tells you they have experienced a great deal of racism in their life while another Black person tells you that they have not, who is telling the truth? The answer can be, and often is, both. That these two life experiences differ does not automatically challenge any claims that antiblackness is a problem in America. Rather, it invites further questions about who these two people are, such as where they live, their social class, their education, and so forth. By acknowledging the diversity of experiences within communities, we gain a better understanding of what bigotry looks like on the ground and the disposition of various communities.

Fifth, we must accept that there is no hierarchy of oppression, but some oppression is more visible than others. Audre Lorde's (1983) idea, that all bigotry is interconnected, is a central belief for opponents of bigotry. That being said, some forms of bigotry are more visible than others for many reasons, including certain groups being actively targeted by bigots and how bigotries can intersect. It is critical to note that just because one form of bigotry is more visible than others does not mean the obscured bigotry is lesser in the harm it causes. For example, while racism, antisemitism, sexism, and anti-queer bigotry are committed to being visible, ableism deals in erasure. People with visible and invisible disabilities are often shoved to the margins of society, and their voices are actively ignored by those in power. Ableism is compounded when combined with other forms of bigotry that increase the erasure. For this reason, opponents of bigotry have to pay attention to the margins of oppressed communities because bigotry seeks to harm all of its targets, regardless of their visibility.

Sixth, we should not use privilege and intersectionality to means test or ration sympathy and empathy (Táíwò, 2022). This walks hand in hand with opposing all forms of bigotry, without exception. Empathy does not mean that we do not hold people accountable for the harm they have done. Rather, it means "the action of understanding, being aware of, being sensitive to, and vicariously experiencing the feelings, thoughts, and experience of another" (Merriam-Webster, n.d.-a). It is a prerequisite for living in a community as well as for combating bigotry. Fred Hampton (1969/2020) articulated this point when he said:

> We got to face some facts. That the masses are poor, that the masses belong to what you call the lower class, and when I talk about the masses, I'm talking about the white masses, I'm talking about the black masses, and the brown masses, and the yellow masses, too. We've got to face the fact that some people say you fight fire best with fire, but we say you put fire out best with water. We say you don't fight racism with racism. We're gonna fight racism with solidarity. (para. 20)

What Hampton is talking about is a radical form of empathy that looks for similarities rather than only focusing on differences. A historical example of this was Martin Luther King Jr.'s Poor People's campaign, which sought to focus on poverty, regardless of race, and was to be the focus of his work before his assassination in 1968. We see this effort continue today with the efforts of people like Reverend William Barber II, who is continuing the work of King's Poor People's Campaign, in highlighting how racism obscures the diversity in the poor community and includes millions of White people (Wilson-Hartgrove & Barber, 2024). Another example of radical empathy is found in how many varieties of feminism articulate that it seeks to save both women and men from patriarchy, because patriarchy seeks to rob everyone of their humanity. It is critical to remember that you can be an oppressor and be oppressed, privileged, and marginalized at the same time. The surest guard against bigotry is empathy for humanity. Bigotry seeks to rob people of their empathy, and a form of that is restricting it only to people who have the criteria of a specific identity. Anti-bigotry requires us to empathize with the suffering of all, including the bigot.

Lastly, hope. All change begins with the audacity to hope that things can be better. Bigotry thrives on despair, desperation, and anger. The antidote to that is hope. All positive cultural change begins with the hope that society can be different and that people are not lost to darkness. The civil rights movement rested on the hope that America would abandon Jim Crow when confronted with the depths of its evil. The women's liberation and queer liberation movements rested on similar hopes. Anti-bigotry rests on the same hope that while things like a post-racial America are magical thinking today, they may be everyday thinking in time. This is what Martin Luther King Jr. spoke about on the steps of the Lincoln Monument in 1963—hope that a dream could be made a reality. Such things take deliberate work. Anti-bigotry is dedicated to making such dreams and magical thinking a reality.

In the end, it is up to you, the reader, to create communities where bigotry cannot find a foothold. It is up to you to challenge bigotry wherever it raises its head. It is up to you to talk to your children about bigotry before a bigot does. The lessons in this book are by no means exhaustive, because as the world changes, so will bigotry. As I wrote in the introduction, this book is a field guide for demystifying how bigotry works and what it teaches. We have a choice of whether to allow bigotry to work its way deeper into our culture until it gains real footholds of power in our communities and our homes, or to recognize how bigotry works and what it teaches, and to drive it into the margins of society, where all their many pontifications, justifications, and deceptions are no more than murmurs lost in noise.

Ultimately, the choice is yours. Choose.

References

Apple, M. W. (2019). *Ideology and curriculum* (4th edition). Routledge.

Browning, C. (1998). *Ordinary men: Reserve police battalion 101 and the final solution in Poland.* Harper Perennial. (Original work published in 1992).

Du Bois, W. E. B. (2007). *Black Reconstruction in America: An essay toward a history of the part which Black folk played in the attempt to reconstruct democracy in America, 1860–1880.* Oxford University Press. (Original work published in 1935). https://play.google.com/store/books/details?id=TXbiAgAAQBAJ

Hampton, F. (2020). *Power anywhere where there's people* [Speech Transcript]. The Hampton Institute. Retrieved September 6, 2024, from https://www.hamptonthink.org/read/power-anywhere-where-theres-people-fred-hampton (Original work published 1969).

Lorde, A. (1983). There is no hierarchy of oppressions. *Interracial Book for Children Bulletin* 14(3&4), 9. https://digital.library.wisc.edu/1711.dl/ZV6IH7UCTMVC28H

Merriam-Webster. (n.d.-a). Empathy. In *Merriam-Webster.com dictionary.* Retrieved November 19, 2024, from https://www.merriam-webster.com/dictionary/empathy

Merriam-Webster. (n.d.-b). Tolerance. In *Merriam-Webster.com dictionary.* Retrieved November 19, 2024, from https://www.merriam-webster.com/dictionary/tolerance

Perry, T. (2020, July14). *Bartender explains why he swiftly kicks out Nazis even if they're "not bothering anyone."* Upworthy. Retrieved September 8, 2024, from https://www.upworthy.com/bartender-explains-why-he-swiftly-kicks-nazis-out-of-his-punk-bar-even-if-theyre-not-bothering-anyone

Popper, K. (1963). *The open society and its enemies: The spell of Plato*, volume 1. Princeton University Press.

Rintels, D. W. (Writer), & Simoneau, Y. (Director). (2000, July 16-17). [TV movie]. In G. W. Abrams, A. Baldwin, M. Boudrias, B. F. Connors, J. Cornick, S. Girard, I. McDougall, & P. A. Sussman (Producers), *Nuremberg.* Alliance Atlantis; British American Entertainment; CTV; Cypress Films; Leahy Ross Conners; Les Productions La Fete; TNT; Warner Brothers.

Táíwò, O. [@OlufemiOTaiwo]. (2022, June 25). "From a comrade: 'Not to be controversial but I think white women and all middle class and even rich women and anyone with a uterus is going to suffer.'" [Post] *X.* https://x.com/OlufemiOTaiwo/status/1540851131806621696

Wilson-Hartgrove, J., and W. Barber. (2024). *White Poverty: How exposing myths about race and class can reconstruct American democracy.* Liveright.

Yep, G. A. (2016). Toward thick(er) intersectionalities: Theorizing, researching, and activating the complexities of communication and identities. In K. Sorrells and S. Sekimoto (eds.), *Globalizing intercultural communication: A reader* (pp. 86–94). Sage.

Zomorodi, M. (Host). (2021, December 3). Loretta J. Ross: What if we called people in, rather than calling them out? [Audio podcast transcript]. In *TED radio hour*. National Public Radio. Retrieved September 8, 2024, from https://www.npr.org/transcripts/1061209084

ableism, 209

accusations, 72

activism: by African Americans, 42;
anti-bigotry, 10–12; Black, 68,
117; in civil rights movement,
107; for marginalized voices,
96–97; MRAs, 185–87; Occupy
Wall Street, 82; psychology of,
12–13. *See also specific activism*

ADL. *See* Anti-Defamation League

advocacy, 82

African Americans: activism by,
42; African American History
Museum, 21; African American
studies, 144; history of, 66–67;
after slavery, 7–8. *See also
specific topics*

Algeria, 125

alienation, 29–30

All Lives Matter, 151

Allport, Gordon, 2–3

American Association of Biological
Anthropologists, 108

American Conservative (magazine),
27–28

The Anatomy of Prejudices (Young-
Bruehl), 2–3

ancestry, 74–75

Angelique, 193

Antebellum South, 71–72

anthropology, 108

anti-Asian American and Pacific
Islander hate, 98

anti-bigotry, 6–7, 38, 42–43, 121–
26, 205–6, 212

anti-bigotry activism, 10–12

anti-bigotry education, 3

anti-Blackness, 50–51, 133–34, 210

anti-CRT, 143–46

Anti-Defamation League (ADL),
185–86

anti-gender ideology, 145

anti-LGBTQ+ bigotry, 124–25,
136–37, 159–60

anti-Pacific Islander hate, 6, 98

anti-queer education, 159–60

anti-Semitism: in culture, 4; in
higher education, 152–53;
history of, 23; by Hitler, 98; after
Holocaust, 50–51; homophobia

and, 209; Islamophobia and, 84–85; in Nuremberg Laws, 169; in popular culture, 92–93, 96–97, 152–53; racism and, 38–39, 75, 89–90; sexism and, 93; stereotypes of, 35; in World War II, 63–64
anti-transgender laws, 143, 146
anti-White racism, 7, 43
Aqua Teen Hunger Force (TV show), 9
Arendt, Hannah, 38–39, 93
Aryan physics thesis, 89–91
Asian Americans, 6, 30–31, 98, 131–32
assumptions, 84–85
Atwater, Lee, 83–84

Baldwin, Alec, 203
Baldwin, James, 32, 53
Ball, Phillip, 89, 105–6
banality, 38–39, 93
Barber, William, II, 211
behavior, 35, 49–53, 113–19, 131–32, 149–54
Benjamin, Walter, 89
Ben-Yehuda, Nachman, 158–59
Berlatsky, N., 149–50
Bernie Moore Track Stadium, 9
bigotry. *See specific topics*
Bigotry and Intolerance (Gay), 2
biology, 108
birtherism, 37–38
Black activism, 68, 117
Black athletes, 10
Black children, 30–31, 53, 56, 87–88
Black culture, 100–101
Black History Month, 58
Black Lives Matter (BLM), 99–100, 124, 151, 193
Black middle class families, xii

Blackness, 42, 50–51, 133–34, 210
Black No More (Schuyler), 135
Black Panther Party, 176–77
Black people. *See specific topics*
Black power, 176–77
Black students, 11–12, 170
Black women, 56, 88, 132–33
Bland, Sandra, 100
BLM. *See* Black Lives Matter
Blue Lives Matter, 166
book burning, 89, 204
Boom, Corrie Ten, 175
Bostock v. Clayton County, 45, 177–78
Boston University, 6–7
Brody, Howard, 174
Bronner, S. E., 115–16
Brooks, Garth, 11
Brown, Michael, 100
Brown, Will, 32
Browning, Christopher, 204
Brown v. Board of Education, 123
Buck, Carrie, 106–7
Buckley, William, 53
Buck v. Bell, 106–7
"Callin' Baton Rouge" (song), 11

Carlson, Tucker, 74
catcalling, 154
Catholicism, xii–xiii, xv, 67, 75
Center for Antiracist Research, 6–7
Centers for Disease Control and Prevention, xvi
Charlottesville, Virginia, 152–53
children: Black, 30–31, 53, 56, 87–88; in childhood, xi–xvi; Delpit on, 168; education of, 22, 204; family and, 119; impressionability of, 207–8; LGBTQ+, 29–30; parents and, 55; sterilization of, 106; White, 194

Christianity, 60, 85, 135
cisgender, 134–35
civility, 198
civil rights movement: activism in, 107; Civil Rights Act, 37, 135–36, 178; culture of, 42–43; humanity in, 199; against Jim Crow America, 55–56; philosophy of, 45–46; politics of, 60; Supreme Court on, 123
Civil War, 43–44, 190
Clark, Kenneth, 32
classism, 4, 66, 91, 100–101
Cline, Natalie, 137
Coates, Ta-Nehisi, 60, 71–72
Cobb, Jelani, 10
Cohen, Stanley, 157–58
collective psychology, 84–85
Combahee River Collective, 115
committed, internalized bigot, 133–34
communism, 64, 67, 158
communities: bigotry in, 41–46; hierarchies in, 129; institutional bigotry in, 56–57; LGBTQ+, 182; loyalty in, 149–50; marginalized, 198–99; marginalized voices in, 101; minority, 132; non-White, 123; reformed bigots in, 200; in US, 113–14; in US South, 63; White privilege in, 73–74
concentration camps, 63–64
concern, 95–101, 181–82
COVID-19, 31, 98, 100, 107–8, 191–92
Craven, Matt, 203
crime, eugenics and, 109
Critical Race Theory (CRT), 57, 67, 143–46, 191
A Critique of Anti-Racism in Rhetoric and Composition (Smith), 2–3

Cross to Bear (Maginnis), xii
CRT. *See* Critical Race Theory
Cruz, Ted, 68
culture: anti-Semitism in, 4; bigotry in, 121–26; Black, 100–101; of civil rights movement, 42–43; cultural marginalization, 175–76; dissenting voices in, 157–58; dog whistling in, 66; double consciousness in, 81–85; false moral equivalence in, 184–85; gaslighting in, 189–94; of Germany, 152–53; global, 81, 109–10; homophobia in, 4, 29–30; intolerance in, 133; of Jim Crow America, 7–8; marginalized voices in, 95–96; of Middle East, 84–85; oppression in, 55–61; Overton Window in, 116–17; politics in, 117–18; public issues in, 142; racism in, xiii–xiv; of religion, 30–31; of social media, 27–28; social mores in, 60–61; in social science, 110; STOP WOKE Act in, 143–44; transphobia in, 4, 31, 61; US, 17, 36–37, 41–46, 206–7; useful idiots in, 129–38; wars, 116

Davis, Angela, 107
Declaration of Independence, 67, 76
dehumanization, 61, 88–89, 91–92, 96–97, 141–42
DEI. *See* diversity, equity, and inclusion
Delpit, Lisa, 168
Democrats, 125, 206–7
denial, 22, 57, 88, 190
Department of Health and Human Services, xvi
Department of Motor Vehicles, 191
DeSantis, Ron, 68, 160–61

disabled people, 107–8, 190–91, 209
disproportionality, 159
disproving racism, 197–201
dissenting voices, 157–58
diversity, equity, and inclusion (DEI), 36–37, 66–68
dog whistling, 66, 82–83, 137–38
double consciousness, 81–85
Du Bois, W. E. B., 81–82, 97
Duke, David, xii, xiii, xiv, 84, 110

education: activism in, 10–11; anti-bigotry, 3; anti-queer, 159–60; bigotry in, 49–53, 55–61, 141–46; Black people in, 130–31; in Catholic schools, xii–xiii; of children, 22, 204; miseducation, 144–45; National Education Association, 144; open bigotry in, xv; race relations in, 11–12; social mores, 58–59; thinking and, 168; wokeness in, 66–67. *See also* higher education
Edwards, Edwin, xii
egalitarianism, 66
Eichmann, Adolf, 38, 93
Einstein, Albert, 89–90
Eisenhower, Dwight, 16–17
empathy, 210–11
Engels, Jeremy, 184
equality, 190
equivalence, 173
Ernst, Rose, 193
ethical dilemmas, 144–45
eugenics, 106–9
Europe, 50–51, 75, 108, 131–32
evil, 203–4, 212
Exxon, 13

faith, 52–53, 133–34
false moral equivalence, 173–79, 184–85, 187

family, 27–30, 36, 99, 119
fascism, 64–65, 162, 183
Federal Bureau of Investigation (FBI), 109
femininity, 98–99, 137
feminism, 114–15, 136–37, 211
Floyd, George, 8, 60, 100, 122
Folk Devils and Moral Panics (Cohen), 157–58
Frank, Leo, 31–32
Fredrickson, G., 73–74
Freire, Paulo, 2
Freisler, Roland, 169
Freud, Sigmund, 89
Friendsgiving, 27–29
Friendsmas, 29

gaslighting, 187, 189–94
Gates, Henry Louis, 135–36
Gay, Kathlyn, 2
gay rights movement, 43
gender: anti-gender ideology, 145; anti-transgender laws, 143, 146; cisgender, 134–35; interracial dating and, 177; oppression and, 185–86; theory, 109–10; vice signaling and, 151–52. *See also* LGBTQ+
generational identity, 96
Genocide Watch, 21–22
Germany: book burning in, 89; culture of, 152–53; history of, 105–6; Nazi marches in, 152–53; in Netherlands, 175; Nuremberg Laws, 169; Nuremberg trials in, 2, 49–51, 106; South Africa and, 21. *See also* Nazis
Gilbert, C. M., 23–24
Gilbert, Gustave, 203–4
Gillon, Raanan, 174
global culture, 81, 109–10
Goldhagen, Daniel, 23

Goode, Eric, 158–59
Gorsuch, Neil, 45
Grant, Madison, 73
Grant, Ulysses, 43
Great Depression, 8, 98, 135
grifters, 133, 137–38
groomers, 160–61
Gross, Jan, 2–3
guilt, 1

Hammer, Fannie Lou, 107
Hampton, Fred, 117, 176–77, 211
Hanisch, Carol, 114–15
Harper, Tyler Austin, 166–67
Harvard University, 37, 58
hate, 200–201
Hayes, Peter, 98–99
Heyer, Heather, 153
higher education: anti-Semitism
    in, 152–53; bigotry in, 13–14;
    friendships in, 29; ignorance
    and, 105–6; after Jim Crow
    America, 16; in Louisiana, 8–10;
    at Louisiana State University,
    8–12; race relations in, 15–16;
    stereotypes of, 169; violence in,
    17. *See also specific schools*
hillbillies, 166–67
history: of African Americans,
    66–67; ancestry as, 74–75; of
    anti-Semitism, 23; of bigotry,
    8–10, 142; Black History Month,
    58; of Black power, 176–77; of
    eugenics, 106–7; of genocide,
    97–98; of Germany, 105–6; of
    humanity, 42–43; of Jim Crow
    America, 13–14; of Ku Klux
    Klan, 43–44; of oppression,
    71–72; of plantations, 21; of
    race relations, 141, 143–44; of
    segregation, 38–39, 90–91; of
    slavery, 17; of slurs, 88–89;

transgender, 2–3; US, 121, 209;
    of violence, 57–58; of White
    supremacy, 73–74
Hitler, Adolf, 63–64, 98
Hitler's American Model
    (Whitman), 169
Hitler's Willing Executioners
    (Goldhagen), 23
Holmes, Oliver Wendell, 106
Holocaust. *See* Nazis
Holocaust Memorial Museum,
    16–17, 21
homophobia: anti-LGBTQ+
    bigotry, 124–25; anti-Semitism
    and, 209; in culture, 4, 29–30;
    groomers, 160–61; sexism and,
    43–44, 121–22; violence and,
    31–32
hope, 212
How Fascism Works (Stanley), 2
humanity: in civil rights movement,
    199; denial of, 88, 197–98;
    hierarchies in, 183–84; history
    of, 42–43; human rights, 49–50,
    109–10; oppression and, 141
Hurricane Katrina, 9–10, 173

identity: bigotry and, 44–45;
    generational, 96; oppression
    and, 42–43; politics, 114–16;
    with popular culture, 95–96;
    psychology of, 81–85, 209–10;
    Queer, 30, 42, 159–60; race
    relations and, 30–31
ideology: of bigotry, 203–12;
    of Civil War, 190; of
    dehumanization, 141–42; of
    hate, 200; of Jim Crow America,
    4–5; of Nazis, 24, 51, 182;
    philosophy and, 113–19; political
    ideologies, 92; politics and,
    73–74, 117–18; psychology of,

87–93; in religion, 52; of White
supremacy, 122
ignorance, 105–6
immigration, 118–19
Indigenous people, 97
inferiority, 129–38
Ingram, David, 175–76
inherent racism, 198–99
institutional bigotry, 23, 37, 56–57,
74
intellect: anti-bigotry and, 38;
behavior and, 35; bigotry and,
165–71; dehumanization and,
91–92; Overton Window and,
118–19; in US, 106–7
internalized bigotry, 134–38
internalized racism, 134
interracial dating, 13–14, 92, 177
Interracial Justice (Yamamoto), 2–3
intersectionality, 96, 109–10
intolerance, 133, 206, 208
Ionesco, Eugène, 161–62
Islamophobia, 4, 84–85
isolationism, 154
Israel, 84–85

Jackson, Robert H., 49–50, 203
Jeffries, Jim, 123
Jehovah's Witnesses, 24
"Jewish Question," 97–98, 171
Jim Crow America: Antebellum
South and, 71–72; anti-bigotry
activism against, 10–12; Black
children in, 87–88; after Civil
Rights Act, 37; civil rights
movement against, 55–56;
culture of, 7–8; Duke for, xiv;
end of, 122–23; evil in, 212;
higher education after, 16;
history of, 13–14; ideology of,
4–5; King on, 207; legacy of, 17;
lynching in, 31–32; marginalized

voices in, 170–71; monuments
in, 59–60; Nazis and, 126, 168–
69; philosophy of, 76; racism
in, 38–39; segregation in, 8, 53;
slavery and, 22–23; violence
in, 4, 7; White people in, 182;
White supremacy in, 57–58; after
World War II, 13
Johnson, Jack, 123
Jones, Robert, Jr., 141

Karen term, 51
Kennedy, John F., 67
King, Martin Luther, Jr.: on Civil
Rights Act, 135; on hate, 201; on
Jim Crow America, 207; legacy
of, 31, 43; Malcolm X and, 116;
philosophy of, 212; on politics,
113; Poor People campaign by,
211
Kruse, Kevin, 73
Ku Klux Klan: activism against, 10;
against Catholicism, 75; Duke
for, xii, 84; history of, 43–44;
Nazis and, xiii; reputation of, xiv

Law for the Prevention of
Hereditarily Diseased Offspring,
106
Lawrence v. Texas, 41–42, 177–78
Lenard, Phillip, 89
Letter from a Birmingham Jail
(King), 31
LGBTQ+: anti-LGBTQ+ bigotry,
124–25, 136–37, 159–60;
anti-queer education, 159–60;
children, 29–30; cisgender and,
134–35; communities, 182; Nazis
against, 64; Supreme Court on,
41–42, 45; TERF movement,
136–37
Liuzzo, Viola, 153

Lombardo, Paul, 106
Lorde, Audre, 42
Louisiana, xii, 8–16, 84, 173
loyalty, 149–50
lynching, 8, 31–32, 60, 122, 150, 153

Maginnis, John, xii
Malcolm X, 116
manifestos, 72–73
Marable, Manning, 4, 87–88
Marcus, Kenneth, 72
Mardi Gras, 10–11
marginalized communities, 198–99
marginalized voices, 95–97, 101, 116–17, 170–71
Marx, Karl, 89
Marxism, 67, 158
masculinity, 92, 98–99, 185–87
mass shootings, 72–73
medieval Europe, 108
meme theory, 51
men's rights activists (MRAs), 185–87
mental health, 143–44
MeToo movement, 186
Mexico, 119
Middle East, 84–85
Mills, Charles, 2–3
minority communities, 132
miscegenation, 75
miseducation, 144–45
misogyny, 43, 98–99, 137
monuments, 59–60
morality: of bigotry, 27–32; definitions of, 27; ethical dilemmas, 144–45; false moral equivalence, 173–79, 184–85, 187; institutional bigotry and, 23; moral panics, 157–62; National Education Association on, 144; of popular culture, 7; public,

160–61; racism and, 4–5; in theology, 116
Morrison, Toni, 24, 55–56, 101, 179–201
Mother Emanuel church shooting, 60, 85
MRAs. *See* men's rights activists

National Association for the Advancement of White People, 84
National Education Association, 144
The Nature of Prejudice (Allport), 2–3
Nazis: Aryan physics thesis, 89–91; Ball on, 105–6; book burning by, 89; Einstein for, 89–90; fascism by, 162; Hayes on, 98–99; ideology of, 24, 51, 182; "Jewish Question," 97–98, 171; Jim Crow America and, 126, 168–69; Ku Klux Klan and, xiii; Law for the Prevention of Hereditarily Diseased Offspring by, 106; legacy of, 167–68; against LGBTQ+, 64; neo-Nazis, xiii, 82; in Nuremberg trials, 2, 49–51, 203–4; in popular culture, 161–62; religion and, 63–64; in Soviet Union, 59; for sterilization laws, 107–8; vice signaling by, 152–53; in war crime trials, 38; in World War II, 175
Neighbors (Gross), 2–3
neo-Nazis, xiii, 82
Netherlands, 175
New York Magazine, xiii
Niemöller, Martin, 63–64
non-White communities, 123
Nuremberg Laws, 169
Nuremberg trials, 2, 49–51, 106, 203–4
N word, 83, 88–89, 130–31

Obama, Barack, 37–38, 60, 122–23
Obergefell v. Hodges, 41–42, 177–78
Occupy Wall Street, 82
On Tyranny (Snyder), 2, 59–60, 161–62, 178
open bigotry, xv
The Open Society and Its Enemies (Popper), 206
oppression: against Black people, 81–82; of Black students, 170; in culture, 55–61; gender and, 185–86; history of, 71–72; humanity and, 141; identity and, 42–43; past, 192; relationships in, 179; visibility of, 210
Ordinary Men (Browning), 204
orthodoxy, 52–53
othering, 99–100
Other People's Children (Delpit), 168
Overton Window, 116–19, 123, 143

Palestine, 84–85
paranoia, 71–77
parents, xi, xv, 27–28, 55, 144–45, 168
Paris Is Burning (documentary), 29–30
The Passing of the Great Race (Grant, M.), 73
past oppression, 192
Pateman, Carole, 2–3
Pedagogy of the Oppressed (Freire), 2
people of color, xv, 76
performativity, 150
Perry, David, 149–50
personality, 114–15
philosophy: of anti-bigotry, 121–26, 212; of bigotry, 49–53, 83, 87–93; of civil rights movement, 45–46; of concern, 95–101, 181–82; of evil, 203–4; ideology and, 113–19; of inferiority, 129–38; of Jim Crow America, 76; of King, 43, 212; replacement theory, 73; of Sartre, 92–93; of slurs, 65–66; of tolerance, 208–9; us/them, 159
plantations, 21
Plessy v. Ferguson, 90–91
police violence, 8, 100, 193
politics: behavior and, 49–53, 113–19; bigotry in, 66, 110; binaries in, 206–7; of civil rights movement, 60; communism, 64; in culture, 117–18; definitions of, 113; DEI, 36–37; dog whistling in, 82–83; false moral equivalence in, 173–79; identity, 114–16; ideology and, 73–74, 117–18; institutional bigotry and, 74; of *Lawrence v. Texas*, 41–42; leadership in, 198; in Louisiana, 84; Overton Window in, 143; political ideologies, 92; in popular culture, 138; psychology of, 121–22; of public morality, 160–61; race relations in, 122–23; of resentment, 183–84; respectability, 100–101; Unite the Right Rally, 152–53; in US, xiv–xv, 37–38, 68, 124–25, 141–46; White supremacy in, 76–77; wokeness in, 45
Poor People campaign, 211
Popper, Karl, 206
popular culture: anti-Semitism in, 92–93, 96–97, 152–53; identity with, 95–96; morality of, 7; moral panics in, 157–62; Nazis in, 161–62; N word in, 130–31; Obama in, 122–23; Overton

Window in, 116–17; politics in, 138; replacement theory in, 74; social science and, 113–14; Supreme Court and, 90–91; Till in, 122–23; in US, 165–66
poverty, 61
power dynamics, 175–77, 194
praxis, 117
Procope Bell, Danielle, 132–33
Protestantism, 67, 84
PRRI. *See* Public Religion Research Institute
psychology: of activism, 12–13; with adrenaline, 14–15; alienation, 29–30; behavior and, 131–32; of bigotry, 63–68, 113–19, 149–54; collective, 84–85; denial, 22, 57, 190; of family, 27–29; of guilt, 1; homophobia, 29–30; of hope, 212; of identity, 81–85, 209–10; of ideology, 87–93; of mass shooters, 72–73; meme theory in, 51; of misogyny, 137; of moral panic, 157–62; of politics, 121–22; of race relations, 8–9, 14–15; of racism, xi–xvi, 14, 129; of sexism, 59; of social justice, 4; thinking, 35–39; victim mentality, 99–100, 181–87; of White supremacy, 175–76
public debates, 199
public issues, 142
public morality, 160–61
public persuasion, 118
Public Religion Research Institute (PRRI), 124–25
Pushaw, Christina, 160–61

Queer identity, 30, 42, 159–60

race relations: Baldwin on, 32; after Civil War, 43–44; in education, 11–12; in higher education, 15–16; history of, 141, 143–44; after Hurricane Katrina, 10; identity and, 30–31; in Louisiana, 9, 14–16; in politics, 122–23; in Protestantism, 84; psychology of, 8–9, 14–15; in US, 10–11, 36; with White people, 12–13. *See also specific topics*
The Racial Contract (Mills), 2–3
racial gaslighting, 193–94
racism: anti-Blackness, 133–34; anti-Semitism and, 38–39, 75, 89–90; against Asian Americans, 30–31; in culture, xiii–xiv; dehumanization with, 97; disproving, 197–201; forms of, 4; inherent, 198–99; internalized, 134; in Jim Crow America, 38–39; language of, 83; morality and, 4–5; Morrison on, 101; against Obama, 37–38; police violence and, 100; psychology of, xi–xvi, 14, 129; in public, 204–5; racism against, 211; in religion, xiv; sexism and, 61, 209; stereotypes of, 166; in US, 122–23; by White people, 31–32, 57, 109. *See also specific topics*
Rajamani, Jaya, 91
rationality, 36
red scare, 158
reformed bigots, 200
religion: bigotry in, 67; Catholicism, xii–xiii, xv, 67, 75; Christianity, 60, 85, 135; culture of, 30–31; ideology in, 52; Islamophobia, 4, 84–85; Jehovah's Witnesses, 24; leadership in, 198; Mother Emanuel church shooting, 60, 85;

Nazis and, 63–64; Protestantism, 67, 84; PRRI, 124–25; racism in, xiv; theology, 116; violence in, 17. *See also* anti-Semitism
replacement theory, 73–77
Republicans, 125, 206–7
resentment, 183–84
respectability politics, 100–101
retribution, 71
Rhinoceros (Ionesco), 161–62
Richard III (Shakespeare), 50
Rodger, Elliot, 31
Romania, 161–62
Roof, Dylann, 30–31, 85

same-sex marriage, 116–17, 177–78
Sartre, Jean-Paul, 92–93
scapegoating, 99, 115
Schmitt, Carl, 162
Schmitz, Matthew, 27–28
Schuyler, George, 135–36, 138
science, 83, 105–10
Scott, Tim, 76
segregation, 8, 38–39, 53, 90–91
Serwer, Adam, 150
sexism: anti-Semitism and, 93; in gender theory, 109–10; homophobia and, 43–44, 121–22; MeToo movement against, 186; MRAs on, 185–87; psychology of, 59; racism and, 61, 209; stereotypes in, 114–15
The Sexual Contract (Pateman), 2–3
sexual harassment, 59, 154
Shakespeare, William, 50
Shelby v. Holder, 123
Shepard, Matthew, 31–32
skullduggery, 179
slavery, 7–8, 17, 21–23, 60, 168–69
slurs, 65–66, 67–68, 83, 88–89, 130–31, 176
Smith, Erec, 2–3

Snyder, Timothy, 2, 59–60, 161–62, 178–79, 194
social-distancing policy, 191–92
social justice, 4, 68
social media, 27–28
social mores, 58–61
social science, 110, 113–14, 182–83
The Souls of Black Folks (Du Bois), 97
South Africa, 23
Southern Poverty Law Center, 73
Soviet Union, 59, 158
Standard Oil, 13
Stanley, Jason, 2, 72, 178–79, 182–83
Stanton, Gregory, 21–22, 57, 96
Stark, Johannes, 89
stereotypes: of anti-Semitism, 35; of Black people, 35; of feminism, 136; of higher education, 169; power dynamics of, 175–76; of racism, 166; in sexism, 114–15; of US South, 166–67
sterilization, 106–8
stigmas, 29–30
stochastic terrorism, 152–54
STOP WOKE Act, 143–44
The Straight Mind (Wittig), 2–3
strategy, of bigots, 165–71
Stryker, Susan, 2–3
students, 11–12, 144–45, 160, 170
Supreme Court: on civil rights movement, 123; on eugenics, 106–7; on LGBTQ+, 41–42, 45; popular culture and, 90–91; reputation of, 116–17; on same-sex marriage, 177–78

Taggert, Michael B., 204–5
Taiwan, 125
Táíwò, Olúfẹ́mi, 91, 149–50
TANF. *See* Temporary Assistance for Needy Families

teachers, 144–45, 160, 168
Temporary Assistance for Needy Families (TANF), 36
TERF movement. *See* trans-exclusionary radical feminist movement
terrorism, 43–44, 152–54
theology, 116
"There Is No Hierarchy of Oppressions" (Lorde), 42
thinking, 35–39
"Tiki Torch Parade," 152–53
Till, Emmett, 4, 31–32, 122–23
tolerance, 208–9
toxic masculinity, 92
trans-exclusionary radical feminist (TERF) movement, 136–37
Transgender History (Stryker), 2–3
transphobia: anti-LGBTQ+ bigotry, 124–25; anti-transgender laws, 143, 146; in culture, 4, 31, 61; scholarship on, 2–3; in sports, 125; TERF movement, 136–37; violence from, 44–45
Trevor Project, 30
Trump, Donald, 45, 76
Tulsa Race Massacre, 57–58
The Two-Party South (Atwater), 83

United Nations High Commissioner for Human Rights (UNHCHR), 109–10
United States (US): African American History Museum in, 21; Antebellum South, 71–72; anti-bigotry activism in, 10–12; anti-bigotry in, 6–7; anti-LGBTQ+ bigotry in, 124–25; Asian Americans in, 131–32; bigotry categories in, 6–7; Black children in, 30–31; Black culture in, 100–101; Black Panther Party in, 176–77; Centers for Disease Control and Prevention, xvi; communities in, 113–14; culture, 17, 36–37, 41–46, 206–7; Department of Health and Human Services, xvi; disabled people in, 107–8; ending bigotry in, 1–3; fascism in, 183; FBI, 109; Great Depression in, 135; history, 121, 209; Holocaust Memorial Museum in, 16–17, 21; ignorance in, 105–6; Indigenous people of, 97; intellect in, 106–7; interracial dating in, 92; Mexico and, 119; misogyny in, 98–99; police violence in, 100; politics in, xiv–xv, 37–38, 68, 124–25, 141–46; popular culture in, 165–66; Protestantism in, 67; race relations in, 10–11, 36; racism in, 122–23; red scare in, 158; same-sex marriage in, 116–17; slavery in, 168–69; South, 63, 166–67; Soviet Union and, 158; stigmas in, 29–30; STOP WOKE Act, 143–44; Unite the Right Rally in, 152–53; in World War II, 43; xenophobia in, 75. *See also* Jim Crow America; Supreme Court
Unite the Right Rally, 152–53
University of Mississippi, 9–10
University of North Carolina, 37
University of Virginia, 152
unreality, 178
US. *See* United States
useful idiots, 129–38
us/them philosophy, 159

verbal violence, 143–44
vice signaling, 149–53
victim mentality, 99–100, 181–87, 192–93

violence: against Black children, 53; in higher education, 17; history of, 57–58; homophobia and, 31–32; in Jim Crow America, 4, 7; in lynching photos, 150; paranoia and, 71–77; police, 8, 100, 193; in religion, 17; stochastic terrorism, 152; from transphobia, 44–45; verbal, 143–44

Walker, Pete, 130
war crime trials, 38
"Watchmen" (TV show), 58
Wendt, Jana, 55–56
"We Shall Overcome" (song), 82
White people: anti-bigotry by, 205–6; anti-White racism, 7, 43; BLM for, 124; classism and, 100–101; Europe for, 131–32; inherent racism for, 198–99; internalized racism by, 134; interracial dating with, 13–14; in Jim Crow America, 182; lynching of, 153; National Association for the Advancement of White People, 84; non-White communities for, 123; people of color and, xv; race relations with, 12–13; racism by, 31–32, 57, 109; self-awareness of, 129; slurs by, 130–31, 176; social justice by, 68; White children, 194;

Whiteness, 207; White privilege, 43, 73–74, 210–11; White women, 51, 91
White Rural Rage (Harper), 166–67
White students, 11–12
White supremacy: definitions of, 73–74; empowerment of, 177; eugenics for, 109; history of, 73–74; ideology of, 122; in Jim Crow America, 57–58; mass shootings and, 72–73; motivation for, 75–76; in Overton Window, 123; in politics, 76–77; psychology of, 175–76; racial gaslighting in, 193–94; as replacement theory, 74–75; slavery and, 60; in Tulsa Race Massacre, 57–58; Unite the Right Rally for, 152–53
Whitman, James, 169
Wilkins, Roy, 135
Wittig, Monique, 2–3
wokeness, 45, 65–68, 143–44
women. *See specific topics*
Woodson, Carter G., 58, 143–44
World War II, 13, 43, 63–64, 175
Wynn, Natalie, 64–65, 200

X (social media), 91, 204–5
xenophobia, 4, 75, 76, 118–19

Yamamoto, Eric, 2–3
Young, Damon, 66
Young-Breuhl, Elizabeth, 2–3

ABOUT THE AUTHOR

Nicholas Ensley Mitchell is an essayist and assistant professor of curriculum studies, courtesy assistant professor of African and African American Studies, and affiliate of the Center for LGBTQ+ Research and Advocacy at the University of Kansas. His scholarship has appeared in the *Journal of the American Association for the Advancement of Curriculum Studies*, the *Journal of Catholic Social Thought*, and multiple edited books. His public scholarship has appeared in The Good Men Project, Blavity, The Conversation, and on MSNBC.com.